CATHOLICITY AND HERESY IN THE EARLY CHURCH

While it has often been recognised that the development of Christian orthodoxy was stimulated by the speculations of those who are now called heretics, it is still widely assumed that their contribution was merely catalytic, that they called forth the exposition of what the main church already believed but had not yet been required to formulate.

This book maintains that scholars have underrated the constructive role of these "heretical" speculations in the evolution of dogma, showing that salient elements in the doctrines of the fall, the Trinity and the union of God and man in Christ derive from teachings that were initially rejected by the main church. Mark Edwards also reveals how authors who epitomised orthodoxy in their own day sometimes favoured teachings which were later considered heterodox, and that their doctrines underwent radical revision before they became a fixed element of orthodoxy.

The first half of the volume discusses the role of Gnostic theologians in the formation of catholic thought; the second half will offer an unfashionable view of the controversies which gave rise to the councils of Nicaea, Ephesus and Chalcedon. Many of the theories advanced here have not been broached elsewhere, and no synthesis on this scale had been attempted by other scholars. While this book proposes a revision in the scholarly perception of early Christendom, it also demonstrates the essential unity of the tradition.

For Mark Allen

Catholicity and Heresy in the Early Church

MARK EDWARDS
Christ Church, Oxford, UK

ASHGATE

Published by
Ashgate Publishing Limited
Wey Court East
Union Road
Farnham
Surrey, GU9 7PT
England

Ashgate Publishing Company
Suite 420
101 Cherry Street
Burlington
VT 05401-4405
USA

www.ashgate.com

British Library Cataloguing in Publication Data
Edwards, M. J. (Mark J.)
Catholicity and heresy in the early Church. 1. Church history—Primitive and early church, ca. 30–600. 2. Church—Catholicity. 3. Theology, Doctrinal—History—Early church, ca. 30–600. 4. Heresy—History. 5. Gnosticism—History.
I. Title
273.1—dc22

Library of Congress Cataloging-in-Publication Data
Edwards, M. J. (Mark J.)
Catholicity and heresy in the early church / Mark Edwards.
p. cm.
Includes bibliographical references.
ISBN 978-0-7546-6291-4 (hardcover : alk. paper) — ISBN 978-0-7546-6297-6 (pbk. : alk. paper) 1. Church history—Primitive and early church, ca. 30–600. 2. Church—Catholicity. 3. Theology, Doctrinal—History—Early church, ca. 30–600. 4. Heresy—History. 5. Gnosticism—History. I. Title.

BR162.3.E39 2009
273'.1—dc22

2009009320

ISBN 9780754662914 (hbk)
ISBN 9780754662976 (pbk)
ISBN 9780754695974 (ebk)

FSC Mixed Sources
Product group from well-managed forests and other controlled sources
www.fsc.org Cert no. SA-COC-1565
© 1996 Forest Stewardship Council

Printed and bound in Great Britain by
MPG Books Group, UK

Contents

Introduction

In academic circles, it is nowadays unnecessary to prove that the teachings of the Christian churches have a history, that the doctrines of the Trinity, of the union of two natures in the incarnate Christ, of the fall and the atonement, of the real presence in the sacrament and of the church itself as the body of Christ were not communicated as a system to the apostles, even by the risen Jesus. Again it is unnecessary to demonstrate that the growth is in part the result of the incubation of the gospel in a particular environment,[1] and not merely the unfolding of an embryonic pattern according to some instinctive or organic principle. Indeed the prevailing notion seems to be that there was at first no line in the development of doctrine, that for three centuries a plethora of antipathetic tenets and speculations fought to maintain themselves until at last the world proved hospitable only to one variety. We might say that a teleological theory of evolution has been succeeded by a Darwinian one, except that the discriminating forces in the evolution of Christian doctrine are generally supposed to have been adventitious rather than endemic. In recent years the narrative has been modified to suggest that the multiplication of 'Christianities' was accelerated rather than arrested by the Council of Nicaea in 325, which is often supposed to have inaugurated the process of unnatural selection which has left us with orthodoxy. Yet since the majority of these experiments too are assumed to have been abortive, the prevailing story is still one that recounts the destruction of a superfluous harvest, a constrained or guided dwindling from the many to the one.

It is not my object in the present study to deny that the norms of Christian thought, as these have been understood by many since the mid-fifth century, are a product of disparate forces, most (to a human eye) contingent, some extrinsic and none perhaps entirely consistent in its operation. I do wish to suggest that the concept of orthodoxy is part of the deposit, that so long as a gospel has been proclaimed it has always been accompanied by harangues against false professors. At the same time, I contend that, while there was evidently some difference of belief and much diversity in the expression of belief, there was no unregulated ferment of opinion such as is posited by those who speak of different and competing Christianities. The *episkopoi* or overseers,[2] who were formidable guardians of a norm which they believed to be that of Paul and the evangelists, were intolerant of locutions or conceits that were not of apostolic provenance; consequently they saw only a polar antitype to the gospel in other systems which, more liberally construed, would

[1] For temperate appraisals of the influence of philosophy see Studer (1998), 170–94; Ramelli (2007), 959–1092.

[2] See Philippians 1.1 and Küng (1968), 399–400.

have been discovered to be largely coextensive with their own. But systems which are mutually reducible are unlikely to remain mutually immiscible. The Gnostics and their dark twins the monarchians answered questions which could not fail to be questions for the episcopate: their premises were frequently alluring, their difficulties unavoidable. It is not surprising, then, that while episcopal theology owed its shape to the exigencies of polemic, it derived its substance from a common patrimony – that Olympus, in short, defended itself with thunderbolts forged by Titans. In Africa and Egypt minor clerics or lay satellites of the episcopate made free use of foreign arsenals, and in consequence were more vulnerable than the bishops themselves to the imputation of heresy in their own time. Yet, deviants and schismatics, though they remain to this day in the eyes of magisterium, are also numbered informally among the church fathers because it was their husbandry that assisted the germination of a new orthodoxy after the Nicene Council of 325. It was fear of the errors that seemed to be still implicit in this inheritance that led others to propose alternatives to the Nicene formula. In many cases, the only result of strife between sees was a hardening of contradictory dogmas; the peace that was concluded at last, however, represented not the ascendancy of a single school, but a confluence of several, including some that, to all appearance, had been abandoned or exploded before the council of 325. It was not so much by attrition as by ingestion that a creed matured which deserved the appellation 'catholic'.

Of the seven tests proposed by J.H. Newman as 'notes' or indices of true development rather than corruption,[3] he himself attached most consequence to preservation of type and continuity of principle. Neither is satisfactory, since there is no early Christian movement which is demonstrably unfaithful to the type laid down by Jesus, and there is no hermeneutic or philosophic principle which yielded only heterodox logomachies without enlarging the catholic proclamation. The test which Newman should have accentuated as a 'note' of catholicity is the power of assimilation, which extends, as I shall hope to prove in the present book, to the assimilation of teachings which to Newman himself seemed aberrant and unworthy of the name 'Christian'. In this introduction, I shall first explain what I understand by 'orthodoxy' in the early church, and then give a brief synopsis of the evidence that I shall adduce to illustrate the workings of the ecclesiastical loom.

The Keys of Orthodoxy

There is scarcely any book of our New Testament which does not contain an invective against false teaching. Even in canonical writings twentieth-century scholars have professed to discover tenets that are mutually inimical, and it has been inferred that the preaching of Jesus, together with his death, gave rise to a constellation of distinct communities, each proclaiming a different gospel. On this view it is possible to contrast the liberal efflorescence of the earliest years with

3 Newman (1845).

the tyrannical pruning of the credal age. It must be observed, however, that not every scholar believes that we have inherited such a heterogeneous canon, and that wherever an open difference of belief is recorded in our New Testament, one belief is deemed to be erroneous. In many cases the author admits that the aberrant view has been defended with eloquence and has proved seductive to many; in no case does he admit any test of orthodoxy but his own conviction. While the term 'orthodoxy' does not occur, we meet its antonym *hairesis* in Paul's letter to the Galatians, perhaps the earliest document in the canon; here and everywhere in Christian literature thereafter, it signifies not the mere choice of a sect or school, but a damnable perversion of the gospel. To require circumcision of neophytes is to spurn Christ's general amnesty to sinners, to maintain that the resurrection is come already is to make shipwreck of one's faith, and to deny that the Son of God came in the flesh as Jesus is to be antichrist. All this is established more by combination than by argument; with the passing of the last apostle, however, those who had hitherto been condemned might urge that no-one now had the power to impose a yoke upon belief.

Although Paul speaks of overseers (*episkopoi*) and servitors (*diakonoi*) in the first verse of his epistle to the Philippians, it is only in the letters that are addressed in his name to Timothy and Titus that we find precepts for the ordination of an official ministry.[4] Because these texts are commonly held to attest a threefold ministry of *episkopoi*, *presbuteroi* and *diakonoi*, it is frequently asserted that they cannot come from the hand of Paul himself, but betoken a subsequent development which could be established only by imposture. This reasoning, however, would appear to be either circular or irrelevant to modern deliberations on the structure of the church. In the present state of our knowledge, to deny that Paul himself could have been acquainted with three orders of Christian ministry is simply to beg the question, unless it is to be taken as an axiom, that such a development cannot have taken place within a single generation. But if this is an axiom, it is so whether God or man devised the three fold ministry; no proof that the God's intending it can therefore be derived from the date of the pastoral letters, or from the erroneous attribution. The puritan who urges that the Church should preach and practice only what is enjoined in the earliest texts must hold that it was possible for all the lasting mandates of the church to be issued in the first generation; in that case, he may not have any safe ground for denying the authorship of these letters to Paul.

The first author who unambiguously speaks of the episcopate, the presbyterate and the diaconate as three orders within the same churches is the happy pilgrim of death who styles himself Ignatius, Bishop of Syria (*Romans* 2); posterity has assumed that his see was Antioch, since he alludes to it as his home. His martyrdom is dated to about 110 A.D., and Walter Bauer, who argues that heretical teaching was everywhere the precursor of orthodoxy in the first century after Christ is therefore

---

[4] For the juxtaposition of the episcopate and presbyterate, which are not yet clearly distinguished see Titus 1.5–8. For the ordination of Titus as bishop see Titus 1.7; for Timothy as presbyter see 1 Timothey 4.14 and 2 Timothey 1.6.

bound to maintain that Ignatius is speaking only for a faction, and that the majority of Christians in the Asiatic towns to which he wrote denied the authority of the bishop.[5] Nowhere, however, do the letters testify to any defiance of episcopacy as an institution; his opponents, who 'acknowledge the bishop in name and yet do everything without him' seem to differ only in contesting the qualifications of a particular incumbent and in claiming the right to gather for worship and teaching in his absence. Ignatius, unacquainted as he is with the constitution of the Roman see, does not refer to the bishop in his letter to that congregation, which is written in a less magisterial character than his letters to the Asiatic churches; but Irenaeus, writing about 180, not only supplies a list of Roman presidents reaching back to Peter and Paul,[6] but assumes in his letter of counsel to Bishop Victor of Rome that the latter is the sole arbiter of practice in the capital.[7] He cites the predecessors of Victor, not to show that Rome had ever been without a monarchical episcopate, but to illustrate the forbearance which these worthies had observed in their exercise of the powers that Victor proposed to wield. When, a generation later, Callistus was pronounced unworthy of the monarchical office by a bilious prelate attached to his communion, the latter could not deny that Callistus was the sole tenant of the Roman see. Of episcopal successions in other provinces we generally have no evidence but the sparse lists in Eusebius; but in the cases where some primary source augments our knowledge – for example, the letter in which the Antiochene bishop Serapion justifies his suppression of the Gospel of Peter – the bishop entertains no doubt of his role as principal officer of the church, with power to license or proscribe (Eusebius, *Church History* 6.12).

Both Victor and Serapion announced their local rulings to other bishops, and communication by official letters, or *formatae*, was considered an ancient practice in the fourth century. Irenaeus speaks of a rule of faith, which is not peculiar to any one see, but a universal adamant which shivers falsehood in Rome as in Lyons, in Antioch as in Alexandria. He does not prove what he asserts – that if we reckon up the incumbents of all the major sees from the time of the apostles, we shall find that all preach the same doctrine – but Tertullian, writing in Carthage and in Latin thirty years after him, also invokes a rule of faith, which for him as for Irenaeus excludes Basilideans, Valentinians, Marcionites and Gnostics. The same four groups are denounced on numerous occasions by Tertullian's younger contemporary Origen; the latter, in the proem to his early work 'On First Principles', sets out what he believes to have been the teaching of the apostles in a series of articles, all of which Irenaeus and Tertullian would have endorsed without misgiving. Clement makes a fourth, and Hippolytus too condemns the same parties that the others

[5] Bauer (1970), 60–80.

[6] For Peter and Paul in Rome see 1 Clement 5; Ignatius, *Romans* 4.3; Irenaeus, *Against Heresies* 3.2.

[7] See *Against Heresies* 3.2 with Molland (1950); Eusebius, *Church History* 5.24 with the commentary of Richard (1965).

deem heretical. Among writers who acknowledge the episcopate we find, if not unanimity of belief, at least consensus regarding the boundaries of the church.

These authors also recognise the same canon of Christian scriptures, which had come to be called the New Testament by the beginning of the third century. According to Irenaeus, the true church knows no evangelists but Matthew, Mark Luke and John. The others signify by their quotations that they agree with him, and even Clement, who draws occasionally on other gospels, did not venture in his *Hypotyposes* to comment on them as he comments on the four that Irenaeus deems inspired. The fourteen texts ascribed to Paul included Hebrews, Titus and the two epistles to Timothy; Origen, who is said to have challenged the authorship of Hebrews, seldom fails in quoting it to advertise his belief in its authority by describing it as the work of the Apostle. In the fourth century, Hebrews and the Apocalypse of John were reckoned among the dubious writings, but the canonicity of the latter was seldom doubted up to the mid-third century. The five great theologians who flourished between 180 and 250 all concur in treating scripture as the sole foundation for argument against heresy; at the same time it is the church (as they understand this term) that furnishes the norms of interpretation, and even Origen never has the hardihood to elicit a sense from the text that contravenes the rule of faith.

It cannot be maintained, then, that before the Nicene Council of 325 there was no magisterial body which purported to define what could be believed and to wield the keys that Christ bestowed on the apostles. It cannot even be argued that the teaching of the episcopate displayed more uniformity after the Council than before it, for in fact it was only after Nicaea that the episcopate crystallized into maledictory factions, each pretending to have the one formula that would encompass all the necessary truths without giving a handle to false speculations. We do of course hear of discord among the bishops before Nicaea, but the feud between Victor of Rome and the Asiatics would appear to have subsided quickly enough (if we may judge by the silence of authors after Irenaeus), and even Hippolytus stops short of pronouncing Callistus a heretic or attempting to dethrone him. When the tenancy of a particular see was contested – as at Rome and Carthage under imperial persecution in the 250s – the charge against the incumbent was that his discipline was too lax, not that his doctrine was unsound. It seems that a bishop might be called to account for his doctrines by another bishop, as, for example, when Dionysius of Alexandria explained to Dionysius of Rome his reluctance to affirm a common essence in the Godhead; but in this case it would seem that the question never became a quarrel.[8] Only one bishop whose tenure had been unopposed at the outset was subsequently driven from his see by the suffrage of his fellow-bishops: Paul of Samosata, bishop of Antioch, was too powerful to be ousted without the assistance of the emperor, and his teaching that the Saviour was no more than a man inspired by God was cherished by a party which continued to exercise legislators and councils for centuries afterwards. Nevertheless his

[8] See Athanasius, *On the Opinion of Dionysius*, with Abramowski (1992a).

departure does not seem to have given rise to any schism in the episcopate, and the story of his dethronement is narrated by Eusebius as an example of the Church's power to act with a common will against the incorrigible (Church History 7.30). Before Nicaea perfect unanimity of doctrine among the bishops was an ideal that had not yet been exposed as a mirage.

Of course there was more dispute when there were more heads to differ and more that demanded public resolution. After Constantine's victory in the east, the formation of parties was encouraged by the multiplication of bishoprics, the suppression of legal impediments to intercourse between Christians and the unprecedented vigilance which was applied to the conscience even of minor prelates. There can be no doubt that the formulations of the conciliar age combine a menacing severity with a superficial clarity of diction that the older rule of faith had exhibited only when it was tempered to the hand of a particular controversialist. Yet the change, so far as change occurred, proved lasting only because it was gradual, undeclared and at first insensible. The Nicene definition of 325 procured twenty years of peace because it defined so little. The poison of Gnostic teaching was assumed to be so inert that one could revive the word *homoousios* with impunity; the Monarchians were tacitly admonished by the juxtaposition of clauses referring severally to Father, Son and Spirit; if individual prelates choose to quarrel about the eternity of the Son or the legitimacy of styling him a creature, the church as a whole remained incombustible. Once a general desire arose to dispel the ambiguities of the creed, this truce was irreparably broken, and no formula that was imposed upon the church between 350 and 361 survived the meeting that proclaimed it.[9] After an unruly moratorium of twenty years, it was partly the fatigue of the disputants, partly the statesmanship of the great Theodosius, and above all no doubt the passing of the principal agitators, that enabled the church to coalesce around an amplified version of the creed of 325.

Systematicians frequently imagine that after 381 there remained but one great schism to be healed, and that the salve was applied in 451 by the Chalcedonian formula which affirms two natures in Christ. In fact, as we shall see in the final chapter, nothing was settled at Chalcedon which had not already been settled in 433 at the Oecumenical Council of Ephesus. The odium which this council had excited in certain quarters of the east was not appeased in 451, though on the same occasion turbulent partisans of Cyril, the victor at Ephesus, suffered a reproof which led within years to a secession. The churchmen whom these malcontents had driven from their sees were temporarily restored, but some were found at a posthumous assize to have been heretics after all. The Council of Constantinople in 553 which vindicated Cyril against his enemies and Chalcedon against its critics was accepted by the Papacy under duress[10] and in defiance of western opinion. During the previous century the best intellects of the east had been intent upon

[9] See Athanasius, *On Synods*; Barnes (1993); Ayres (2004).

[10] The role of coercion in previous councils seems to me to have been exaggerated by Macmullen (2006) and De Ste-Croix (2006).

the defence, the supersession or the rebuttal of the Chalcedonian formulae; the cunning elucidations which were ratified at last in the Byzantine church were seldom read by the western clergy, and have never been reduced to a creed for the laity in either half of Christendom. The un-reconciled Nestorians of Syria and the discontented Cyrillines of Egypt ceased to molest the Emperor's counsels only when they had been irrevocably torn from his dominion by the Arabs. In the west his writ was dead without the assistance of the Pope, and the Pope in turn could wield no power except by making a tool of princes who desired him as a talisman against their own rivals or against Byzantium.

We must remember that laws in the ancient world were not published with the celerity or the ubiquity that a modern legislator takes for granted, and that, outside a few great cities, they could not be enforced with universal rigour. Even before the extinction of Roman government in the west, the decrees of an oecumenical council laid no burden on the incumbent of a minor see or even the dissident patriarch who commanded the seamless loyalty of his province. Those who had not been present at a council were unlikely to see a copy of its rulings; the majority of the people, who (in common, no doubt, with many of their clergy) were illiterate, were allowed to believe or disbelieve in silence. If by orthodoxy we mean an opinion which was held without demur by the entire body of the faithful, there was no orthodoxy – and hence, if you will, no church – from the time of Jesus; if we mean the expressed consensus of those prelates who were summoned to general councils, it is easier to discover orthodoxy before Nicaea than in any subsequent period of ecclesiastical history, from the fourth century to our own.

Plan of the Work

Orthodoxy is thus whatever is taught in any epoch by the majority of bishops, and to be catholic is to concur with this majority. It does not, however, follow that we ought to begin, as conventional genealogies of doctrine do, with the first acknowledged representatives of episcopal teaching, for that would be to forget the provisional character of the norm in each generation and its capacity to grow by the assimilation of tenets that had not been fathered by the episcopate. In any case, it has seldom been found profitable to look for intimations of a future orthodoxy in the writings of the apostolic fathers or the apologists, as the latter wrote primarily to deflect false accusations while the former touch on doctrine only so far as is necessary to arm the faithful against temptation or distress. The pioneers of Christian speculation, as I shall argue in the first chapter, were Basilides, Valentinus and Marcion – authors who are often relegated to the hinterland of ecclesiastical history because they appear in the guise of heretics even in our earliest testimonies. Whether the myths to which they appealed were of pagan or Christian provenance we need not determine here, since when a Gnostic is named the teachings attributed to him purport invariably to be readings of or supplements to the gospel. We cannot, on the other had, point to a catholic antecedent for their reflections on the loss of the heavenly archetype in man, the eternal sonship of the Redeemer and the omnipresent ministry of the Cross. In Chapter 1 I shall trace the incipient lines of catholic dogma in these innovators and their anonymous mentors; in Chapter 2 I shall argue that their principal critic, Bishop Irenaeus of Lyons, could not pursue them except by shadowing their manoeuvres, and that where he fails to anticipate the consensus of later times, it is because he has been guided by their premises or deterred by their example. Like many a notable piece of Christian music, his theology is the orchestration of an existing score.

In Chapter 3 I shall argue that the Alexandrian catholics Clement and Origen both took booty from their Valentinian neighbours, building systems which were partially homologous with those that their faith required them to eschew. This was the heresy of heresies for all Alexandrian catholics of this Monarchian confusion of Father and Son, but in this chapter I shall canvass the possibility that the dispute between Trinitarians and Monarchians was inflamed, if not occasioned, by the misunderstanding of an ambiguous watchword. No spokesman of the episcopal consensus could deny that Jesus of Nazareth was one person (*hen prosôpon*) with the incarnate Word, whom some Trinitarians styled the second hypostasis and others the second *person*a or *prosôpon* of the Godhead. The same Formula that was anathematized when it seemed to reduce the Son to an appurtenance of the father became a touchstone of orthodoxy when it signified that there is one Sin and not two. But in the third century those who detached themselves from the Monarchians were inevitably suspected of making terms with the opposite heresy, and we shall find in Chapter 4 that even Origen's apologists, within sixty years of his death, were so afraid of following him into the Valentinian camp that they conspired with his detractors to intercept the approach to Nicene orthodoxy.

The Nicene settlement, as will become apparent in Chapter 5, did not result in a formal vindication of Origen, but in persecution from another quarter. Nevertheless he must be counted among the progenitors of the Trinitarian doctrine that is now considered orthodox. So too perhaps should the Gnostics, some of whose speculations can be shown to have been adapted for catholic use against the Arians. One extant tract suggests that a Gnostic group was at war with those whom the Nicene party stigmatized as Anomaeans; the latter kept half their arsenal for the so-called homoousians, who, in contrast to the Nicenes with their Gnosticizing fables of emanation, preached two equipollent gods. The homoousian legacy to the Church is thus no compromise (as is commonly alleged), but an augmentation of Nicene teaching on the Son's divinity. In Chapter 6 I hope to refute another theory of accommodation. When the Chalcedonian Council of 451 affirmed the coexistence of two natures in the Saviour, it corrected a false interpretation of Cyril of Alexandria, but did not redeem any portion of the teaching of Nestorius, whose condemnation Cyril had secured some twenty years earlier at the third oecumenical council. On the contrary, in predicating a real birth and real death of the Nazarene who was also God, it ensured that Cyril's teaching on the passibility of the incarnate Word would not be invidiously conflated, as Nestorius and his allies wished, with the heresies ascribed to Apollinarius. The salutation of Mary as

Theotokos or Mother of God, the assertion that it was God who died on the Cross and even the formal attribution of two natures to the Son were all Apollinarian tenets to Nestorius, and the canonisation of Cyril's letters in 451 entailed a tacit rehabilitation of hitherto controverted teachings. On the other hand, Apollinarius' substitution of the Word for the human soul in Christ remained as unpalatable to the Chalcedonian fathers as to Cyril; neither would appear to have been aware that by insisting on the presence of this element, they were bringing a suit on Origen's behalf against the catholics who had first put him in the dock.

The term 'catholic' (from the Greek *kath' holou*) seems to have been intended at first to comprehend the whole body of the elect,[11] as opposed to the local congregation. As early as the third century, this body was so divided that the catholic church was merely one of a number of communions – the sole communion, as its champions boasted, which was never called by another name even when it was persecuted or impugned.[12] One proof of its catholicity, they urged, was that, in contrast to its rivals, its was represented in every proportion of the inhabited world; another was its willingness to tolerate the tares alongside the wheat, and to offer terms of readmission to those whom others put beyond the reach of mercy. The present study suggests that it was catholic in a sense that it might have preferred to disown, since, notwithstanding its fanciful claim to preserve the one truth handed down to the heirs of the apostles, it was the church that lent its countenance most readily to the mingling of the old and the new, as liberal in receiving the chastened form of an idea that it had once declared unlawful as in taking back the excommunicate who abjured his sin.

---

[11] Zisioulas (1988), 144 denies that it has this meaning in the proem to the *Martyrdom of Polycarp* (Lightfoot, 1885–1890, vol. 5, 948) on the grounds that it would be pleonasm to speak of a universal church 'throughout the world'. But if the term 'universal' indicates merely that the whole church is spoken of, it says nothing about the dimensions of that church.

[12] Augustine, *On True Religion* 7.12; *Martyrdom of Pionius* 9.6 at Knöpf (1901), 65.

Chapter 1
The Gnostic Beginnings of Orthodoxy

Notwithstanding all that chance and scholarship have brought to light in the last hundred years, it is probable that Marcion, Valentinus, Basilides and the Gnostics will continue to be known to us primarily through the philippics of Irenaeus and his younger contemporaries, who, from their own time to the present, have been regarded as the architects of catholic theology. Eulogists the heretics have in plenty today, but not among those who wish to uphold the traditions that have now become normative; they are praised instead, as they were once condemned, for the intrepidity and diversity of their experiments on the gospel. Books which follow the hegemonic line in the 'development of doctrine' may concede in a parenthesis that these thinkers had a catalytic role in the framing of orthodox thought, as Irenaeus would not have put any systems on paper had he not felt obliged to contradict them; but, so long as it is assumed that he arrived at his own beliefs without their counsel, it will always appear that his thought emerged from theirs like a ray from darkness rather than as sunrise after dawn.

The aim of the present chapter is to show that each of the names that I have cited can be associated with the first expression of a principle which has become an axiom of catholic doctrine. This project will require us to take account of salient differences between Gnostics, Basilideans, Valentinians and Marcionites, which have often been obscured by the broadening shadow of the term 'Gnostic'. Once the embryonic presence of orthodox norms in one or more of these groups has been established, it will be possible, in the next chapter, to examine the survival and germination of these precepts in episcopal writers of the second century. We shall see in later chapters that the content of orthodoxy, as it is now defined, was augmented by the recrudescence of thoughts that seemed at one stage to have died of vigorous pruning, while, on the other hand, some tenets advanced at first by catholic writers either in deference or in opposition to 'Gnostic' reasoning were at last proscribed by creeds which purported to represent the immutable teaching of the Church.

Taxonomies

'Gnostic' has become a term of abuse in modern theology, but only by an abuse of its primitive sense in Christian circles. Outside the church in antiquity, the epithet *gnôstikos* was applied more often to human faculties or their objects than to agents, and was not nearly as common in either sense as the noun *gnôsis*, which means 'knowledge'.[1] In the modern age, when faith does not sit well with academic theology, and the academy itself is wary of all claims founded on metaphysical reasoning, the 'Gnostic' is characterized as one who professes to have an advantage over the common mind of the Church by virtue of esoteric knowledge or cryptic reasoning. They take as their foundation neither the plain text of the scriptures nor the content of any traditional creed – though 'plain sense', 'tradition' and 'creed' are all words more often vociferated than examined. His cardinal tenet is supposed to be that God is remote and inaccessible to any mind that thinks itself at home in the mutable world. Whereas Christianity preaches the goodness of creation and the redemption of the material realm from evil, Gnosticism is seen as the first, illicit inroad of a pagan discipline which teaches us to neglect our earthly neighbour and his sufferings in the hope of emancipating some inner man. Orthodoxy is defined as the religion of divine love mediated by the suffering of Christ, and hence the religion of the material sacrament, corporate salvation and the vindication of God in the mundane.

There are scholars and theologians who have thrown the word 'Gnostic' at everyone who affirms the transcendence of God or exhorts the Christian to live for another world.[2] It is not my business here to determine whether this cult of the immanent, this disdain for the other-wordly, is the result of an unavoidable metamorphosis of Christian thought in the light of philosophical reflection, historical criticism and scientific discovery.[3] My purpose is only to show, as a matter of history, that the principles marked for ostracism in many current systems of theology – the doctrine of divine transcendence, a strong antithesis between flesh and spirit, a low estimation of all that is mutable – are those that the early Christians whom we term catholic and orthodox professed to have received from the apostles. In their eyes, the imputation of passibility and change to the Godhead, with the related notion of a natural affinity between the divine and the mortal, were the characteristic blasphemies of the heretic. The evidence also requires us to add that 'heretic' is the only compendious name available to us in this discussion, since, in contrast to both their critics and their champions today, the heresiologists of the first three centuries never used the term 'Gnostic' to stigmatize an opponent but only to identify those who had used it of themselves.[4] They do not say of anyone 'I call him a Gnostic, though he denies it'; they do assert from time to time, 'They style themselves Gnostics, though I have another name for them.'[5] The opposite position is commonly held today by those who, while admitting that 'Gnosticism' is an artificial category, lay the artifice at the door of Irenaeus, the first heresiologist, on the grounds that he charges all his adversaries with an affectation

[1] See Pétrement (1960).

[2] On Harnack's enmity to 'Gnostic' thought in his own communion, see King (2003), 55–70.

[3] For a critique of the modern position see Gunton (1993), 74–100.

[4] Casey (1935); Edwards (1989); Pétrement (1991), 1–26.

[5] See for example Hippolytus, *Refutation* 5.2; Irenaeus, *AH* 1.25.6.

of 'gnosis falsely so called'.[6] But if the logic of this argument were sound, it would yield two unpalatable inferences: firstly that even heretics who maintained the full humanity of Christ fell under the appellation 'Gnostic' in the ancient world, and secondly that, since the locution 'gnosis falsely so called' implies that there must be a *gnôsis* truly so called, Irenaeus considered himself a Gnostic. In fact the logic is poor, as Greek does not form adjectives from nouns by a universal algorithm, and we have noted above that the usage of the noun *gnôsis* is not coterminous with that of its derivative. One orthodox writer, Clement of Alexandria, exhorts the Christian to become a Gnostic if he can, and thus to cultivate a purity of doctrine and an integrity of life that will confound the 'so-called' Gnostics whom the Church anathematizes.[7] The latter are distinguished from other groups professing *gnôsis*, and the rider 'so-called' implies that they have no right to term 'Gnostic'. It is not so much that Clement is purloining a designation that had hitherto been the property of a heretical group, but rather that the name was there to be employed by controversialists of either party, provided that they were addressing an audience learned enough to tolerate refinements of the Greek vernacular.

It was not in the interests of heresiologists to represent their enemies as a numerous cohort, united in the defence of a single system opposed to theirs. Like the apologists of the Roman Church in the sixteenth century, they found it more expedient to magnify contradictions between two schools, or within the same school, as an illustration of the discord which inevitably follows when a Christian sets his own gnosis against the consensus of the apostles and their successors. Such unity as the different schools exhibit – and here again the polemic anticipates that of the Reformation era – is not so much generic as genealogical: as all Protestants can be said to spring from Luther, so the aberrations of a Marcion, a Basilides or a Valentinus are traced by their ancient critics to the pride of Simon Magus or the notorious absurdities of the Gnostics strictly so called. What it is to be a Gnostic strictly so called in the eyes of those outside the Church we learn from the neoplatonist Porphyry: it is to hold that the demiurge of the visible cosmos is malign.[8] This definition fits those groups whom Irenaeus, Origen and Clement describes as Gnostic, though not perhaps the Gnostics of Hippolytus, the most prolix and least typical of our Christian witnesses. The named heresiarchs who now pass for Gnostics all approximate to this definition, but none fulfils it exactly, and each differs from the rest in points that cannot have seemed inconsequential to their contemporaries, since (as we shall see) their peculiarities frequently align them with the episcopal church against one or more of its rivals.

This chapter will examine four developments of Christian thought in the second century. Each falls under the modern taxonomies of Gnosticism, though only one – the one without a named heresiarch – was called 'Gnostic' in its own time. I shall argue that the elements in each which seemed most foreign to its first

6 See in Smith (1981), King (2003), 31.

7 See *Stromateis* 7.8.82 amongst others, with Ashwin-Siejkowski (2008), 152–87.

8 See the title of *Enneads* 2.9, with Porphyry, *Life of Plotinus* 16 and Edwards (1990a).

critics are not baseless innovations, that in each case we observe a natural ripening (or at worst a hypertrophy) of motifs that belong to the earliest proclamation of the Gospel. It was by the domestication, not by the mere rebuttal, of their conjectures that produced its earliest system of theology. It was the Gnostics strictly so called – the *Gnostici Barbelo*, as Irenaeus styles them (*AH* 1.30) – who first reasoned that if humanity is made in the image of God, the Godhead must contain the image of humanity, in body no less than in soul. This, I shall argue, is a mythological intimation that the fall is anticipated in the Godhead, and that its suffering is the predestined instrument of our redemption. I shall then go on to show that Basilides was the first to harmonize the different senses of the term 'sonship' in the New Testament, making the eternal filiation of Christ the paradigm of his earthly ministry and the saint's election. Next we shall see that this teaching on the prefigurement of the temporal in the eternal was confirmed by the Valentinian myth of the fall and redemption of Wisdom before the ages. We shall briefly examine Marcion's emaciated version of the Gnostic myth, which, because it excluded suffering from the Godhead, obliged the church to find other means of reconciling the fall with the goodness of the creator.

The Image of God in Gnostic Thought

To discover what the catholic tradition owes to the Gnostics, we must collect the same materials for a theology of the image from the source that Christians now call the Old Testament. At Genesis 1.26, a passage all the more famous because it lacks a parallel in the Old Testament, God undertakes to 'make man in our image and likeness'. Two verses later, man is made in his image, but with no mention of the likeness, though with the rider that he is created male and female (Genesis 1.28). Since God cannot lie, this silence is an enigma, which admits of two solutions. Either the *complementarity* of the sexes is the ground of our resemblance to God (in which case it would seem that God himself is to be conceived hermaphroditically[9]), or else he has yet to communicate the likeness, and in the meantime the *differentiation* of sexes remains as a sign of our imperfection.

To any ancient Christian who acknowledged this dilemma, it would have seemed that Paul had seized the second horn of it. He extols Christ as the image of God at Colossians 1.5, and the male, in contradistinction to the female, as the image and glory of God at 1Corinthians 11.7. He nowhere, on the other hand, accords the likeness of God to a creature, and any likeness to which he alludes is assumed or superimposed at the cost of glory. The Son of God is said at Romans 8.3 to have come in the likeness of sinful flesh, to ransom those who, flouting a positive ordinance, have sinned after the likeness of Adam (Romans 5.14), together

[9] See *Bereshith Rabba* 8, in Freedman and Simon (1977), 54. For Christian specimens of this conceit see Clement of Alexandria, Rich Man's Salvation; Gregory of Nyssa, Commentary on the Song.

with those who, spurning natural revelation, mocked the creator under the likeness of a four-footed beast (Romans 1.23). Far from positing any fusion of sexes in the Deity, Paul exclaims that in Christ there is neither male nor female, and exhorts a mixed congregation to reap the fruits of Christ's descent in human likeness by growing up into the form of a perfect man (Ephesians 4.9).

Nor does Paul join some of his fellow countrymen in reasoning that when God employs the plural at Genesis 1.3 – 'Let us make man in our image' – he is deputing the formation of Adam's body to the angels.[10] Yet this is what he is willing to say of the Law – that it was delivered not by God, but by the angels, through the 'hand of a mediator' (3.20), which is to say, not from one but from many.[11] While this tradition is cited in commendation of the Law at Acts 7.53, Paul uses it to reinforce his argument that the Jew who rests his hope of election on this fragile instrument is as much an idolater as the pagan devotee of the 'weak and beggarly elements' (Galatians 4.3, 4.9). He none the less concedes that the Law, when rightly construed, is spiritual, and here at least he seems to be at one with James the apostle of works, for whom righteousness proceeds from the contemplation of the 'perfect law of liberty' (James 1.25). James contrasts the student of this law with the man who passes on unmindfully after gazing upon his own face in a mirror. Paul likewise speaks of our knowledge in this world as a dark simulacrum of that which awaits the saints after death; it is by gazing 'with open face on the glory of God' that we are translated, little by little, into his image, until the body itself becomes one in form with the glorious body of Christ (2Corinthians 3.18; cf. 4.18).

No work of a self-styled Gnostic was so widely disseminated in antiquity as the one called the *Apocryphon of John*. The Nag Hammadi Library, a cache discovered near an Egyptian monastery in 1945,[12] contains two versions of unequal length, while a third, the Berlin Codex, has been known since the last years of the nineteenth century. The Christian world has long been in possession of a fourth, the derisive and meagre, but (as it now proves) not inaccurate synopsis in Irenaeus, who gives the name Gnostic Barbelo to its votaries (*AH* 1.29). It has been alleged that the text in its primitive form had no peculiarly Christian traits,[13] yet the John of its title is clearly the apostle, and there is nothing to show that it ever bore another, or that the introductory dialogue between John and the Pharisee Arimanius is an accretion.[14] There are many works of early Christian literature, some later than

[10] See Pétrement (1991), 51–74.

[11] Paul says of the gift on Sinai what an Israelite would say only of legislation to the Gentiles: Gaston (1987), 43.

[12] For a review of theories regarding the genesis of this library, together with some original speculations, see Goehring (2001).

[13] Tardieu (1984), 26–45 has offered perhaps the strongest argument for a non-Christian prototype; for criticism see Logan (1996), 15–17 and 21.

[14] II 1, 1–30. Arimanius is the evil deity of the Zoroastrians, and we find an appeal to a book of Zoroaster in a section which describes the formation of the human body by the archons (II 1, 19.10, p. 111); but this section is absent from all other versions.

the *Apocryphon*, which cite no other scripture than the Old Testament, neglect the material sacraments and speak of Christ, if at all, only under a cryptic and impersonal nomenclature: we are not justified in assigning a Jewish or pagan milieu to every work that clothes its teaching in the Jewish or pagan vulgate. The doctrine of God with which the cosmogony of the book commences[15] is of that negative or apophatic kind which holds that nothing can be predicated truly of the first principle except that it does not possess the predicates of any lesser being. So much has already been affirmed by a number of devout philosophers, though not perhaps by any that was wholly untouched by Biblical teaching on the inscrutability of God;[16] of all religious movements, Christianity was the one most likely to cultivate such a vein of thought, for in proclaiming Christ as the image of the invisible God, it implied that the Father, as archetype, must transcend what was visible in the image. If it was in Christ, as Paul averred, that the 'fullness of God dwelt bodily' (Colossians 2.9), something greater than fullness, greater than all that we can imagine of power and knowledge, must be attributed to the Father. The *Apocryphon* is perhaps the first text to assert that even the axioms of logic cannot circumscribe the inscrutability of the first principle:[17]

> He is ineffable, being perfect in incorruptibility. He is not in perfection nor in blessedness, nor in divinity, but he is far superior. He is not corporeal nor is he incorporeal. He is not large nor is he small. There is no way to say 'What is his quantity?' or 'What is his quality?' for no-one can know him. He is not someone among other beings, for he is far superior, not as being superior but himself. (NHC II 1, 3.19–29, p. 25, Waldstein and Wisse with editorial annotation removed.)

Scholars who take the negative theology of the Platonists as a touchstone see here only an idle superfoetation of tenets which have lost their intellectual pedigree. How can it be said coherently of any being that it has neither a given predicate not its contrary, and how could it be said of the divine without blasphemy that it is 'not incorporeal'?[18] A historian's, if not a philosopher's, answer will begin by

[15] The translation followed here is that of M. Waldstein and F. Wisse (1995), in Robinson (2000), vol. 2, 1–209, where the Coptic of the three Nag Hammadi versions is printed in parallel with that of the Berlin Codex, with English rendering below. The pagination of the original cited here is that of Nag Hammadi Codex II.2.

[16] Whittaker (1969) adduces parallels from Seneca, *Epistle* 58, and Philo, *Rewards and Punishments* 30, but neither is so willfully paradoxical as the *Apocryphon*.

[17] The Berlin Codex, printed on p. 24 Waldstein and Wisse, reads: 'He is neither perfection nor blessedness nor divinity, but he is something far superior to them. He is neither unlimited nor limited, but he is something superior to these. For he is not corporeal; he is not incorporeal. He is not large; he is not small. He is not quantifiable, for he is not a creature. Nor can anyone know him. He is not at all someone who exists, but he is something superior to them, not as being superior but as being himself'.

[18] See for example Dillon (1999).

noting the presence of a complementary doctrine in Christian literature of the early second century. By this time, there were some who affirmed, in a zealous spirit of orthodoxy that Jesus Christ was God and man, at once begotten and unbegotten, of God and of Mary, passible then impassible[19] – in short that the irreconcilable qualities of creature and Creator had been, in this case, only, united in one person. The Christian could not, therefore, join the Platonist in affirming that God can never possess a body, though at the same time he would think it no less impious to assert that the Godhead possesses a body by nature. The apophatic formula that God is neither corporeal nor incorporeal has, of course, never become the norm of Christian belief, and it is not the only vehicle for talk of God in the *Apocryphon*. The text shifts within a few paragraphs to an anthropomorphic idiom, for which no Jewish, Greek or pagan source can provide a cognate.

The Father is characterized as the primal man, ineffable and immaculate (NHC II 1, 2.15–25, p. 19 Waldstein and Wisse). He acquires the capacity for procreation by emitting, as his first thought or Ennoia, the aeon Barbelo, who appears to derive her name from the first two words of the Hebrew scriptures,[20] and can be described indifferently as a female power or as a dyadic unity of the feminine and the masculine (NHC II 1, 5.7–32, pp. 35–7). God's abstraction of Eve from the side of Adam in Genesis 2 is commonly, and rightly, adduced as an analogue; we have no record, however, of any Jewish tradition that this earthly miracle had been foreshadowed by a bifurcation of sexes in the Godhead. On the other hand, it was not foreign to Christian thought, when it passed as orthodox to picture the Holy Spirit as a feminine emanation from the Father, and among the religions of the ancient world there is only one that regards virginity as a good superior to conjugal union. Christians know, not only by Paul's admonition but by the example of their founder, that it was better for a man not to touch a woman (1Corinthians 7.1); a letter ascribed to Clement of Rome, which is generally reckoned an orthodox, though inauthentic composition, quotes as a saying of Christ himself the precept that in order to be saved the male and female must become one.[21]

The *Apocryphon* goes on to recount the birth of the divine Autogenes from the Father and Barbelo (II 1, 7.1–18, pp. 45–7). We must seek the antecedents of the name in Greek philosophical works which represent the creative power as at once self-generated and dependent on an ineffable predecessor.[22] But the title 'Christ' is also accorded to him (II 1, 8.1–2, p. 49), and, while this might be an epithet of any anointed or 'messianic' figure, it was only the Messiah of the Gospels who was said to have been born of the Holy Spirit. Even in the fourth century, as we shall see

---

[19] Ignatius of Antioch, *Ephesians* 7. Ignatius will be considered in the next chapter.

[20] Harvey (1857), 221 suggests an etymology which would signify 'God is four'; cf. Pearson (2007), 88.

[21] 2 Clement at Lightfoot (1885–90), part 1 vol. 2, 239; cf. *Gospel of Thomas* logion 105.

[22] See Whittaker (1975), 207 on the 'disrepute' that accrued to the term among Christians as a consequence of its popularity in Gnostic literature.

when we come to Marius Victorinus, it was not patently unorthodox to maintain that the nativity on earth was anticipated in the procession of the Word from the Holy Spirit and the Father, and the eternal anointing of the Second Person by the Third within the Trinity was affirmed by the unimpeachably orthodox Gregory of Nyssa.[23] What follows in the *Apocryphon*, on the other hand, could not fail to offend the stewards of orthodoxy in every religious and philosophical school of the ancient world, for none of these, however low a view they held of the physical creation, traced its origin to an error or trespass in the supernal realm.

The evolution of lesser deities from the first triad begins with the spawning of four aeons, whose names and characters need not concern us here, except to note that they emerge with the full consent of the higher powers, for the completion of the intellectual realm and not with any intention of framing a world below (II 1, 8.4–9.24, pp. 49–57). After a further series of proliferations, the aeon strangely named Sophia, or Wisdom, excites a rupture in the Godhead by endeavouring to create without a male consort (II 1, 9.29–38, pp. 59–61). There are other Gnostic records in which Sophia is inveigled from the higher sphere by a luminous projection of her own image on to the surface of the underlying waters;[24] here, however, the first inferior object of her gaze is her shapeless progeny, Yaldabaoth, who assumes in consequence the form of a lion-headed serpent.[25] With a retinue of archons who administer the seven planets, and therefore the seven days of the mundane week, he fashions a cosmos from vestigial memories of the plenitude above, which he knows only at second hand (II 1, 11.4–13.6, pp. 67–79). Imagining this facsimile to be greater than the original, he proclaims: 'I am God, and beside me there is no other' (II 1, 11.20, p. 71). This is the premise of divine legislation in the Old Testament (Exodus 20.2–5; Isaiah 45.5); it is also the boast of the potentate or angel who aspires to dethrone his Maker. Yaldabaoth is rebuked from above by Sophia, who informs him that his superiors are 'Man and the Son of Man' (II 1, 14.14–18, p. 88; cf. 13.9, p. 71).

These two were venerated, to the exclusion of all other objects, by a group whom our informant, Bishop Hippolytus of Rome, lampoons as Naassenes or worshippers of the snake, though he believes that they were the first to coin the name 'Gnostic' for themselves. Whether or not the author of the *Apocryphon* belonged to this sect, there is only one source in which he or they would have come upon 'Son of Man' as the sobriquet of a being entitled to worship. God, supernatural agents or exemplars of humanity in the Old Testament could be introduced by locutions such as 'one like a son of man' or 'the likeness of the similitude of a man';[26] but it is only with respect to Christ, that 'the Son of Man'

---

23 Gregory of Nyssa, *Against the Macedonians* pp. 102–3 Mueller.

24 See for example Plotinus, *Enneads* 2.9.10.

25 II 1, 10.5–28, pp. 61–63. On the origin of the name see Scholem (1974, and on the iconography Jackson (1985).

26 Daniel 7.13; Ezekiel 1.28. See Quispel (1980) on the seminal importance of the latter text in Gnostic thought.

becomes an appellation in its own right. In works that now form part of our New Testament, 'man' as a common noun and 'son of man' as a proper designation are applied to Christ successively, in the order that is repeated in Gnostic texts. At Mark 2.27–8, he himself avers that as the Sabbath was made for man, so the son of man is Lord of the Sabbath. At Hebrews 2.6 the author quotes the Psalmist's question, 'What is man that thou art mindful of him, a son of man that thou visitest him?' (Psalm 8.4). Then he explains that, whereas Jesus, like all men, has been made lower than the angels for a season, he has now been raised above them as a pledge and a foretaste of our exaltation (Hebrews 2.9).

The *Apocryphon* goes on to relate that the rulers of this world were dismayed to behold in the waters a luminous duplicate of the heavenly androgyne, or Anthropos (II 1, 14.28, p. 87). They produced their own clay-copy in emulation, but this remained a mere idol until Sophia filled its nostrils with her own spirit (II 1, 15.10–13, p. 89).[27] This spirit – which is not to be confused with the one that moved on the face of the waters at the creation[28] – pervades this lower world as a solvent to the obesity of matter and the arbitrary rigour of the Law. It gave the fruit of knowledge to Adam and Eve in the teeth of Yaldabaoth's prohibition, and shielded their descendants from the perennial ebullitions of his wrath (II 1, 21.17–23.37, pp. 123–37). This sedulous inversion of the Biblical narrative shows that the author was writing for a circle in which the Book of Genesis could not be neglected. Pagans of this epoch might be acquainted with its first chapter, but for them it was Homer and Hesiod who were canonical. Jews devised fantastic pictures of Adam, corrected or elaborated the history of the patriarchs and adapted the chronology of the sequel to the fall in order to justify new calendars. But it is in the letters of Paul, the converted Pharisee, that the image of God at last becomes a cardinal motif, and it is in the Gospels written for his generation that the plenipotentiary of God the father is declared to be at the same time Son of Man.

Against the Christian provenance of the *Apocryphon*, it can be urged that its nearest cognate is the *Poimandres*, the first text of the Hermetic corpus, which is widely assumed to embody the syncretistic thought of Greek-speaking Egyptians in the Hellenistic era.[29] The *Poimandres* begins, as in fact the *Apocryphon* also does,[30] with the apparition of a celestial messenger, followed abruptly by the liquefaction of heaven and earth in a riot of mingling images.[31] Within this chaos

---

[27] For a rabbinic parallel see Urbach (1975), 231.

[28] For a contemporary reading of the same passage see Numenius of Apamea, as reported by Porphyry, *Cave of the Nymphs*, p. 63.12 Nauck. On the kinship between Numenius and the Gnostics see Edwards (1990b).

[29] Reitzenstein (1904) discovers that the matrix of Christian Gnosticism in the Poimandres and other texts that are not of Jewish or Christian provenance. But the Jewish antecedents of this text are exposed by Dodd (1935) and Pearson (1981).

[30] NHC II 1, 1.30–2.3, pp. 16–17 Waldstein and Wisse. Cf. Jeremiah 4.23–6.

[31] *Hermetica* I (*Poimandres*) 1–4. For translation and commentary see Copenhaver (1992), 1–7 and 93–124.

the visionary becomes conscious first of the fathomless immensity of the Godhead, then of the evolution of its demiurgic powers under the masculofeminine aspect of the Anthropos, or primal man.[32] In this text it is the man who is engulfed by his own reflection, and there is no such opposition as in the *Apocryphon* between the myopic demiurge and the penitent Sophia. Nevertheless, it has seemed to many scholars that the Poimandres is the nucleus from which the Christian tractate grew by accretion. It has never been compellingly shown, however, that the *Poimandres* is the older of the two: why should it not have been a strategic abridgement of the *Apocryphon* by a Christian who, like many apologists of the second century, preferred to omit whatever seemed calculated to excite a hostile predisposition in the pagan reader? Affinities between this work and Genesis are so numerous that the author has been credited with a sympathetic knowledge of that volume; nor can we explain how he and Paul could both profess to reveal the mystery that was hidden before the ages, unless one had read the other or they consulted a common source. If the Hermetica originated in a milieu that was neither Jewish nor Christian, nothing survives of this but the texts themselves; the *Apocryphon*, on the other hand, is explicable as the tumid but natural of a movement that, from its very inception, had read the Law and the prophets with great vigilance and a peculiar disdain for the natural sense.

Sonship and Salvation in Basilides

The Christianity of Basilides, the first of the named heresiarchs in the second century, is not contested, though we cannot be certain whether Irenaeus, who aligns him with other 'Gnostics', considers him an apostle or a disciple of that sect. He is credited in one source with a commentary on John's Gospel in twenty-four books;[33] our oldest witnesses ascribe two systems to him, which are generally agreed to be incompatible.[34] The prolix and dramatic system expounded by Hippolytus is certainly the product of an energetic Christian mind, and illustrates the general truth that even the anomalous speculations of this era do not sprout from nothing or die without progeny. My thesis will be that one of its principal aims is to distil three senses of sonship from the Gospel of John – the text on which Basilides, as we have just observed, is the first known commentator. It will be useful to offer a

32 *Poimandres* 14–15. On Jewish parallels see Scott (1925), 37–45.

33 Eusebius, *Church History* 4.7, strangely ignored in Hill (2004), 224–6.

34 Quispel (1948) prefers the testimony of Hippolytus is at variance to its incompatible rival in Irenaeus; Löhr (1996) demonstrates that other patristic notices of this heresiarch may be tendentious or fictitious, while some perhaps attribute to him the views of his putative disciples. For our purpose it is sufficient to observe that no catholic author would have invented the system paraphrased by the author of the *Refutation*, and that no date later than 250 A.D. can be plausibly assigned to the latter work.

prefatory survey of the evangelist's usage, so far as this can be divined, without appeal to any confessional premises, from his own Greek.

We read in the opening verses of a Logos or Word that was 'with God in beginning' (John 1.2), and through which, as 'what God was the Word was', all things came to be (1.3). Of the origin of the Logos nothing is said, but when at 1.14 he 'becomes flesh', the author purports to have seen his glory as the Father's *monogenês* or 'one of a kind'. The translation 'only-begotten', though superfluous, is almost warranted by the juxtaposition of this epithet with the noun *huios* (son) at 3.16, and perhaps at 1.18, though here there are reputable witnesses who read *theos*, or 'god', instead. The incarnate Word habitually addresses God as 'Father', and alludes at 10.35 to his own (unattested) use of the title 'Son of God', which the Jews regard as a sacrilege punishable by stoning. While this Gospel nowhere styles him the image of God, he asserts that 'he who has seen me has seen the Father' (14.9), while in the first epistle ascribed to the Evangelist we are told that to know the Son is to know the Father, and that the true believer is known by his confession of Jesus Christ as Son of God. The titles Word and Son are never predicated of Jesus simultaneously, but he speaks the words of eternal life, and likens the revelation of his own sonship to the coming of the 'word of god' to those who lived before him (John 6.68, 10.34–35). If the glory that he professes to have enjoyed in the Father's presence before the ages (17.5) is the same glory that awaits him in the hour of death, it would seem that his filial ministry consists in the surrender and restoration of the divine estate that belongs to him by nature as the Word.

There is another kind of filiation which the incarnate Word confers on his disciples: 'to as many as received him, to them he gave power to become the children of God, who were born not of flesh and blood but of the Holy Spirit' (John 1.13). Before his crucifixion, he reserves the term 'Son of God' for himself, and even the appellation Son of Man invests him with a unique authority both to save and to judge (John 3.19, 5.27). At the same time, he intimates, by denouncing his accusers as sons of the devil, that his followers can aspire to a better patrimony, and after his resurrection he says to Mary 'I do to my Father and your Father, to may God and your God' (20.17b). Thus we can distinguish a latent sonship before the ages, the consummation of that sonship in his appointed work on earth, and the delegation of sonship to 'as many as receive him' (1.1.2) after his re-ascent to glory.

In the system that Hippolytus attributes to Basilides, the Word, the Saviour and the Elect form a catena of three sonships. The source of all three is the hidden Father, who is so far above all description or the thought of it that Hippolytus sarcastically declares him to be a mere tissue of negations, and thus in reality nothing at all.[35] In this abyss, however, slept the seed of all that was to be, and the first efflorescence of it was the command 'let there be light',[36] which is none other (says the Hippolytan Basilides) than the 'light which lighteth every man'

---

[35] Hippolytus, *Refutation of all Heresies* 7.21.1, following a polemical but not uninformed burlesque of Aristotelian metaphysics.

[36] *Refutation* 7.22.3, citing Genesis 1.3.

in the prologue to the Fourth Gospel (7.22.4, citing John 1.9). Yet the two, if not distinct, are not quite identical, for the sonship that accompanies the creative light resides above the firmament, while a second sonship sinks below for a season until it escapes the nether darkness on the wings of the Holy Spirit.[37] It is the sonship alone that completes the ascent, while the Spirit) who, not being a son, is not of the Father's substance) must remain as a divisor between the higher realm and the sphere of mutability (*Refutation* 23.1). In this domain a third sonship remains in bondage to the Great Archon and his acolytes, who have forgotten that they owe their own generation to the descent of the second sonship (23.4–6). The third sonship can be liberated in stages, as the words of Christ awaken it to the light (25.1–5).

The Biblical allusions here are manifold and subtle. The ascent of the earthbound Son to his father, foretold at John 20.17a, is narrated at Luke 24.50–53, and appears to be preceded in both cases by a refinement of the gross body (Luke 28.31, Luke 20.19). The detachment of the sonship from the Spirit is implied by Christ's assurance that he will send a new paraclete, or comforter, to his orphaned followers (John 14.16), and again by his exhalation as he imparts the gift at John 20.22. Not only in John's prologue but in a hymn familiar to Paul, Christ is invoked as the bringer of light to those who sleep (Ephesians 5.14). That the archons of this world procured his death (1Corinthians 2.8), that the evil proceeds from invisible powers stronger than flesh and blood,[38] that Satan is the true god of this world, are all notions attested in different letters of Paul. And while it is convenient, in the light of its clear citations of the Fourth Gospel, to treat this myth as a fugue on that text, the Apostle too can be claimed as a witness to the three modes of sonship. According to one construction of Romans 8.3, Christ was already the son of God before his mission; at Romans 1.3 the resurrection proclaims him the son of God on earth, and we read in numerous passages that the elect are his fellow-heirs (for example in Galatians 4.4–7).

These testimonies are easily collated now, not so easily in the days when Christians lacked not only concordances, but the codices which made the concordance possible. Early theologians therefore taught compendiously by other means. Myth was the recognised vehicle in antiquity for thoughts that were peculiarly arcane, or for speculations that could be mastered only by disciplined fusion of the imaginative and intellectual faculties. Plotinus the Neoplatonist speaks of timeless truths concealed in a temporal narrative,[39] but where such biblical episodes as creation, the fall, the incarnation and the resurrection are read as history, it might be more true to speak of a synchronism of the eternal and the

[37] *Refutation* 21.10–11, alluding to Genesis 1.2. For the spirit as intermediary between God and inchoate matter see Genesis 1.2; for his detention in the world after Christ's departure see John 14.16–18.

[38] Ephesians 6.12; see further Caird (1956).

[39] *Enneads* 3.5.9. See Tarrant (2000), 44–6 and 54–6 for other Platonic Testimonies, and Edwards (2001) for a sustained application of these principles to the Valentinian cosmogony.

temporal. Whether Basilides took the gospels to be accounts of actual happenings in this world we cannot say, but his linear narrative enables him to harmonize John with Paul, and to discern a common principle in their varying uses of the same locution. In imagining the drama of our salvation to have been played out in the Godhead, he is elongating the plain but gnomic statements of canonical texts – that Jesus was the lamb slain before the foundation of the world (Revelation 13.8), that those who chose him were already chosen (John 15.16) and that their lives are presently 'hid with Christ in God' (Colossians 3.3).

Valentinian Wisdom

We saw above that the hermaphroditic Anthropos, or primal man, who is entombed by his own reflection in the *Apocryphon of John*, is replaced in other Gnostic texts by a figure who bears the female eponym Sophia, or Wisdom. Few scholars doubt that her literary ancestor is the wisdom of Proverbs 8, who enters the text as a personification of the human virtue but at 8.22 declares herself the first creation of God and his associate in the fashioning of all other things from the heavens to the deep. If there was ever a notion of a female deity yoked to the God of Israel, the only trace of it in this eulogy is the boast that 'I was daily his delight' (8.30); but in the much younger Greek text called the Wisdom of Solomon, where the sage pronounces her dearer than light, the most vital of vital forces, the interpreter of all sempiternal mysteries, she is described as an exhalation of God's power, the effulgence of his glory, and a mirror of his brightness (7.25–6). The God of this author is not the primal man of Gnostic thought and is not seduced by his blameless image. In an intermediate book, Ecclesiasticus or Sirach, it is Wisdom – the very wisdom that issued from the mouth of God to frame the heavens – who irradiates the temple, quickens prophecy and consecrates the Law.[40] In the writings of our New Testament her accolades are transferred to Christ: as Logos he was with God in the beginning (John 1.2), as Son he is a ray of the Father's brightness (Hebrews 1.3), and as Saviour he is the image of the invisible God and the firstborn of creation (Colossians 1.15–18). A union of these traditions might produce a bisexual luminary, though not one who would suffer a fall like that described in the Gnostic *Zostrianus*:

> When Sophia looked at [...] them she produced the darkness. [The lost text must have described the generation of the Demiurge] ... He saw a reflection. In relation to the reflection which he saw in it he created the world. With a reflection of reflection he worked at producing a world, and then even the reflection belonging to visible reality was taken from him. But to Sophia a place of rest was given in exchange for her repentance (Nag Hammadi Codices VIII.1.9–10, trans. J. Sieber).

[40] See Ecclesiasticus 24.5–32 with Davies (1965), 147–76.

How to account for this catastrophe? We must remember that Proverbs deifies wisdom, not to unlock the secrets of creation, but to set up a changeless norm of rectitude for the people of Israel. The Mosaic law is the natural law, because it is the testament of the same power that informs the heavens (Psalm 19.1–8). But because transgressors are legion, even in Israel, the Book of Proverbs draws the picture of folly as a meretricious antitype to Wisdom, irresistible to her besotted suitors, who do not perceive until they cross her threshold that they have entered the 'depth of hell' (9.18). Inordinate love impairs the wisdom even of a Solomon, while Israel, which often functions as a paradigm for humanity, is represented ideally as the bride of God (Hosea 2.19) and pejoratively as a whore who deserts her husband for a multitude of lovers (Ezekiel 16.15 and 45; Hosea 2.5). Since worship of the illusory or diabolical gods of neighbouring peoples was the usual form that apostasy took in Israel, idolatry and fornication coalesce in prophetic symbolism. In the Septuagint, the Greek name for a maker of idols – *demiourgos* rather than *ktistes*, the designation of God himself[41] – is the one the Platonists gave to the artificer of the visible world. The sophist, or charlatanical philosopher, is satirically compared in Plato's *Republic* to a man who pretends to create new objects merely by catching the images of natural phenomena in a mirror. The false image, or *eidôlon*, is habitually contrasted in his writings with the *eikôn*, or true likeness, the world itself being styled a true icon of the eternal in the *Timaeus*. But in common Greek the noun *eikôn* denotes an effigy of the kind that Jewish and Christian writers stigmatize as an idol.[42] Paul came to hold that idolatry consisted not so much in the veneration of stocks and stones, not even in substituting the creaturely likeness for the unseen creator, but in worshiping the weak and beggarly elements.[43] Paul does not espouse the view – so alien to all religious sentiment in antiquity – that the author of the cosmos is malevolent or deluded; the 'god of this world' (2 Corinthians 4.4) who blinds his own devotees is not the true sovereign but a tolerated rebel. But if the delinquent Sophia of the Gnostics represents the fallibility of human reason, as her ancestor in Proverbs is the mouthpiece of obedience to the divine law, the Biblical pedigree of the myth is clear enough. Sophia, on this interpretation, stands for the temerity of the human mind, which, rather than wait for a perfect revelation, takes its measure of the world and its own capacities from some fleeting counterfeit.[44]

One may protest that this reading is arcane, that it eluded both the Platonists and the catholic theologians of antiquity. But if we eschew any figurative reading, it will be hard to explain how Platonists and catholics alike could regard the Gnostics of their own day as a Christian sect. Narratives of the estrangement

41 On the salience of *ktizô* and its cognates in the *Hermetica* see Zuntz (1955).

42 See for example the Letter of Jeremiah and Isaiah 44.9–20 on the absurdity of a manufactured god.

43 That is, to say, the *stoikheia* (elements, letters) of the law are to Jews what an idol or heavenly body is to the pagans: Galatians 4.9.

44 Burkitt

and redemption of humanity are the staple of Christian thought, and in a newly-discovered text from Nag Hammadi, the *Exegesis on the Soul*, Sophia becomes a universal paradigm of delinquency, the counterpart of Odysseus in a fanciful gloss on Homer.[45] Similar experiments on the *Odyssey* are ascribed to the philosopher Numenius of Apamea and to Valentinus,[46] a Christian innovator who, though not strictly a Gnostic, is credited with an ornate redaction of the Gnostic myth. The few fragments that survive from his hand[47] reveal some knowledge of Plato, who admitted that his own confabulations lacked the certainty of dialectical or deductive reasoning. While some of Plato's adepts read his myths as literally as any Christian read the scriptures, it was widely agreed that myths like that of Atlantis could mean one thing to the plain reader and another when parsed esoterically as essays in cosmology or the analysis of soul.[48] Such legerdemain was not always forbidden to Christians, as we learn from Augustine's commentary *On Genesis against the Manichaeans*, in which Eden stands for the fecund soul, its fountain for the Spirit and its four out-flowing streams for the cardinal virtues. We may be sure that the original meant no such thing; the myth of Valentinus, on the other hand, abounds in reminiscences of both Platonic and Biblical anthropology, sometimes perpetuating a metaphor common to both traditions, sometimes using the lexicon of one or the other as an Esperanto.

The myth, like its Gnostic precursor, begins by tracing all existence to an unfathomed and ineffable fatherhood, conceived as the *buthos* or abyss of pure negation.[49] From this proceeds first a consort, Sigê or Silence, then from the coupling of these two a succession of three further syzygies or conjugal unions. Nous and Aletheia (Mind and Truth) give rise to Logos and Zoe (Word and Life), and these in turn to Anthropos and Ecclesia (Man and Church). The first alliance represents the informing action of mind on its objects, according to the principle (nearly ubiquitous among Platonists of this epoch, as opposed to Pythagoreans) that the ideal forms of being are the progeny of the demiurgic intellect. The coherence of Word and Life is attested in the prologue to the Fourth gospel: 'in him was life and the light was the life of men' (John 1.4). That man should contain the church might seem a strange conceit, but Paul, who regards the growth of the church as the realisation of Christ's own fullness, expresses the hope that his congregation

---

45 See the edition with translation by W.C. Robinson in Robinson (2000), vol. 2, 135–69. The citations of *Odyssey* 1.48–59 and 558 and *Odyssey* 4. 260–64 appear on p. 167 (NHC II 6, 136.28–137.5).

46 For Numenius, see Porphyry, *Cave of the Nymphs*; for Valentinus see Irenaeus, *Against Heresies* 1.9.4.

47 See Stead (1980). Markschies (1992) maintains that the system ascribed to Valentinus in catholic writings is the invention of successors who may not have been his pupils; but it was certainly not fabricated by the heresiologists.

48 See Tarrant (2003), 60–84.

49 In this and the following paragraph I have conflated the synopses of Irenaeus and Hippolytus.

in Ephesus will attain the maturity of a 'perfect man' (Ephesians 4.9).[50] There is more than a casual miscegenation of systems here: Valentinus is drawing up a pedigree for his church by resting its testimony upon the Word and this in turn on the intellectual knowledge of himself that God vouchsafed to philosophy after an aeon of silence. Revelation thus falls into three phases, natural, positive and spiritual, each new disclosure illuminating the last. But it is only in the man of the church – that is, in the Valentinian elect – that the mystery hidden before all ages becomes a Gospel.

To understand this gospel, which at first sight seems to have little good news in it, we must remember that, just as all healing implies a sickness, so all redemption implies a fall, not only for Valentinus but for all Christian writers since the time of the apostles. Paul argues that, in the wake of Adam's sin, all his descendants suffer death as the penalty of their own transgressions (Romans 5.12ff). He does not say whether the first offence engendered a sinful propensity in the race, but he speaks of the flesh as the seat of a law opposed to that of God, and as the receptacle of a wisdom which is 'death' (Romans 7.23–4, 8.6). This wisdom induced both Greek and Jew to murder Christ when he came in the fullness of ages, and to reject him when he rose from the dead as the firstfruits of salvation. The task of the evangelist is not to bring Israel home to her old fidelity, but to teach the Jews not to stumble at Christ's death, and to persuade the Greeks that his suffering was not (as they think) mere foolishness but the checkmate to their own wisdom (1Corinthians 1.21–4). Between this moribund wisdom and the fullness of God (Colossians 2.9) stands the Cross, exposing the vanity of all that is done in the service of the archons or the weak and beggarly elements. We meet the same antithesis, though without the concomitant imagery, in other texts which are now canonical. James contrasts the wisdom that is from above with that which is earthly and from the devil (3.15); in the third gospel Jesus either professes to quote the 'wisdom of God' or receives that sobriquet from the evangelist when he denounces the specious knowledge of the Pharisees and custodians of the Law (Luke 11.49).

In the system ascribed to Valentinus[51] there is no simple polarity between the wisdom of God and that of the creature. The two Wisdoms of his myth are both imperfect, both estranged, the difference being that the archetype repents while the copy remains incorrigible. In his myth the eight transcendent aeons form an Ogdoad, or group of eight; the fullness or pleroma of the Godhead is further ramified by the emergence of ten aeons from the second syzygy and twelve from the third. Sophia is the last of these twelve aeons, and her defection is said in a number of accounts to prefigure that of the twelfth disciple, Judas Iscariot. Her motive is given either as a desire to exceed the knowledge of the Father that is

---

50 Paul's term is *andra*, strictly denoting the male. All 'Gnostic' thought assumes the superiority of the masculine to the feminine: see for example *Gospel of Thomas* 105 on 'making Mary male'.

51 As Stead (1969), Markschies (1992) and many others have noted, even Irenaeus appears to contrast the developed system with the primitive teaching of Valentinus at *AH* 1.11.1.

allotted to her station (Irenaeus, *AH* 1.2.2) or an ambition to create without her male consort, Thelema, who personifies the divine will (Hippolytus, *Ref.* 6.30.7). In both these overweening aspirations she is a type of Eve, as many scholars have noted, and Valentinus may not have been the first Christian to see in Eve's seduction a proof of the universal infirmity of her sex.[52] But whereas Eve and her progeny are redeemed by the pains of childbirth, Sophia owes her reformation to Christ and the Holy Spirit, two aeons who are brought forth as firstfruits by the whole *pleroma* or fulness of God in the aftermath of her transgression (Irenaeus, *AH* 1.25; Hippolytus, *Ref.* 6.31.3). To protect the *plêrôma* from further loss or debilitation, a boundary is created under the name of Stauros, or Cross (Irenaeus, *AH* 1.2.4; Hippolytus, *Ref.* 6.30.5). Sophia takes up residence by this boundary, though she is not allowed to cross it, and the story of her contrition and return has something in common with rabbinic accounts of Israel's restoration. In the period of her apostasy, however, she has produced a pale facsimile of herself, called Achamoth or Sophia Prunicos,[53] who, being the child of a feminine perturbation without male intercourse, is a mere abortion, as Paul confesses that he too was in the time of his unbelief (1Corinthians 15.8).

This deformed being has vigour enough to produce another scion, here considered temporarily as a male and called, in Platonic nomenclature, the Demiurge. He fabricates a world in imitation of the *plêrôma* which he knows only at first hand, using as matter the tears of the penitent Sophia. It cannot, therefore, be said that the material world is evil in its conception; it is, however, defective in its materials, and it becomes a prison for souls when he creates the seven planets and subjects each to the rule of an archon blinder than himself. The demiurge and his retinue form a group of eight, the Ogdoad; although this term which could be used to denote the Sabbath or the complement of the ark which saved humanity from the Flood, it here implies the subordination of the physical world to the revolutions of the heavenly bodies. Philosophers and occultists alike believed that these were inexorable, except for those who had liberated the soul or spirit from its mortal envelope. The Demiurge, being no philosopher, cannot apprehend anything superior to his own creation, and fondly proclaims, 'I am God, and there is no other.' The offspring of false wisdom is the idolatry of oneself and one's own handiwork, as the scriptures of old declared; for Valentinus, however, the God who is celebrated in these scriptures is the father of all idols. His world would be in bondage to his ignorance for ever, were it not that Sophia (whose functions are now androgynous) is able to impregnate it with her own spirit, which survives in matter sporadically as the substance of elect souls. The gospel of truth (as Valentinus

---

52 See Stead (1969, 102; Macrae (1970); 1Timothy 2.13–14.

53 Irenaeus, *AH* 1.4.1; Hippolytus, *Ref.* 6.31.7. Stead (1969) and others regard the duplication of Sophia as a late accretion to the myth, but it seems to me quite possible that the prototype already contrasted the wisdom of the penitent with false sagacity of the carnal mind. The story has much in common with the allegories of fall and restoration (tikkun) in later cabbalistic thought. See for example Luzzatto (1997), IV.5.7–8.

styles it[54]) is the disclosure to the elect of their heavenly origin, the knowledge of which enables them to escape the toils of matter, leaving to annihilation the merely psychic or hylic being, that is the human without a spark of celestial wisdom, who is merely a wandering soul if his faith is weak or a tenanted corpse if he has none.

Although it is widely perceived that Sophia's fall represents the abuse of human wisdom, the interposition of the Cross goes unexplained, or is explained by appeal to sources that have little to do with primitive Christianity.[55] It ought by now to be clear that it was Paul, before Valentinus, who set the benighted world to one side of the Cross and the fullness of the Godhead to the other. It should also be clear that nothing could be further from the truth than to describe the pleroma as a sort of shield or sanitary cord between the transcendent and the mundane,[56] for it is only the procession of named aeons from the hiddenness of the Father that brings the mundane into existence. What is not so Pauline is the shift from earth to heaven, the location of the fall within the Godhead, and the prefigurement of repentance and the Cross in the first creation. These were not, so far as we know the tenets of Christ or of any creed that might be reckoned catholic; yet the catholic tradition holds that all that comes to pass in the present world was foreseen, and thus in a sense condoned, by God when he first divided the heaven from the earth. Again it holds that God elected to fight the evil that he foresaw by a self-bereaving love, an indefatigable suffering that entailed no change in his nature or his purposes, because it was the manifestation of his essential character. The myth of Valentinus may mean more than this, but it cannot well mean less, and the cosmic tragedy that he imagined is no substitute for, but an adumbration of, the historical ministry of redemption. So much is now apparent from a text discovered in 1945 at Nag Hammadi, commonly known as the *Gospel of Truth*.[57]

For this reason error grew angry at him, persecuted him, was distressed at him and was brought to naught. He was nailed to a tree and became a fruit of the knowledge of the Father. It did not, however, cause destruction because it was eaten, but to those who ate it gave cause to become glad in the discovery (NHC I 3, 18.21–31, p. 85, Robinson).

This conceit is founded on Paul's description of Christ as the firstfruits of the resurrection at 1Corinthians 15.23; error personifies the benighted servants of the Law, and the tacit contrast between the Cross as the tree of life and the tree which Adam robbed in Eden is foreshadowed at Philippians 2.6, where Christ is said to

---

[54] See NHC I 3, 16.31 at Robinson (2000), vol. 1, 83. This exordium has induced the majority of scholars to give the Name Gospel of Truth, attested at Irenaeus, *AH* 3.11.9, to the entire text, which, like other contents of the Jung Codex, is untitled. I am not aware, however, of any text in the Nag Hammadi corpus whose original title, when it can be ascertained, coincides with its opening words.

[55] Bousset (1911), 855.

[56] Grillmeier (1975), 98.

[57] Translation by H. Attridge and G. Macrae, in Robinson (2000), vol. 1, 55–122.

have been in the form of God but to refrained from any seizure or *harpagmos* of equality with his archetype.

Among the few quotations ascribed to Valentinus himself, there is one in which he professes to see 'all things suspended upon the Spirit, all things borne upon the Spirit, the flesh suspended from the soul, the soul depending from the air, the air suspended from the aether, and fruits brought forth from the abyss, the young from the mother's womb' (Hippolytus, *Ref.* 7. 37.1–7). We may ask whether this is the idiom of theology, but we should not forget that associative thinking and florid diction are also characteristic of catholic writers in the second century. It was quaint but not unorthodox of Justin, an apologist admired by Irenaeus, to see a premonition of the Cross in a passage of Plato, where the Demiurge forms the soul by placing otherness and sameness into the shape of a letter X. Nor was any new doctrine introduced by the episcopal martyr Ignatius of Antioch when he spoke of Christ as the Logos who proceeds from silence. From his usage elsewhere it is clear that Ignatius means by silence the secret preparation of the world for the nativity, and hence that he is alluding here, as Paul did, to the failure of the archons to anticipate the advent of the saviour (1Corinthians 2.8). These antecedents show at least that the system of Valentinus came into being by increments, not by a wilful betrayal or abrogation of all that had hitherto passed for Christian belief. From Ignatius he took a verbal conceit, from Justin a view of history in which the Cross is the scaffolding of creation. But the acme of Valentinus falls some twenty-five years before that of Justin, and no catholic writer before him had said so clearly that the last things are adumbrated in the first.

Marcion and the Law

The relation between the deliverance and the origin of the soul in Valentinus resembles that between a photograph and its negative, or between a finished portrait and a poor sketch. Sophia brings forth the oppressor of the world by her temerity, and rescues the elect by a second, surreptitious act of procreation; the cross which severs the Godhead from the world in the higher plane acts in the lower plane as a conduit for souls aspiring to rise above the material sediment of thc fall. In Marcion of Pontus, who began to teach a little later than Valentinus, the figure of Sophia disappears and the seductive apparatus of myth gives way to a bald antithesis between the myopic justice of the demiurge and the benevolence of a higher deity, father of Jesus Christ, who employs his son to bring enlightenment and liberty to the elect. God is spirit, the Demiurge merely psychic, the world a carnal prison for soul and spirit, from which only the latter escapes. Matter is irredeemable, and Christ came not in the flesh but (as Paul discloses at Romans 8.3) in the phantasmal likeness of flesh. For Marcion the first trespass and its remedy are no longer the work of one agent; the Old Testament is no longer, as the Valentinians held, a chequered source of illumination prefiguring the Gospel, but an inventory of the vain laws and tyrannical interpositions which the Gospel came to undo. Paul is no longer one of a number of witnesses to Christ's ministry, but the sovereign interpreter of the Gospel, which, when it takes the form of narrative, can be trusted only in Luke's recension, and only when all passages that imply a real incarnation have been excised. The same instinctive principle of emendation also enables Marcion to acquit Paul of any statement which would imply the collusion of spirit in the creation of the material universe. Marcion was, so far as we know, the first to define a New Testament, with a more restricted canon than any subsequent compilation, and the first to establish a visible rival to the episcopal communion represented by Ignatius of Antioch, Justin Martyr and Irenaeus. If he is none the less considered by many to be more orthodox than Valentinus or Basilides, that is no doubt because he adopted a purely didactic mode of exposition, in which nothing is said ambiguously or hidden under fantastic narrative. And while he parted company with the majority of Christians, then as now, in what he denied, he is often praised today for having affirmed, more clearly than any reader of Paul before him, the incompatibility of faith in Christ with the doctrine that salvation depends on sedulous obedience to the Law.

One can illustrate the dichotomy between faith and works in Paul without deciding whether or not he taught justification by faith without works, or whether any doctrine of justification is at the heart of his theology. There is no doubt that he inveighs against the preachers of circumcision on the grounds that they measure righteousness by servitude to the Law and do not perceive that the Law is an implacable master. Moses, as Paul observes, declared that one who offends the law in any point is guilty of all; if we add Paul's own rider – deduced from experience and the Psalms – that 'all have sinned and fallen short of the glory of God',[58] it will follow that, since all have offended in some point, none will be saved by works of the Law. The Law is set against the promise, the covenant of bondage, given through Moses, against the covenant of sonship, made with Abraham on behalf of many nations (Galatians 3.16–21). The Law is so poor a custodian of the first covenant that it put the prophesied seed of Abraham under a curse, and thereby made an end of its own authority (Galatians 3.13). It has not escaped either ancient or modern readers that the Law performs the same work as the archons who, according to Paul, betrayed their own ignorance when they crucified the Lord of glory (1Corinthians 2.9). While Paul himself insists that the Law is spiritual, he confesses that its ordinances give rise to the very sins that they are supposed to avert, so long as those who try to obey them are under the dominion of the flesh (Romans 7.7–15). Marcion was not to first to conclude that the Pauline corpus offers contradictory judgments on the Law, and while most modern critics do not obelise the text as freely as he did, they remove a number of difficulties by denying his authorship of half the corpus, and are willing to entertain the possibility that the shorter version of Romans used by Marcion is more faithful than the one that

58 Romans 3.23, citing Psalm 14.

we now divide into sixteen chapters.[59] Even these expedients do not, in the eyes of many scholars, render Paul's teachings perfectly consistent; Marcion's theories of interpolation show that he did at least accept the assumption of his contemporaries that the Apostle was incapable of error.

Paul's estimate of the body may also seem to us ambivalent. The works of the flesh are at odds with those of the spirit, and it is because 'I am carnal, sold under sin', that the spiritual mandates of the Law become my temptations. While it better that the law should be inscribed on a heart of flesh than on a heart of stone, the term 'flesh' almost always denotes in Paul a state of infirmity and moral blindness, inimical to the freedom of the elect. This inward morbidity takes the form of a 'law in the members', inclining the will to sin and sometimes prevailing even against the regenerate mind. One the one hand, the flesh contemns the precepts of the Law; if, on the other hand, these precepts are honoured, they become fetters to the spirit, as the mere observance becomes a source of boasting in the flesh. The body that encumbers us will not survive natural death, but will give way to a house not made with hands; it is sown a psychic body, but raised a spiritual body. While many, including Paul, have ocular proof of Christ's resurrection, there is nothing in Paul's own testimonies, or in the accounts of his conversion in Acts, to imply that it was a body that he saw. In his letters he almost always means by 'body of Christ' the church in the present world. Of course we may say that the body has been debauched by the sin of Adam and his descendants, that it came perfect from the hand of its creator, that what rises again is still a body of some kind; but much of this is rather inferred from Paul than stated clearly in his own writings. A zealot who was more like Paul than Paul himself might urge that, since idolatry of the Law and faith in bodily resurrection are both Pharisaic traits, a convert from that sect would renounce them both in embracing Christ.

Marcion was in ancient times the most notorious advocate of the view that Christ came only in spirit, and only to emancipate the spirit from the body.[60] The same position was widely imputed to the Valentinians – at times with the mocking caveat that they admitted the resurrection of a spiritual body – but, as many modern commentators have noted, there is little in the Valentinian doctrine that could not have been substantiated from the letters of Paul. There was dispute within the school as to whether Christ had come in a psychic or a spiritual body – that is, whether his body was governed by the soul or by the spirit – but it was not alleged that his body was a phantom. As to the resurrection of others, the question for Valentinians was not 'will it happen?', but 'will it be in the flesh?'. An answer in the affirmative is given in one text, the *Letter to Rheginus*, and it is frequently

---

59 See Sanday and Headlam (1907), xc–xcviii, citing Origen, *Commentary on Matthew* 10.43 and Tertullian, *Against Marcion* 5.4. Some MSS have an Amen at the end of Chapter 15 and the greetings in Chapter 16 have often been thought irreconcilable with a Roman venue.

60 Though even this tenet does not entail the renunciation of material sacraments: see Stewart-Sykes (2002).

assumed that this is the Pauline answer. In fact it is not, for Paul nowhere affirms the resurrection of the flesh and states distinctly at 1Corinthians 15.52 that 'flesh and blood will not enter the kingdom of heaven'. The *Letter to Rheginus* seems to take sides, against literal readings of this verse, with the tradition now called catholic, according to which the body that rises will be of a similar texture to that of the body that goes to earth. Marcionites, on the other hand, said flatly that nothing rises but the spirit. Marcion himself incurred the ridicule of Tertullian when he explained the words of Christ at Luke 24.40. – 'a spirit has not flesh and bones, as you see me having' – to mean not 'you see that I have flesh and bones', but 'you see that I have the character of a discarnate spirit'. But his true preceptor is Paul, not Luke, and the strength of his position is revealed by the strange constructions that his adversaries put on Paul's exclusion of flesh and blood from the kingdom of heaven.

It cannot be said that Marcion offers a comprehensive reading of any unmutilated text. He not only opposes Paul to the Law and the Sermon on the Mount, but opposes letter to letter within the Pauline corpus, verse to verse within the same letter. His legacy to the catholic tradition is his choice of Paul as a privileged amanuensis of the mind of Christ, his perception that any theory of obligation to the Law involves a theory of human nature, and his insistence that when Paul hailed Christ as the end of the Law he did not mean simply that Christ fulfilled the prophecies of the Old Testament and left us an example of righteous works.[61]

Conclusion

We have seen in this chapter, therefore, that the Gnostics of modern scholarship are often Gnostics falsely so called, that their thoughts are not of all of a piece and that they do not combine on every point against the catholic teaching of their own or a later epoch. None of them fits the caricature of the dualist who crudely divorces matter from God and denies that any divine work can be accomplished through the body; on the contrary, it can be said of all but Marcion that they people the void between the corporeal and the incorporeal, whereas catholics held the Creator to be of a nature that does not admit of mixture with that of his creatures except by miracle. It was easy enough for the Gnostic who subscribed to this confusion of matter and spirit to maintain that the fall and redemption of the divine image are eternally foreshadowed in the Godhead; it was easy again for Basilides to hold that our election to sonship recapitulates the descent and return of the Son of God in both the heavenly and the earthly plane, and for Valentinus to imagine that the whole cosmos owes not only its restoration but its origin to the passion of the Godhead. On the other hand, all these systems join with Paul and the Jesus of

[61] I have dealt more summarily with Marcion, since his influence on the church has been recognised since Harnack (1990), first published in German in 1924. For the view that he was the author of the term 'New Testament' see Kinzig (1994).

the Gospels in denying any value to the soul's contrivances for its own salvation; in Marcion's antithetical construction of this premise, the carnal law is dethroned and with it all the embarrassments of matter. The task of catholic teachers was to accommodate these sound readings of the New Testament to a scheme in which the world is the product of God's will and does not result from an accidental hypertrophy of his substance. We may say that they could have arrived at the same positions without a heretical interlocutor; but that would be almost to say that these positions follow inevitably from the witness of the apostles. If that is so, we must ask why, as we shall see in the following chapter, that catholics sometimes beat a path of their own which proved to be a cul-de-sac, and sometimes followed a 'Gnostic' path into territories that were later deemed to lie outside the domain of orthodoxy.

Chapter 2
The Catholicity of Irenaeus

We have seen in the previous chapter that the Gnostics (as we loosely term them) defined and developed a number of speculations which are now cardinal postulates of catholic thought. This chapter is concerned with the apologists and dogmaticians of the next generation, some of whom borrowed materials that the Gnostics had already hewn, while in others the determination not to make use of such materials shaped the contours of an original system. In neither case would it be enough to say that the Gnostics forced the orthodox to raise walls against them; we must grant them a hand in the masonry of those walls. At the same time, it is evident that the first Christian philosophies were not coterminous with those that followed and survived them, and my object, in the first section of this chapter, is to ascertain why, if there was a shared foundation, it was not the foundation of a united church.

The Errors of the Gnostics

Because the sects called Gnostic agree in denying the resurrection of the gross body, and the majority of them derive the material cosmos from a schism or aberration in the higher realm, it is commonly supposed that they vilified matter and identified the good with incorporeal. Because some are represented as libertines others as vegetarians and celibates, all are charged with a detestation of the body. Because the term 'Gnostic' is formed from the word for knowledge, it is assumed that they hoped to be saved by the solipsistic cultivation of this faculty, without material sacraments or physical association in ministry or worship. Gnosticism thus becomes a microcosm of heresy for the modern age, when preaching and theology are hostile to otherworldliness, fearful of singularity in morals and accustomed to identify the historical with the quotidian. In an age that excels all others in the writing of history, Christianity is acclaimed as a historical religion, which is taken to mean a religion of immanence rather than transcendence. The presence of 'Gnostic' features in catholic teaching is explained as a corollary of the same contingent factors which gave rise to the Gnostic flight from the world: the apathy and pessimism of the Greek philosophers were too strong to be resisted, or an era of plagues and warfare, aggravated by a sense of political deracination, begot a ubiquitous hatred of the world.[1]

---

[1] See Jonas (1963), 1–27. Historians today are apt to dwell on the resilience of the Empire, and the durability if ancient norms; see now Heather (2005), 110–19.

It is true that there is no Christian precursor of Valentinus, Basilides and the *Apocryphon of John* who asserts so garrulously that God can be spoken of only in negations. It is true that Biblical testimonies to the solitude, the ubiquity and the changelessness of the Father are not framed as paradoxes or embellished by metaphysical casuistry. By the end of the second century, however, catholic teaching on the nature of the Godhead was as floridly apophatic as that of any Gnostic, and catholics were the self-anointed prophets of divine ineffability. Having kidnapped an arsenal of privative terms from the Greek philosophers, they complained that pagans used them as temporal and contingent predicates, as though it were only for want of discipline that the mind remained ignorant of God.[2] Nor did any catholic tax the Gnostics with an exaggeration of divine transcendence, with an arbitrary widening of the gulf between the creator and his creatures. On the contrary, the Gnostics were accused of making a hybrid of spirit and matter, of subjecting God to the possibility and vicissitude of the lower realm. One early sect (whom Hippolytus labels Naassenes, or snake-folk, while confessing that their name for themselves was Gnostics[3]) substitute monism for theism, representing spirit and matter as the upper and lower branches formed by the parting of an original *askhêmosunê* or formlessness.[4] The soul, partaking of both spirit and matter, is apt to pass from one to the other in perpetual undulation, though the Gnostic (whose knowledge seems to lie in the divination of a common nucleus in diverse religious teachings) will be aware that repose and freedom await him only in the upper realm while in the lower his body will remain in thrall to the fiery demiurge Esaldaios. The Naassene sermon recorded by Hippolytus is built on a hymn to Attis, a Phrygian deity or hero whose death was commemorated in a pagan mystery.[5] The homilist holds that the content of this hymn is recapitulated in the Greek rites of Samothrace and Eleusis (5.7.33; 5.8.9–12), in the Egyptian myth of Osiris (5.7.23–6), and in the transmutation of Adam, whose name denotes a kind of rock, into Jesus Christ, the stone whom the builders rejected.[6] All these cultic figures are epiphanies of primal man, who is at once the redeemed and the redeemer, the true self and the saviour of the errant soul. If any Christian group in the ancient world proclaimed the humanity of God, it was the Naassenes: Hippolytus observes that they had so little notion of anything superior to the human that they worshipped none but Man and the Son of Man (5.6.4–5).

---

[2] See especially Origen, *Against Celsus* 7.42.

[3] *Ref.* 5.2, 5.6.3, exemplifying the law that 'Gnostic' in early Christian literature is always a self-designation, not a pejorative epithet.

[4] *Ref.* 5.7.18, oddly citing Romans 1.27, where *askhêmosunê* (formlessness) means sexual dissipation. On the fusion of moral and metaphysical categories in alchemy, see Jung (1967), esp. 145ff on the Naassenes.

[5] *Ref.* 5.7.13–15 and 5.9.7–9.

[6] *Ref.* 5.6.2–6, 5.7.3–5 and 5.8.1–4, citing Psalm 117.22 as at Matthew 21.42 and assimilating Adam to *adamas*, 'adamant'.

The phrase 'son of man' and its cognates are used of Jesus in the New Testament, most commonly on his own lips, and can be construed in many passages as a synonym for 'man' or as a circumlocution for the personal pronoun. In the Old Testament, a 'son of man' is always an individual human, and even the vindicated sufferer who is 'like a son of man' at Daniel 7.13 appears to be a representative either of humanity in general or of Israel as the remnant of humanity. There is some contestable evidence that a heavenly redeemer was awaited under this name in the time of Jesus, but not that this redeemer was divine or that he lacked the finite attributes of a person.[7] While the locution 'man and the son of man' in Gnostic documents follows a sequence which is exemplified in a number of scriptural passages,[8] there is no precedent for the use of either term to denote an object of devotion. Yet the Naassenes are not alone, for in a number of Gnostic texts, including the *Apocryphon*, the Demiurge who declares himself the sole god is at once confuted by Sophia's admonition 'Man exists and the Son of Man'.[9]

To a catholic it would seem that the capital error of the Gnostics is to deify the human, to conceal the ephemerality and finitude which are germane to our condition, and which teach us that we cannot be our own saviours. The Valentinians, according to Irenaeus, veer to the opposite pole by robbing God of the attributes which force us to confess our dependence on him, while assuring us that his saving purpose cannot be deflected or revoked. If God is to be God, he says, his will must be imperturbable, and hence immune to passions (*AH* 2.14.8; 2.28.6); his freedom from change and death imply that his attributes are inalienable and his substance uncompounded (2.13.3); since he is invisible, he can neither possess a body nor occupy space (2.13.6–7). In words that were supposed to be older than Plato, he declares that God is all mind, all spirit, all intellection[10] – in short, that whatever he is is identical with his essence and whatever is truly predicated of him is true eternally. Valentinus, by contrast, imagines a growth to plenitude by increments (2.13.2), and in a sequence which repeatedly makes the better a tributary of the worse. Sige or silence, the consort of the Father, is also represented in the Valentinian myth as his inchoate thought, his *ennoia* or *enthumêsis* (*AH* 2.13.1), and even if this term need not connote any interior motion, as Irenaeus alleges, it certainly implies that reason is not the first act of God. Had he been more of a Platonist, Irenaeus might have admitted the propriety of deriving Logos from Nous, as the latter term was used of the mind in its unfettered contemplation of the eternal, whereas Logos is the discursive action of minds that have still to escape the bounds of sense. On the other hand, his objection that Anthropos should precede Logos, since a man is the progenitor, not the offspring of his own word,

---

[7] The texts commonly adduced, as Borsch (1967), 132–53 concedes, are all likely to have been adulterated in the interests of the Church.

[8] Psalm 8.4–6; Mark 2.27–8; Hebrews 2.6–8.

[9] For an inventory of parallels see Borsch (1970), 38–75.

[10] *AH* 2.28.4; cf. Xenophanes, Fr. 24 DK, cited in Sextus Empiricus, *Against the Astrologers* 9.144 and Diogenes Laertius, *Lives of the Philosophers* 9.19.

would have been endorsed by the majority of philosophers and is ascribed by Irenaeus himself to another freethinking brotherhood, 'their progenitors, falsely styled Gnostics' (*AH* 2.13.10). The bishop makes satirical play with the adjective *endiathetos*, which may have been coined by his adversaries, but was already being employed in orthodox casuistry to distinguish the Word meditated from the Word uttered:[11]

> If they assert that the Word is *endiathetos* [immanent to the Father's being], Silence will be so also, and none the less she will be distinct from the *endiathetos logos*. That she is not in fact endiathetos is sufficiently revealed by this very term of theirs, ennoia [consideration]. Let them not say, therefore, that the first and primary Ogdoad is constituted by passion and Silence, but let them disown either Word or silence (Irenaeus, *AH* 2.12.5–6).[12]

The progenitive action of Sige or Silence, the consort of the Father, is here assumed to arise, like that of Wisdom, from a fault or perturbation. There is little warrant for this assumption, or for the stipulation that if both Silence and Word are immanent to the Godhead, they can not be distinct. A Valentinian sees no bar to the evolution of one term from another within the same immaterial habitat; but although Irenaeus simply ignores the premise of his opponents here, he argues elsewhere that they entail three blasphemies. Their system, he maintains, conceives the powers of God as accidents in a substrate, thus denying him the divine simplicity that logically pertains to him (*AH* 2.13.5); it is used of a latent property that is destined to emerge, whereas in God there is neither transience nor duration (2.13.3); it implies that there is that in God which might be outside him, and hence that there is a boundary to the infinite (2.13.5–6). According to the Valentinian narrative, what emerges is not merely an accretion to the Godhead, but the protoplasm of psychic and hylic substances below. It follows that the human soul and its captain in heaven are *homoousioi* or consubstantial, though this predicate was applied before the third century only to beings of the same corporeal species:[13]

> First they say that she (Sophia) formed from the psychic substance the Father and king of all, and the things *homoousios* with him – that is, the psychic entities – which they call the right-hand things, and also of those left-hand things, as they call them, which proceed from passion and matter (Irenaeus, *AH* 1.5.1; cf. 1.5.5, 1.56).

---

[11] For the complementarity of the *endiathetos logos* (immanent word) and the *prophorikos logos* (spoken word), see Theophilus, *To Autolycus* 10; Origen, *Against Celsus* 6.65, though Origen, here and elsewhere, applies this Stoic nomenclature only to human speech.

[12] According to Rousseau and Doutrelaeu (1982), 1, 393, Irenaeus himself will have spoken in Greek of an *endiathetos logos*, parent of the emitted logos, at *AH* 2.13.2, where the Latin speaks of a word abiding in the mind.

[13] For a collection of Valentinian references see Stead (1977), 190–202.

Here it may be noticed that, while matter itself is supposed to be an efflux from Sophia, the flesh that inhabits matter is not said to be consubstantial with the spirit. We have seen above, however, that in the epistle to Rheginus the elect are promised flesh of a different texture in the aeon, while both psychic and pneumatic flesh are acknowledged in Valentinian debate on the incarnation. Marcion is said to have considered matter and spirit to be immiscible, admitting only a spectral incarnation; not so Apelles, his putative disciple, who won evergreen notoriety by maintaining that the body of Christ existed before the nativity in heaven, as material spirit or spiritual matter.[14] The sect properly called docetic (from the Greek verb *dokeo*, 'I seem') held not that the flesh of Christ was a mirage but that he created it from the darkness at the limits of the universe (Hippolytus, *Ref.* 8.10). Thus a kind of solidity is accorded to mere privation, and the Docetae function (at least in heresiology) as the antitype to such figures as Apelles and Valentinus, who attach the properties of an extended substrate to the opposite pole of being.

By contrast, a strict dichotomy between the corporeal and incorporeal was observed in the episcopal tradition, which regarded all these sects as aberrations. While its representatives have seldom been of one mind as to the status of saints and angels, the premises that whatever is corporeal is created has been unanimously interpreted to mean that the visible cosmos and its denizens were created with a purpose, that they came unblemished from the hand of God, and that whatever ill befalls the body does not proceed from the mere fact of embodiment. The opponents of the catholic view, although they did not associate mere extension with defect or vice, regarded what in this world is called body as a sediment or concretion of the extended and passible subject which they called spirit in the aftermath of schism or perturbation. This theory implies a natural affinity between the Creator and the created body, though no bond of will or love. Evil thus arises from the same fault that engendered matter, not (as a Platonist might have argued[15]) from the seductive or entropic character of matter itself. The position that traces evil to the miscarriage of free will, which is now the orthodox one, acquits both matter and flesh without excluding either from the divine economy. Its partisans held that the body is neither good nor evil, neither a part of God nor an indigent copy of him, but the substrate of an existence that is distinct from God's yet destined to share his glory.

Between the New Testament and Irenaeus

Nevertheless, affinities between catholic and Gnostic thought before Irenaeus are not far to seek, if we mean by catholics those whose names are applauded in the episcopal tradition, and by Gnostics those who are generally ranged against them in our textbooks. Ignatius of Antioch is the earliest writer who professes to be a

---

14 See Tertullian, *On the Flesh of Christ* 1.3 and passim. Tertullian's aim is not to prove that Christ had flesh, but that his flesh and soul were two unmingled substances.

15 See Plotinus, *Enneads* 1.8 and 2.4 and for modern bibliography O'Brien (1996).

bishop, perhaps the first of that profession to be martyred. Resolved as he was to imitate Christ's obedience to the point of death, he held that there was no more pernicious error than to deny that the Saviour had come as man and undergone a bodily crucifixion (*Smyrnaeans* 4.2). Yet this same man who suffers to expiate the sins of the world (*Smyrnaeans* 2.1) is also extolled, in the letters of the same Ignatius, as the companion of the Father before the ages (*Magnesians* 5.1), God for us if not God himself,[16] whose birth from Mary required no human seed and whose death imparted the divine prerogative of immortality to his elect (*Ephesians* 7.1; *Trallians* 9.1). It is mere delusion, he urges, to trust a delusive Christ with our salvation. If the Judaism of the uncircumcised to which he alludes in certain letters is not a different heresy, it seems probable that his adversaries regarded Christ as one of those manlike surrogates or epiphanies of God that were commonly known, and sometimes venerated, as angels.[17] As we see from the mistakes of the first disciples, a Jewish Christology would be one that represented Christ as an angel or an incorporeal demon;[18] in an age of persecution, the adoption of this Christology, together (as Jerome says) with outward marks of Judaism such as the keeping of the Sabbath, would enable the timid Christian to reconcile his apostasy with his conscience.[19] By denouncing such evasions and affirming the real humanity of Christ, Ignatius proves that he is neither Jew nor Gnostic; yet there are elements in his teaching which, had the letters been composed or forged at any time after 150 A.D. would have savoured of heterodoxy to another bishop.

Irenaeus and others, for example, were later to speak of a rule of faith that taught the Church to read the Old Testament as the promise of the Gospel and the Gospel as the fulfilment of that promise. Ignatius, on the other hand, when he is asked for a demonstration of the gospel from the archives, retorts that he has no need of one, since 'Jesus Christ is the archives' (*Philadelphians* 8.2). Against the Judaizers he avers that the Israelite prophets lived according to the Lord's Day, not the Sabbath (*Magnesians* 9.1), but his claim is not supported or explained by any text. He goes so far as to say that the nativity, the virginity of Mary and the passion, though they are mysteries that 'cry aloud', were matured by God in silence so that the devil would not be aware of them (*Ephesians* 19.1); thus he sets aside the ancient testimonies to the Messianic role of Christ, and cannot maintain, as some apologists later did, that pagan rites resemble those of Christianity only because the demons tried to forestall what they were permitted to foresee. The Incarnation itself he conceives as an issuing of the Word from silence, evidently meaning that the Word became flesh to manifest what had hitherto been

16 Proem to *Romans*, proem to *Ephesians*, *Ephesians* 15.3; but at Smyrnaeans 1.1 he appears to be simply 'God'.

17 Marshall (2003).

18 Ignatius, *Smyrnaeans* 3.2; cf. Luke 24.39 with Mark 6.49 and Hebrews 1.5.

19 Edwards (1995); Jerome, *Commentary on Galatians* 3.6.12 at Edwards (1999), 96.

concealed.[20] Yet the same terms, as has often been remarked, could have been employed by a Valentinian in describing the proliferation of aeons from the silence is coupled with the Father; some editors find the affinity so disquieting that they insert a 'not' and juggle with chronology to turn the passage into a refutation of this conceit. Such expedients need not detain us if we assume that the Valentinians treated Ignatius as they treated Paul and John, translating cryptic but intelligible locutions into the deliquescent imagery of myth.[21]

It is true that such coincidences of imagery and language have been cited to show that the letters ascribed to Ignatius depend on 'Gnostic' sources, and hence cannot be authentic.[22] But why should it be more likely that a forger in the catholic interest borrowed from the Gnostics than they should evolve their own figures from the tropes that an eminent churchman had drawn from Paul? When the Apostle styles himself an *ektrôma* or abortion at 1Corinthians 15.8, he means that he was the last, belated witness of the Resurrection; in the Ignatian letter to the Romans the word *ektrôma* has become a generic symbol of humility; finally in the Valentinian system it is transferred to the aftermath of fallen Wisdom (Irenaeus, *Against Heresies* 1.1). We can trace a similar pattern for the verb *husterein*, which at Colossians 1.24 denotes what 'falls short' in Paul's afflictions. Ignatius holds that anyone falls short if he is found 'outside the altar', while in the Valentinian lexicon the noun *husterêma* signifies want of power and understanding in the alienated soul (Irenaeus, *Against Heresies* 1.2.4). In each case the progression is from a Pauline aphorism to an Ignatian metaphor, then to the Gnostic cipher: the logical sequence matches the order of composition.

Tatian is believed by Robert Grant to picked the purse of Valentinus; Hunt's reply that the Gnostics and the apologist worked on irreconcilable on irreconcilable premises will be valid so long as one adopts a parsimonious reading of both systems.[23] Tatian was Justin's pupil, and it is often surmised[24] that the Ptolemaeus whose martyrdom Justin commemorates in his *Second Apology* is the Valentinian of that time. A recent study suggests that the work that now goes by this title was not conceived as an integral text, but is the sediment left by the application of a catholic filter to a lost archetype, which propounded doctrines akin to those of Valentinus as ecumenical tenets of Christianity.[25] The *First Apology*, on this hypothesis, is the product of a studious contraction in Justin's sympathies; nevertheless, it upholds positions dangerously similar to those of groups whom

---

[20] *Magnesians* 8.3; Schoedel (1985), 120–22. On the interdependence of the texts that speak of silence in Ignatius see Chadwick (1950).

[21] Edwards (1998).

[22] See further Edwards (1998).

[23] Grant (1964); Hunt (1964), 22–50; see following chapter on Theodotus.

[24] See Parvis (2007), 32, citing most recently Lampe (2003), 239–40. But an author who held the views analysed by Markschies (2000) is unlikely to have been recognised by Justin as a co-reigionist.

[25] Parvis (2007).

the rule of faith excludes. Thus, although it proclaims the immutability of God and mocks the Greeks for worshipping deities who are born of other deities, it does not maintain that God is eternally one or eternally there, but asserts that the Son, having first existed as the latent thought of the Father, came forth as a discrete hypostasis only for the creation of the world. This savours of Valentinus, though not as strongly as the nomenclature of Theophilus of Antioch, a bishop contemporary with Irenaeus. Far from sharing the latter's aversion to the epithet *endiathetos*, Theophilus applies it to the Son in his latent phase before he issues from the Father with his wisdom (*To Autolycus* 2.10). In the usage of the Stoics these terms are not complementary but antithetical, as every sound produced by a larynx, including the inarticulate din of animals, falls under the locution *logos prophorikos*, while the *logos endiathetos* is the faculty of communing with oneself which is peculiar to humans. In adapting them to describe the evolution of a plurality from the primordial monad, Theophilus does not mean to concur with the Stoics in attributing passibility or materiality to the governing principle of the universe; at the same time, he does not feel bound, as Irenaeus did, to countermand the heretical notion of change in God by postulating an eternal Trinity.

The Shape of Irenaean Theology

The *Refutation of Knowledge Falsely* so Called by Irenaeus of Lyon, composed about 180 A.D. is the first surviving inventory of heresies, and perhaps the only one from the patristic age whose arguments against the rejected doctrines are not wholly devoid of intellectual or forensic merit. The outlines of the theology which he expounds as a vindication of the apostolic doctrine against its fraudulent expositors can be found in any textbook: he asserts that the word and spirit are coeternal with the Father, that the three constitute an incorporeal Godhead which produced the corporeal realm by an act of will, that the lower hypostases served the father as his two hands in the creation of humanity, and that God imparted his image to Adam but either withheld the likeness or denied him the secure possession of it in order that Adam and his posterity might learn through disobedience the merits of obedience. While he does not expressly describe the theft from the tree of knowledge as a fall, and even intimates that the plan of God could not have been accomplished until the knowledge of good and evil was vouchsafed to his creatures, he treats the eating of it as a transgression, commends God's edict of death as a means of saving Adam and his posterity from the pullulation of sin, and explains Christ's sacrifice as the consummation of an obedience which disarms the wiles of Satan and restores to humanity all that was lost in Adam. The death of Christ occasions the release of the Holy Spirit in power, and those who desire salvation are led by the Spirit to the eucharist, which, by making them participants in the body of Christ, not only delivers them from captivity but enables them to attain that likeness to God which was promised to Adam but exhibited for the first time in the Incarnation of the Word.

The defence of the 'rule of faith' (as he styles it) thus required Irenaeus to demonstrate:

a. the sovereignty of the triune God in the disposition of all things earthly and heavenly;
b. the integrity of the human composite which was framed in the image and likeness of God from body, soul and spirit;
c. the perfection of this image in Christ the incarnate Word, which enabled him to recapitulate all that was lost in Adam;
d. the manifestation of God's benevolence in the history of the patriarchs and the covenant with Israel; and
e. the reality of the death which Christ accepted on behalf of Adam's seed as the consummation of his obedience to the Father.

It is widely assumed that his teachings were antithetical to those of his opponents, who will therefore have argued:

a. that there is some principle of evil or dissipation in this world that did not originate in the Father;
b. that the image of God resides only in one portion of the human subject;
c. that the coming of Christ in the flesh, if it happened at all, does not redeem but abrogates the first creation;
d. that there is no preparation in history for the gospel and therefore no historical content to the knowledge that brings salvation; and
e. that as Christ came neither to fulfil the law nor to save the flesh, he did not undergo a bodily crucifixion, though he may have seen fit to feign one.

There is evidence that each of these tenets was held by one or more of the parties denounced by Irenaeus; at the same time, it can be shown that there were other parties, equally inimical to his rule of faith, who held positions that foreshadow his and are not expressly maintained in this era by representatives of his own tradition. It is only part of the truth to say that controversy forced him to enunciate a hitherto latent system; we must add that his system appears to derive its shape and tenor from those of his opponents, that he not only sets out to explain anew what they were the first to explain, but is indebted to them for some ingredients of his explanation. It is often the case in intellectual history that acrimony blooms between those who would otherwise have been allies: thus the frequency with which the name of Valentinus appears in the following study need occasion no surprise.

1. The paradigmatic forms of Gnostic thought would appear to be dualistic myths which represent the world as a cockpit of unlike and unequal forces, tracing the good in it to the higher god and the evil to some blind or jealous marplot. For Platonists, if not for Plato himself, the adverse principle is matter; the difficulty of

taming it is sometimes blamed on the working of a malignant soul,[26] more often on its amorphousness and promiscuous receptivity to change. In the earliest Gnostic systems also matter, though not endowed with an evil will, is opposed to spirit, either (as the Naassenes teach) by virtue of being the lower branch of a forking stream, or else (as in the *Apocryphon* and related texts) by acting as a mirror to the most susceptible element in the Godhead. The physical world, according to the *Apocryphon*, is a hybrid of flux in matter and perversity in the Godhead; the Naassenes appear to have regarded the alternation of the soul between spirit and matter as a blessing to the lower realm, though the soul cannot but feel her own descent as an affliction (Hippolytus, *Ref.* 5.8.22–30). Later than both is the Valentinian myth, in which there is no independent nursery of evil, as the matter which stands between the soul and knowledge is itself a precipitate from the tears of Wisdom. There is no evidence in this myth of a penumbra or void around the expanding Godhead, and *topos* or 'place' is among the appellations of the Demiurge, who is born as a result of Wisdom's fall.

The genesis of the aeons thus appears to precede the creation of space and matter. If none the less we are apt to imagine a kind of spatial intumescence (as Irenaeus does, mischievously likening the *plêrôma* to a swollen gourd), this is because in embodied beings imagination is the pupil of the senses. Valentinus anticipates the objection of Irenaeus, that since there is nothing outside God there would be no room for expansion; his strictures would have more weight, on the other hand, against the catholic apologists of the second century, all of whom attribute a period of latency to the Logos or second person until he issues from the Father as the instrument of the latter's desire to create. Justin carries back the history of the second person to his emergence from the Father before the ages (*Trypho* 83.4 amongst others), while his pupil Tatian speaks of his leaping forth from the Father's head in a metaphor that perhaps alludes to the eruption of Athene from the head of Zeus in a celebrated myth.[27] Athenagoras, urging that although Christ is the offspring of the Father he is not one of the things that come to be, explains that he was eternally in the Father's mind, but tacitly contrasts this inchoate twofoldness with the clear numerical difference that is entailed by his procession.[28] Theophilus borrows technical terms from the Stoics to express the same distinction, characterizing the word within as the *logos endiathetos* or immanent reason of God and the begotten word as his *logos prophorikos* or determinate utterance (*To Autolycus* 10). Half a generation after Irenaeus, Tertullian of Carthage, though asserting that the Father is never without his Son, divides his

---

26 See Plutarch, *Isis and Osiris* 369e and 372e, commenting on Plato, *Laws* 898b. On the turbulence of the receptacle in Plato's *Timaeus* see Plutarch, *On the Soul's Creation in the Timaeus* 1026ef and 1072a, with Festugière (1949), 114–52.

27 Tatian, *Oration to the Greeks* 5; cf. Harris (1923). Note here an early appearance of the term *hypostasis* in Christian teaching on the Logos and perhaps an implicit distinction between the *logos gennêtheis* (begotten) and matter which is *genêtê.*

28 *Embassy* 10, explicitly contrasting the *gennêtheis* with the *genêton*.

existence into the same two phases, representing *logos endiathetos* by ratio or 'reason' and *logos prophorikos* by *sermo* or 'speech' (*Against Praxeas* 5.3).

Tertullian and Irenaeus are often said to have been the first Christians to enunciate a doctrine of creation out of nothing,[29] since the biblical proposition that the world was made from things which are not does not exclude creation from unformed matter, and Genesis 1.2 can be read to imply that this was the first creation of God. Tatian and Theophilus appear to have drawn this inference,[30] while Justin, who gives no account of the origin of matter, may have understood this verse as an amplification of the words 'God created the heaven and the earth' in the previous one, with no other purpose than to explain that God used matter as a substrate.[31] If he assumed, with the Platonists, that matter requires no author, he posits something eternally outside God and is therefore vulnerable to the charge of having circumscribed the infinite. Marcion would have pleaded guilty to this imputation, for in his system matter is independent of the redeeming God, who acts upon it for the first time through the mission of his Son.

There is thus no single opinion among catholics or among their opponents whom we now call Gnostic: if Valentinus agrees with Irenaeus in one point in which they also agree against Justin – that is to say, if they both maintain that there was nothing outside the Godhead before the generation of matter – we can say that there are catholics and Gnostics on either side of a line bisecting both traditions. And in fact they agree in idiom more closely than they would have done had Irenaeus in fact said 'out of nothing'. His words at *AH* 4.1.20 are not *ex nihilo* but a *semetipso*, 'from himself', because his aim is not to enunciate a system of catholic doctrine but to refute his interlocutors by parody. As they affirmed that the stuff of the world was produced by a wandering satellite of the Godhead, he retorts that its true progenitor was the one Father of all that exists in earth or heaven. The antithesis would have been maimed had he added at this point that the Father produced by fiat and Sophia by an involuntary alienation of her own substance. On the one hand, then, he rejects the term homoousios, which was later to become the palladium of orthodoxy; on the other he can adopt a Valentinian locution which, if literally construed, would imply that God and his creation are of the same stuff.

The Son and the Spirit function in Irenaeus as the two hands of God when, as Genesis 2.7 relates, he kneaded the first man from the clay of Eden (*AH* 5.17.3 amongst others).[32] Baptism in the name of Father, Son and Holy Spirit

---

[29] May (1994), 164–78 awards the palm to Irenaeus alone, but does not find an attestation of the phrase 'out of nothing' either at *AH* 2.10.3 or at 4.20.1–2. For *ex nihilo* in Tertullian (who, in contrast to his Greek precursors, could not have elected to say 'from things that were not'), see *Against Hermogenes 1*.

[30] Tatian, *Oration* 5; Theophilius, *To Autolycus* 10.

[31] *First Apology* 10.2. Athenagoras, *Embassy* 19 implies that either God creates matter or they are coeval.

[32] At *AH* 2.2.5, citing Ephesians 4.6, the Father is above all, the Son the one through whom all was made, the Spirit the power within all. See Steenberg (2008), 66–84 on apparent inconsistency in the distribution of roles.

is enjoined at Matthew 28.19, and the three are joined in Paul's doxology at the end of 2Corinthians 13. Justin testifies that the church of his day honoured first the Father, then the Son with his angelic retinue, and in third place the 'prophetic Spirit' (*First Apology* 6.2); Athenagoras celebrates the Father, the Son and the Spirit in succession (*Embassy* 10); Theophilus is the first to adopt the word triad to denote the Trinity of three divine powers, though his names for them – God, Logos and Wisdom – are not attested elsewhere in the Greek tradition. Since all these authors held that the Son emerged from the Father only for the purpose of creation, it would seem that for them the Three supervene on the One; for Irenaeus, however, the premise that there can be no division or increment in God entails that if he had not been a triad from the beginning, he would never have become one, and hence that all three persons of the Trinity are eternal and eternally distinct. Neither an essential nor a supervenient threefoldness in God is maintained by any of the great heresiarchs in this period, but the Son and the Spirit appear in the Valentinian myth as firstfruits of the pleroma, who combine after Wisdom's fall to restore the form that has been defaced by her transgression and expulsion from the Godhead. The procession of these two emissaries from the Godhead thus gives rise to a triad consisting of the fullness of God, the Son and the Holy Spirit, a triad which, like that of many Christians in the age of Irenaeus, is not coeternal with the transcendent Father but antedates the creation of the present world.

In the Valentinian myth known to Irenaeus, the pullulation of aeons before the fall produces a fullness or *plêrôma* too multitudinous to be expressed as a Trinity of Father, Son and Spirit. There is, however, another Valentinian text, of uncertain date, in which the God assumes a threefold character at the outset which remains exempt thereafter from increment or perturbation. The Tripartite Tractate (as it is called, for want of any title in the manuscript) maintains that the only Father who deserves this appellation is the progenitor of the aeons, as his homonyms are invariably the offspring of other fathers. But the logic of this nomenclature entails that the ingenerate one will generate another, for there can be no father where there is no son:[33]

> He existed before anything other than himself came into being. The Father is a single one, like a number, for he is the first one and the one who is only himself. Yet he is not like a solitary individual. Otherwise how could he be a Father. For whenever there is a father, the name Son follows (NHC I 5, 51.8–16, p. 193 Robinson).

The tract goes on to proclaim the ineffability of the Father and to declare, in picturesque variant of the formula which Irenaeus borrowed from the Greeks, that he is 'his own mind, his own eye, his own mouth, his own form' (55.8–9, p. 199 Robinson). Next we hear that, just as there was none before the Father, so

[33] For edition and translation see H.W. Attridge and E. Pagels in Robinson (2000), 1, 158–337).

there was none who precedes the Son in the temporal order (57.15–19, pp. 201–3 Robinson); firstborn though he is, however, he has a sibling:

> Not only did the Son exist from the beginning, but the Church, too, existed from the beginning. Now he who thinks that the discovery that the Son is an only Son opposes the statement (about the Church) – because of the mysterious quality of the matter it is not so. For just as the Father is a unity and has revealed himself as Father for him alone, so too the Son was found to be a brother to himself alone, in virtue of the fact that he is unbegotten and without beginning (NHC I 5, 57.33–58.10).

Such orthodox paladins as Alexander of Alexandria and Tertullian also urged that if the Father is always Father there must always have been a Son;[34] both, as we shall see, were taxed with Valentinian sympathies by their opponents. It was an axiom for all parties after Nicaea that the Father alone is ingenerate, and the difficulty for catholics in the fourth century, as for the author of the Tractate, was to reconcile his primacy with the eternal coexistence of the three persons. The Tractate couples not the Spirit but the Church with the Firstborn; while there is no catholic doxology in which this substitution occurs, the two are overtly or tacitly equated in the work of catholic authors, and Paul himself avers that the saints are chosen before the foundation of the world (Ephesians 1.4). There can be no question of tracing the catholic doctrine of the Trinity to a Valentinian source, but if something so like it can be adumbrated in such a text – which goes on to extol the threefold glory of the transcendent sphere – it would seem that Gnostic and catholic thought were subject to analogous developments.[35]

2. The doctrine of the Godhead thus appears to have been subject to analogous developments in episcopal and Valentinian circles, and we need not suppose that either was the cause or explanation of the other. Regarding the creation of humanity in the likeness of God, on the other hand, Irenaeus adopts a position so unusual, so much at odds with that of any catholic writer for centuries after him, that it is difficult to account for it except as a by-product of his controversy with the Gnostics. In his fifth book *Against Heresies*, where he undertakes to show that the embodiment of the Word was the predestined consummation of his own handiwork, he maintains that it was the whole person of Adam, the body no less than the incorporeal elements soul and spirit, that was moulded by the Son and the Spirit in the Father's likeness.

The posterity of Adam since his expulsion from Eden, are said to consist of soul and body alone until, through incorporation into the visible body of the risen Christ on earth, they receive a new birth through the Holy Spirit who restores to them the third element that was forfeited by Adam, and perfects the likeness of

---

34 Tertullian, *Against Praxeas* 10; see *Against Hermogenes 1.*

35 Attridge and Pagels favour a dating of the *Tractate* to the third-century at Robinson (2000), 1, 178.

which he seems to have had but the promise or foretaste.[36] This passage implies that the image is retained by all, but elsewhere it is implied that neither the image nor the likeness could be communicated in full before the eating of the fruit and the manifestation of the Saviour (*AH* 4.38.4). It is not clear whether the body retains its portion of the likeness after the spirit is withdrawn,[37] but it is evidently the chief goal of Irenaeus, in the theodicy which he sketches in opposition to the Gnostics, to show that the end is prefigured in the beginning, that nothing has been imparted to the redeemed that abrogates or supersedes the design of the creator. This premise, of course, was endorsed by his successors in the catholic tradition, yet they were of one mind in holding that it was the inner man alone who participated in the image and likeness of God. If it was not enough to cite the philosophical platitude that God is incorporeal, so that nothing could be more foreign to his essence than the body, they could appeal to the testimony of scripture itself, which after describing the creation of all humanity in the image and likeness of God, tells a second story in which the first man and his consort are formed, in two discrete and unlike stages, from the clay of Eden.[38] There is no contravention of the general teaching on the incorporeality of God in Irenaeus, for he explains that it is not insofar as Christ is God but insofar as he condescends to a lower state that he wears a body which stands to ours as archetype to ectype (*AH* 5.16.2). This reasoning, however, shows no more than that the likeness *can* be exemplified in the body, not that it *must* be; we have still to ask why Irenaeus was almost the only catholic not to deduce from the Mosaic account that embodiment was an adjunct or appendix to the creation of humanity in the image and likeness of God.

Comparison of his arguments with those of his interlocutors suggests that he hoped to come at truth by steering as far as possible from error. The *Apocryphon of John* represents the body not only as a supervenient creation, but as a fruitless one, for this counterfeit of the heavenly man produced by the archons remains a moribund image of an image until it is secretly imbued with life by Wisdom. Rather than concede the inferiority of the second creation, Irenaeus subsumes the human body into the archetype, declaring that the inner and outer man were formed as one. At the same time, whereas his adversaries dub the face of Adam on to the Godhead in the very hour of creation, Irenaeus posits only a proleptic conformation of Adam's body to the image which was later to be exhibited in Christ the Word incarnate. Thus he inverts the anthropomorphic theology of the heretic, explaining the creation of Adam's body not as a fall from divine perfection but as an earnest of perfection yet to come.

---

36 See *AH* 5.6.1, with 16.1 and 3.18.1.

37 Behr (2000), 94–121 distinguishes the spirit vouchsafed at creation, which survives the fall, from the vivifying spirit that Christ imparts to his elect. Orbe (1969), 131 distinguishes the assimilating Spirit of God, the assimilated body and the organ of assimilation.

38 See for example Origen, Homilies on Genesis 1.13, Dialogue with Heraclides 15–16, Commentary on Romans 7.4, with Jacobsen (2008).

Yet this is not all: there is more in common between him and the Gnostics than the symmetry of opposites. For them as for him, the body is the portal of salvation, for had not the archons forged this shroud of clay for the image of God, there would have been no conduit for the breath of Wisdom, and hence (so far as our narrative goes) no means of rescuing the inmates of the lower realm from ignorance and subjection. In this tradition, not only the first enlightenment but the subsequent deliverance of humanity were frequently attributed to subterfuge: the birth of the Saviour results in Gnostic texts from the impregnation of a surrogate of Wisdom by the archons whom she dupes into coupling with her, while in Valentinian literature a paradoxical shift of roles enables Wisdom to father a son on the Demiurge by stealth. Catholic exponents of the virgin birth proceed with more decorum, but it was a truism for Paul and for his admirer Ignatius of Antioch that Christ assumed his carnal guise to elude the powers of darkness,[39] while orthodox writers from Origen to Augustine proclaim that since the fall the knowledge of God has reached the soul only through media that are palpable to the senses. Both catholic and heretic – again we are using modern terms – see the body as an organ of divine intrigue, though the one relates as a fact of recent history what the other depicts in myth as a concomitant to the creation of the first man.

3. It was an evergreen complaint that those who denied the incarnation and the real suffering of Christ not only made liars of his evangelists but stole the hope of an afterlife from the martyrs who died invoking his afflictions. This protreptic reasoning gives way in Irenaeus to a rich and seminal theodicy: only by the assumption of full humanity, he argues, was it possible for the Word to expiate the disobedience of Adam and restore the physiognomy of God to his descendants. To this end it was necessary for him to pass through every age from infancy to maturity; it was necessary again that he should bear the pains of grief, fatigue and hunger at the pleasure of the same enemy who seduced Adam and oppresses his posterity; it was necessary at last, as the consummation of his obedience, to embrace the death that other humans suffer as the penalty of sin (*AH* 2.22.3–4, 3.20.3 amongst others). Of these three tenets, the second and third are vigorously upheld by every catholic writer after him. The first remains peculiar to him, and neither catholic nor heretic in the ancient world embraces his corollary that, in order to recapitulate every stage of a normal life, Christ died a little before his fiftieth year and not, as Luke implies, soon after his thirtieth. Against the Valentinians, for whom the thirty years of his life on earth signify (or are signified by) the procession of thirty aeons in the *pleroma*, Irenaeus cites the admonition 'Thou art not yet fifty years old' from John 8.57, and argues that his detractors would have made capital of his being younger than forty if they could (*AH* 2.22.5–6). The conjecture that he was closer to fifty than forty (maybe forty-six years old, the age of the temple) has impressed a number of modern commentators in the Gospel,[40] but Irenaeus adopts it only to confute the Valentinians. This, then, is another instance of his making it a

---

[39] 1Corinthians 2.9; Ignatius, *Ephesians* 19.

[40] Notably Kokkinos (1989).

condition of good theology that it should be antipodal to bad theology; at the same time, it can be argued, in this instance as in others, that the conclusion requires assent to premises that were never catholic, but characteristic of schools that he considers heterodox.

The blasphemy that Irenaeus has tempered here is attributed in his work to a more obscure sect than the Valentinians, not attested in independent sources. The Carpocratian teaching, as he reports it, is a seminary of errors all to itself: no other heresy of his acquaintance tolerates either a female clergy or the veneration of images (*AH* 1.25.6), but that is no doubt because no other heresy maintains as a cardinal doctrine that the way to salvation opened to us by Christ consists in flouting every ordinance of the written law and tasting every variety of sin (1.25.4). Yet it is not so hard to believe that such a philosophy could be held if we regard it as another form of the doctrine of recapitulation, in which sin is identified not with the breach of the law but with the vain attempt to observe a law that can never be satisfied in the flesh. Paul's famous account of the origin of covetousness in Romans 7.8 can be construed with little violence to mean that the Law is the cause of sin and not its antidote; the collateral belief that Christ had saved the world by the boldness of his trespasses can be derived from a literal reading of 2Corinthians 5.21, where 'he who knew no sin' is 'made sin for us', or of Galatians 3.13, where Christ is said to have incurred the malediction pronounced by Moses on 'him that hangeth on a tree'.

In a romance entitled the *Acts of Peter* which is agreed to exhibit traits that would now be termed Gnostic, Jesus assumes the aspect both of a boy and of an apostle, and it may not be out of place to observe that similar metamorphoses are ascribed to Eros or Eros in the pagan novel Daphnis and Chloe.[41] Plato declares that Eros is at once the eldest and the youngest of all things (*Symposium* 178c; 194e–196a), while the religious verse that passes under the name of Orpheus gives this appellative, along with Protogenes or 'first-begotten', to an androgynous demiurge. Ignatius of Antioch can say of Christ, 'my *eros* is crucified' (*Romans* 7), while a Gnostic or Gnosticizing text, the *Origin of the World*, describes the creation of a hermaphroditic Eros who receives his soul from one of the lower avatars of Wisdom and whose blood is then dispersed throughout the cosmos to purify its Stygian passions.[42] It may have been the equation of Christ with love that made it possible to endow him with this polymorphic character, and that Irenaeus saw, in his being all things to all, a soteriological function that is obscured by the more superficial application of this conceit in works that he, like the modern church, considered heterodox.

It may be said that allotropy of this kind can be attributed only to a mythical Christ or to one whose body is a phantom. But that is untrue, since none of the

---

[41] *Acts of Peter* 17 and 21–22, in Elliott (1993), 411–15; [Longus], *Daphnis and Chloe* 2.3–5.

[42] *Origin of the World* 109.1–110.1, pp. 53–5 in Robinson (2000), vol. 2, trans. H.G. Bethge.

writings cited in the last paragraph denies a real body to Christ or to the primal man whose foreshadows him. Nor can it the body allotted to Christ in Valentinian systems be judged unreal, for there would not then have been a schism between the eastern and the western Valentinians as to whether the flesh of Christ was psychic or pneumatic.[43] Although it was the custom of catholic authors to insinuate that a pneumatic body is much the same thing as no body at all, the term originates in the letters of Paul to Corinth where the psychic body is plainly our present domicile in the flesh (1Corinthians 15.44) and the pneumatic or spiritual body a 'house not made with hands' (2Corinthians 5.1) resembling the glorified form of Christ (1Corinthians 15.45ff; cf. Philippians 3.21).[44] According to a tradition relayed by Clement, the Valentinians supposed the flesh of the risen Christ to be penetrable to the hand, but that is to say that its matter was subtle, not that it was illusory. If there is any text in which the Valentinians speak for themselves, it is in the *Tripartite Tractate*, which reveals that more than a specious condescension to the human state was required for our salvation:

> He it is who was our Saviour in willing compassion, who is that which they were. For it was for their sake that he became manifest in an involuntary suffering. They became flesh and soul – that is, eternally – which things hold them and with corruptible flesh they die. And as for those who came into being, the invisible one taught them invisibly about himself. Not only did he take upon himself the death of those whom he thought to save, but he also accepted their smallness to which they had descended when they were born in body and soul. He did so because he had let himself be conceived and born as an infant in body and soul (NHC I 5, 114.31–115.10, pp. 299–301 Robinson, deleting critical apparatus).

Mingled with the descent of the soul, which Irenaeus could not affirm, is a skeletal doctrine of recapitulation and an echo of his belief that to be compounded of body and soul alone is to be dead in spirit. It is through the Saviour;s assumption of a body that the elect 'become exalted in the emanation according to the flesh' (115.37); another Valentinian text, the Treatise on the Resurrection sometimes called the Epistle to Rheginus, premises not the dissolution of the flesh but its sublimation:

> So, never doubt concerning the resurrection, my son Rheginus. For if you were not existing in flesh, you received flesh when you entered this world. Why will you not receive flesh when you entered into the aeon? (NHC I 4, 47.1–9, p. 153 Robinson, vol. 1, trans. M.L. Peel).

---

43 Hippolytus, *Ref.* 5. 35.5–7, though his testimony is judged to be baseless by Jacobsen (2008).

44 The spiritual body and the church are more distinct than Robinson (1952) allows, since Paul does not say that the first exists before or the second after the consummation.

To speak of a resurrection in the flesh is to contradict Paul, though not perhaps the prevailing view among catholics in the second century.[45] It is equally heretical to endow Christ with a pneumatic body before the resurrection, if we mean by this a body of subtler texture than ours, but this is not the heresy that the ancients knew as 'docetism'. As the Gnostics were at one with Irenaeus in maintaining that the outer man bears the image of his divine prototype, so the Valentinians agree with him in holding that the Word put on flesh in order that the flesh might be redeemed with the inner man.

4. Apostles and defenders of the Christian faith proclaim that it is founded on events, that the salvation which it promises is the flowering of a historical process, not an emancipation or flight from history. On inspection, the events that announce or impart salvation prove to be of a kind that seldom detains the modern historian, and it is therefore common to use the term 'myth' to indicate that they harbour truths of such high moral or pedagogic value that any question of historicity would be a cavil. If there were any Christians in antiquity who employed the term 'myth' in this sense, they were those whom we now call Gnostics; it is Irenaeus, however, who is regularly extolled as the first expositor of 'salvation history'. His landmarks – the fall, the flood, the incarnation – are those that punctuate the narratives of his latter-day admirers, though for him they are simply more salient, and not more providential or less historical, than the tribulations of Israel or the miracles of Christ. But they are landmarks also for the Valentinians and the *Apocryphon of John*, and, whatever else may be symbolic or fictitious in the latter text, it seems to espouse the historicity of these episodes as strongly as any work in the catholic tradition. It assumes that the Moses who wrote the book of Genesis received the Law from the Demiurge, that the latter shaped a garden for Adam and Eve but forbade to taste the fruit of knowledge, that when they broke this command he drove them from the garden, and that when their descendants moved him to wrath again, he released a flood upon the world. Much that he asserts as fact they too assert, but what he depicts as masterful benevolence they construe as tyranny.

In one respect these historians agree with Irenaeus against the catholic norm: he and they are equally loth to allow that a just creator would wish his creatures to remain perpetually ignorant of good and evil. Gnostics protest that the Demiurge withheld the fruit of knowledge, and that God would not have done so; Irenaeus answers that, since God would not have done so, it cannot have been the purpose of the Demiurge to withhold it. If it was forbidden to Adam and Eve, the reason must be that preparation was required before the knowledge of good and evil could be a means to God's perfection of his image and likeness in humanity:[46]

---

[45] See Pagels (1979), Chapter 2.

[46] Thus at *Against Heresies* 4.38.3, it appears that the acquisition of this knowledge was the penultimate stage in a process which was to end with the consummation in humanity of the image and likeness of God.

> It was necessary that the human being [or humanity] should first come to be, and having come to be should grow, and having grown should be fortified[47] and having been fortified should be multiplied, and having been multiplied should grow in strength (*eniskhusai, convalescere*), and having grown in strength should be glorified and having been glorified should see its own Lord (4.38.2).

That *convalescere* means 'grow strong' can be proved by reference to a surviving excerpt from the Greek. It is unfortunate that the best-known English version should translate it, in the teeth of ancient usage, as 'recover', thereby intimating (as the translator adds in a parenthesis) that humans were predestined to contract 'the disease of sin'.[48] If that were the sense, the sin would have to consist in something other than the eating of the fruit, as the outcome of this – our being able to distinguish good and evil – is the immediate prelude to the consummation of God's design. Nevertheless, it is evident from what follows that for Irenaeus we come at perfection only by the discovery of our imperfection – that is to say, we learn what it is to be righteous by the *experimentum mali*, a more than notional apprehension of our freedom to violate the divine command.

Thus Irenaeus teaches that we cannot be delivered from sin except by sinning – a tenet that brings him closer to Carpocrates than to any writer of the catholic fold. There are other Greeks – Theophilus, Clement and Origen, for example[49] – who assert that something remained to be accomplished after the first creation, but none of them suggests that Adam's crime was ineluctable. To Irenaeus himself it is barely a crime, as it is no more than the unseasonable performance of an act that, at a later stage, could not have been left undone if the education of the race was to be completed. His strongest term of reprobation, therefore, is *parekbasis*, which signifies a mere divagation or trespass; within a century of his death, however, it had become the custom, even in the eastern world, for catholics to describe the impetuosity of Adam as a fall.

5. Irenaeus believes that the incarnation of the divine Word was ordained from the beginning, as a disclosure of the perfect image and likeness of the Father to the maturing human race. In the wake of Adam's trespass, it became also a work of mercy, though it seems that no two interpreters of Irenaeus ascribe the same theory of the atonement to him. All agree that the Word in his earthly ministry is a vessel of edification, in accordance with the original plan of God, and that, by virtue of his capacity to subsume or recapitulate the whole progeny of Adam, his obedience is in some degree redemptive; but what further good was effected by his suffering on the Cross? Hastings Rashdall[50] makes him a pioneer of the ransom

---

[47] The Greek *andrôthenta* means literally 'made male', perhaps an allusion to Ephesians 4.9, if not another instance of the 'Gnostic' residue in Irenaeus.

[48] This rendering, from volume 1 of the Ante-Nicene Library version (regularly reprinted now by Hendiksen) has been canonised for English-speaking readers by Hick (1968), 219.

[49] See Tennant (1968), 275–306 and materials examined in the next chapter.

[50] Rashdall (1919), 243–4, citing *AH* 5.1.1; cf. 279, citing 5.2.1 and 280, citing 5.21.3.

theory, according to which his blood is the price that God paid to the devil for our release; but the text advanced to show this, from *Against Heresies* 5.1.1, does not refer to the devil by name, and argues only that it is was fitting for God to overcome 'apostasy' by suasion rather than by a reciprocation of the force and guile that had been employed by his enemy. While the devil is styled the 'apostate' elsewhere in the work, it is also said, without ambiguity, that the outcome of Christ's struggle with him is the subjugation of force by force, the reduction of the captor to captivity (*AH* 5.21.3). It therefore appears more probable that apostasy here is not the jailer himself but the inward spirit of collusion which must be exorcised by cajolery, even after the jailer is vanquished, if the prisoner is to walk free.

Gustave Aulen,[51] writing in opposition to Rashdall, justly observes that deliverance is achieved not by suborning the adversary but by worsting him in the open; but when he maintains that the battle is won on the cross, his eye has shifted to a Pauline text, Colossians 2.14, which is never adduced by Irenaeus. For Irenaeus himself the wilderness is the scene of victory (*AH* 5.21), and when he speaks of the Cross in another place (*AH* 5.16.1), he commends it only as the summit of obedience, with a corroborative citation of Philippians 2.8 (*AH* 5.16.1). If anything is transacted there that was hitherto wanting in the work of Christ, it was the 'propitiation' of the insulted Father, for this is the term that we find in the Latin text of the paragraph which immediately succeeds the quotation of the Philippian hymn. Yet the biblical text that Irenaeus is glossing here (1 Timothy 2.5) salutes Christ as the mediator of God and men with no explicit mention of the Cross, and in the absence of the Greek or of any supporting reference to the crucifixion, we must be careful not to hear more than is said.

Even the heretics, Irenaeus declares, admit that the Lord was crucified (*Against Heresies* 5.18.1), but even they must see the absurdity of supposing that the paltry fruit of ignorance and defect could have been his scaffold. The Word who contains all things did not cease to fill his own handiwork when he was crucified, and the Cross itself, although it was a thing of wood set up in a particular locality, can also be said, by virtue of its burden to have spanned the entire creation (*Apostolic Demonstration* 34). Antecedents to this conceit can be found in Paul and Justin,[52] but none so striking as the Valentinian conception of the Cross as the *horos* or boundary between the soul's peregrinations in the lower world and its homecoming to the plenitude of the Godhead.[53] It can be said indeed that his heretical interlocutors[54] made more of the Cross than he did. We have seen in the previous chapter that the Cross first enters Valentinian myth as a *horos* or boundary to protect the remaining aeons against the turbulent aftermath of Wisdom's fall. We have seen that it may provide the unseen scaffolding from which all things depend

[51] Aulen (1951), 33–52.

[52] Ephesians 3.18; *1Apology* 60. See previous chapter.

[53] See Tiessen (1993), 146–52.

[54] He seems to be alluding to the *Gospel of Truth* when he urges that the Cross in Valentian thought is the fruit of defect and error.

in a Valentinian hymn, and that, according to the *Gospel of Truth*, the Saviour became the firstfruits of the *plêrôma* when he suffered crucifixion in this world. It is pertinent to add here that, because the events of his ministry are otherwise adumbrated only in ciphers and abstractions, this Gospel accords a prominence to the Cross that it does not enjoy in the works of Irenaeus, who dwells at greater length on the miracles and the temptation in the wilderness. In the *Gospel of Truth* the crucifixion is not only the summit, but almost the whole of the ministry:[55]

> Just as there lies hidden in a will, before it is opened, the fortune of the deceased master of the house, so it is with the totality, which lay hidden while the Father of the totality was invisible, being something which is from him, from whom every space comes forth. For this reason Jesus appeared; he put on that book; he was nailed to a tree; he published the edict of the Father on the Cross. O such great teaching! He draws himself down to death though eternal life encloses him (NHC I 2, 20.16–29, pp. 87–9 Robinson).

The heavenly Cross, or Stauros, is a boundary between the material and the immaterial; the *Tripartite Tractate* explains the descent of the Saviour as a division of his own person into Word and Son (that is, into a divine and a human element), in order that his passion may force humanity to the right or the left, the elect on the right hand constituting the image and those on the left the mere likeness (98.12–26, p. 271 Robinson). Although Paul used the term 'likeness' to mean a counterfeit at Romans 1.23, this is plainly not the sense intended at Genesis 1.28, and the catholic tradition could not accommodate this nomenclature. But if (to use Newman's term) it is a 'note' of catholicism to grant the Cross a peculiar efficacy in restoring sinners to God, it would appear that the Valentinians possessed this note at a time when it was not so characteristic of the episcopal church for which Irenaeus constructed his theodicy.

Who is a Catholic?

Of course it is Irenaeus, as the one bishop in the fray and the defender of the fourfold gospel canon, who wins the suffrage of every churchman from antiquity to the present; but in their own time Valentinus and the Gnostics passed as Christians, or it would not have seemed necessary to unmask them; the Nag Hammadi codices, together (as we shall see below) with the fragments of Theodotus and Heracleon, reveal that their theologies were not always couched in narrative; and even their myths resemble those of the Platonists, which were always understood to be cryptographic representations of ideas that admitted of rational defence . It is thus not illegitimate to ask whether the creed of such a group, considered under the five heads that we set out above when examining the catholicity of Irenaeus, would be

[55] There seem to be allusions here to Hebrews 9.15–17 and Colossians 2.13–14.

more or less orthodox than his – or to put the question accurately, whether theirs or his approximates more closely to the creed professed by later exponents of the catholic norm before the fall of the western empire.

1. In ridiculing the Valentinian notion that divinity can expand, evolve or engender a new divine subject Irenaeus disowns that concept of the Word as an emanation from the Father which is commonly advanced by apologists in the catholic interest up to the Council of Nicaea. Whatever the Christian doctrine of God may be in certain quarters nowadays, it is this mouthpiece of the episcopate, and not its Gnostic rivals, who regards the impassibility of God as an indefeasible premise of the catholic faith.
2. Against the Gnostic teaching that the human form is an effigy of a luminous silhouette in the heavens, Irenaeus contends that body, soul and spirit were framed as one in the image and likeness of God. The vehemence of his opposition to heresy has thus led him to conclusions which found no other champion in the patristic era.
3. In order that Christ's ministry may comprehend a diversity of human types, Irenaeus has him live almost to his fiftieth year, but eschews any speculation that makes him subject to metamorphosis or capable of sin. The greater part of Christendom, including the Valentinians, disagrees with him in assigning a little over thirty years to the life of Christ in accordance with the testimony of Luke.
4. The Gnostics and Irenaeus address the same nodal points in history, though one is apt to read black where the other reads white. Irenaeus concedes to his opponents that humanity could not have escaped its childhood but for the knowledge of good and evil; he differs in maintaining that the interdict on the plucking of the fruit was provisional and imposed by God, whereas his adversaries ascribed it to an envious subaltern.
5. The crucifixion occupies a terminal, but not a climactic position in the ministry of the Saviour as Irenaeus conceives it; in Valentinian literature the passion is almost coextensive with the ministry.

Irenaeus would think it an infringement of the rule of faith to postulate emanation within the Godhead, to identify the image of God with the inner man alone or to suppose that our parents in Eden came so perfect from the hand of the Creator that no profitable increment to their knowledge was conceivable, and no incarnation would have been necessary but for their sin. For churchmen of the third century, none the less, the first two tenets are phylacteries of the catholic faith, and if the third was never universally held, it would have appeared more orthodox to most than any theory which implies that God did not mean to prevent what he explicitly forbade. Thus the work of Irenaeus serves as a matrix for later catholic systems only when it is fused with elements that he considered foreign or repugnant to the teaching handed down by the apostles.

Chapter 3
The Foundations of Catholic Teaching in the Third Century

Christian texts of the second century perished, except for those that were addressed to Jews or polytheists of the ambient society. Irenaeus himself would not have been spared but for a translation into Latin. The first speculative writer whose works survive in any quantity is Clement of Alexandria, who seems to have reached his acme as a teacher at the end of the second century after quitting Athens for Egypt in his boyhood.[1] Even of his voluminous works a mere three survive entire: the *Protrepticus* is an exposure of pagan superstition, the *Paedagogus*, or Governor, a manual of conduct and the *Stromateis* a miscellany of excerpts from Greek poets and philosophers to illustrate both the truth and the antiquity of the Christian revelation. The last work being by far the longest and the least imitable of the surviving there, we are apt to think of Clement as a philosopher; we might have a different notion of him, for all that, if we still possessed such works as his *Hypotyposes*, an summary of doctrine from the New Testament,[2] or the Canon in which he harmonized the teachings of the New Testament with the ordinances and prophecies of the Old (Eusebius, *Church History* 6.13.3). Even in his *Stromateis*, it is obvious that Clement is no satellite of the schools, as he contends that all philosophers are plagiarists, and that only the scriptures furnish us with the axioms of faith, on which true knowledge of God is founded.[3] Where common sense, morality or the weakness of the flesh preclude a literal application of the scriptures, he will interpret them symbolically according to methods authorized by the most pious of the philosophers, he does not, however, take up a theological position from any Greek source which fails to confirm or elucidate the truths communicated in the scriptures.[4] His thought on secular matters he admits to be an 'eclectic' blend of

---

1 *Stromateis* 11.1; on his death c. 212 see the letters preserved in Eusebius, *Church History* 6.11.6 and 6.14.9. On what is known of his biography see Osborn (2005).

2 See the edition of the fragments by Stählin and Früchtel (1970), with Duckworth and Osborn (1985). Eusebius, *Church History* 6.14 reports that the work consisted of exposition of every book in the New Testament canon, 'including those that are controverted'. At 6.13.2 he indicates that this work, like the Stormateis, was divided into eight books.

3 *Stromateis* 5.26.1 on gnosis as the perfection of faith, with Osborn (1994). Torrance (1995), 155 cites *Prophetic Excerpts* 28.3: 'there is no faith without catechesis, no comprehension without gnosis'.

4 On the primacy of the Word in Clement see Torrance (1995), 152. De Lubac (1949), 171–5, examines the theory that Clement pursues a fourfold exegesis – literal, symbolic, moral, prophetic.

the best that is taught by doctors in the practical and liberal arts,[5] but even to Plato he cannot grant that direct inspiration which he accords to certain prophets of the Greek world.[6] The philosopher is at best the refractory servant of an unacknowledged master; he cannot be a master in his own right.

Omnivorous as Clement is, he seldom returns empty-handed from an encounter with those whom he regards as heretics. Where he finds licensed turpitude, as in the case of the Basilideans, he does not temper his condemnation;[7] Valentinian tenets, on the other hand, he cites frequently and not always with reproof. He can entertain reports that the body of Christ, though not phantasmal, was immune to hunger and pentrable to the hand, while his *Excerpts from Theodotus*, which tell us almost all that we know of this Valentinian of the 'eastern school' are punctuated only by occasional strictures. To Clement 'we' are the catholic or Episcopal church, and Theodotus is of another persuasion; yet comparison of the *Excerpts* with the *Stromateis* suggests that he may have learned more from Theodotus than he was able to see or willing to confess.

I shall argue here that Origen, Clement's younger contemporary if not his pupil, was another beneficiary of this local influence. I shall go on to contrast them with men of a different stamp, Tertullian and Hippolytus, who applied the winnowing-fan to the heretic rather than the heresy. Both tried to secure the boundary between the rule of faith and aberrant teaching by upholding or rejecting certain formularies; posterity was to find, however, that words are too protean and too easily suborned to serve as guardians of doctrine. No adamantine shibboleths were devised to mark the line between orthodoxy and heresy in Alexandria, though this need not imply, as many assert, that the line was vaguer or more vulnerable to trespass. The frontier between Scotland and England is not vague because it now appears only on maps and nowhere coincides with the fixed opacity of Hadrian's Wall.

Theodotus

Theodotus was a contemporary of Clement, whose birth is dated to about 160 A.D.[8] Thus he belonged to the first or second generation of Valentinian teachers,

---

5 *Stromateis* 1.37.6. Edwards (2002), 20 argues that the 'eclectic' is not an amalgam of teachings peculiar to the different schools, but a consensus of teachings on ethics and the sciences.

6 See *Stromateis* 6.42.3 on the Sibyl and Hystaspes, the same prophets whom Justin names at 1Apology 44.12 as recipients of direct inspiration. All the works attributed to them are now agreed to be Jewish or Christian forgeries.

7 See especially *Stromateis* 3. Nautin (1974) treats the Alexandrian testimonies to the teaching of Basilides with assiduous scepticism; his position is tempered by Löhr (1996) 138–51.

8 Clement is perhaps our only witness to his teaching. Edwards (2000) suggests that he may be the same man as Theodotus of Byzantium whom Hippolytus denounces at

and the rudiments the system are discernible in the Excerpts, though it is also clear at times that he is not adduced by Clement as a typical representative of the school. Crude notions of a dichotomy between flesh and spirit in Valentinian doctrine are dispelled by the first of the excerpts, where, in commenting on the ejaculation 'Father, into thy hands I commend my spirit', Theodotus declares that the 'pneumatic seed' which the Saviour returns to the Father on the Cross is the fleshy integument, the *sarkion*, with which Wisdom apparelled him for his descent. The flesh that he relinquished at his death was not an individual carapace but the whole body of the elect – the masculine seed, or angelic emanation, which the Word implants in the sleeping soul to unite the two creatures of Wisdom, soul and flesh, which have hitherto retained their particularity. The Gnostic is therefore not the one who escapes his corporal tenement, but the one in whom the outer and inner man are no longer at war. The achievement of this harmony is gnosis or knowledge, according to *Excerpt* 78, the transformation of the unformed progeny of the female into a man, that one may become the 'son of the bridegroom' (*Excerpts* 68 and 79). Although these sayings imply that the works of Wisdom are imperfect without the infusion of masculine power, we learn in *Excerpt* 53 that she herself is the one who projects the pneumatic seed into the 'osseous' soul, here characterized as the heavenly seat of intellection. *Excerpt* 62 implies that 'osseous' is a figurative epithet for the soul encased in flesh, and at this point we revert to Christ's words 'into thy hands I commend my spirit', only to be told that it was the labouring soul that yielded herself to the Father, while the spirit, pent in its osseous frame, was not released but brought release to others.

Wisdom is thus represented there both as the redeemer and as the one to be redeemed; it is now the pneumatic, now the psychic element of Christ that is restored to the Father in death. The apparent contradictions could be mitigated at least, if not resolved, by the supposition that Theodotus is not the only speaker in the excerpts, for on a number his opinions (or those of another teacher) are juxtaposed with those of the Valentinians,[9] and we are never informed that he and they maintained the same philosophy. More probably (since we can hardly doubt that all the opinions broached in the excerpts proceed from Valentinian circles) the discrepancies arise from the practice of tempering the same doctrine to different levels of understanding, in accordance with the example of the Saviour himself, who taught his apostles 'the first things in types and mysteries, the second in parables and enigmas, the third in private without dissimulation' (*Excerpt* 66).

Just as he entertains no strict antithesis between flesh and spirit, so Theodotus cannot posit a Demiurge who is simply depraved or at odds with the incorporeal. As he explains, the latter term is often used of beings who are neither strictly bodiless nor encumbered by a gross vehicle; the Demiurge, who belongs to this class, inhabits the psychic realm which is at once a bridge and a barrier between the Godhead and the lower cosmos. In a number of *Excerpts* (34, 35, 38, 39) he

---

Refutation 7.35.1–36.1.

[9] For the Valentinians see *Excerpts* 2.1, 6.1, 16.1, 17.1, 21.1, 23.1, 24.1.25.1, 28.1.

is all but identical with place, or Topos, an appellative of the true creator in Philo of Alexandria. In the Timaeus of Plato a term of similar import, *khôra* or space, denotes the undulating manifold from which the Demiurge creates the visible cosmos, using soul as his instrument of governance and formation. To make the artificer himself a psychic being, as Theodotus does, is of course to degrade him; at the same time, it can be said that Theodotus ennobles space, for in contrast to Plato he distinguishes it from the substrate in which Place or the Demiurge shapes the astral bodies to act as bailiffs of Heimarmene or Fate. While no region is devoid of soul, the soul that animates the denizens of this region is 'choic' or earthy and doomed to perish. That there is in each of us such a principle, consubstantial with the souls of beasts, is indicated by the creation of man from earth in Genesis 2.3 (*Excerpt* 50), but the infusion of divine breath into Adam's nostrils at 2.7 represents the gift of a higher soul, consubstantial with the Demiurge. Although his administration is marred by *apotomia*, or undue severity, the Demiurge is the lawful master of this soul, which exhibits his likeness and is thus superior to the outer man, or earthy soul, which is said to be made 'according to the image'. Neither of these souls, however, bears the image of the true God, which resides in the spirit vouchsafed to the elect (*Excerpt* 86).

According to Theodotus, creation and redemption populate more than one plane of being. The universal demiurge is the Saviour, who, as the image of the Father, assumes the paternal role by sending forth the psychic Christ as his image. (*Excerpt* 47). This Christ, who sits at the right hand of the Demiurge (*Excerpt* 62), is the vesture for Jesus when he descends from the Place (*Excerpt* 59). Jesus is the paraclete, who issues from the *plêrôma*, big with the fullness of the aeons, in answer to the petition of Christ on behalf of his mother Wisdom (*Excerp*t 23, 40). The Christ who makes this prayer is said in *Excerpt* 32 to proceed from the meditation of Wisdom as an image of the *plêrôma*, and to receive election in Jesus as the firstborn of creation. We must suppose him to be pneumatic rather than psychic, and he seems not to be identical with the Christ who resides eternally in the Monogenes, the unique or only-begotten one, who is equated in *Excerpt* 6 with the beginning in which the Logos came to be. At this altitude, Christ is both the Word and the Life of the prologue to the fourth gospel (*Excerpt* 6). Jesus is, according to *Excerpt* 35, the light who empties himself by quitting the pleroma. In baptism he submitted to dispersal in order to reunite the dispersed elect (*Excerpt* 36). Above he is the supernal church (*Excerpt* 17); below he assumes the church is assuming Christ (*Excerpt* 58). While Christ is the head of the church, it is Jesus who, by shouldering the Cross, sustains 'the seed' (*Excerpt* 42). It was the better powers of the universe, those of 'the right', who foresaw his coming (*Excerpt* 43), and the prophecy that all Israel will be saved refers allegorically to the Israel of the spirit (*Excerpt* 56). Souls who have faith without knowledge become companions to the Demiurge in his intermediate heaven, but it is in the higher Ogdoad – comprising, not the earth and the seven planets, but the Father, his consort Silence and the first six emanations – that the rest decreed for the spiritual church will be enjoyed as a *kuriake*[10] – no mere Sabbath or weekly octave, but the eternal day of the Lord (*Excerpt* 64).

Even in these abstruse and gnomic utterances we see anticipations or refinements of conjectures that we should now associate with orthodox circles. The notion that the saints' rest in the Ogdoad is the Lord's Day echoes the assertion of Ignatius that the prophets lived according to the Lord's Day, not the Sabbath. This is an illustration of a rule that we have already noted, according to which a conceit in Ignatius becomes a concept for the Valentinians; there is nothing in him, however, to anticipate the doctrine that Monogenes is a title of the first emergent power in the Godhead, even before the assumption of flesh or the creation of a world outside the pleroma. Theodotus here approaches the later orthodoxy more closely than many apologists of his own period, for whom the sonship is not an eternal property but a supervenient function of the one who was 'with God in the beginning'. On the other hand, the uncoupling of creation and redemption, the fissiparation of Christ at different levels, and the identification of Jesus with the paraclete rather than Christ would seem to be almost calculated provocations to the episcopate. If they are taken literally – if more saviours than one are postulated, and not merely one Christ in sundry apparitions – it is also impossible to reconcile them with the first premises of John and Paul, whose words are cited as freely in these *Excerpts* as in all remains of Valentinian teaching.

Theodotus and the Catholic Norm

Whenever the defence of a putative heretic survives, his plea is that each of his own propositions is the logical antitype to one whose falsehood is already perceived by all good Christians Thus he can represent himself as the victim of a private suit whose sponsors, whether or not they know it, are making common cause with public enemies of the church. There may have been no tribunal to hear an impeachment against Theodotus in his lifetime, but if an apology had been required of him, he could have framed it as a syllabus of errors, comprehensive enough for its times:

1. Against the monarchians, he insists that the Logos resides eternally in the bosom of the Father as the *monogenes*, or only-begotten, and hence as one distinct from his progenitor. In his devolution to lower planes, the *tautotês* or fixed identity that he possesses in the fullness of his communion with the Father is never compromised. Nor does the Logos forfeit his divinity though the primordial divinity of the Father cannot be ascribed to him. If the Logos is *theos*, the Father is *autos theos*, God himself.

[10] Perhaps a transmutation of the word which denotes the Lord's Day in contradistinction to the Sabbath at Ignatius, *Magnesians* 9.1. They may be another echo of Ignatius (*Ephesians* 19) in Theodotus' meditation on the star which apprised the magi of Christ's birth (*Excerpt* 75.2).

2. Against the Carpocratians, he denies that the soul of Christ passed through a series of embodiments, shedding one place for another. '*Topos*' or 'place', an appellative of the Demiurge in Theodotus, denotes for him that realm of pure extension which is not yet matter but the condition of materiality. Into this realm spirit descends by taking on the properties of soul, and it is through this coarser medium that Christ –or rather his image – effects the deliverance of the psychic beings who people the first creation of the Demiurge. To enter the lower realm he must suffer a further determination of his nature, becoming flesh in the creation of the world and the inspiration of the prophets, but only once putting on the envelope of *sarkion pneuma* 'spiritual flesh' which renders him apprehensible to our grosser organs. Thus Christ adapts himself in each plane of being to the faculties of its denizens, but in each he remains the one saviour, never quitting his adopted domicile. So far as we can ascertain, Theodotus holds (in contrast to the Basilideans as well as the Carpocratians) that each souls falls but once into the present world, and on leaving it is irrevocably one of the lost or one of the elect.

3. Against the Naassenes, for whom spirit and matter are the upper and lower branches of an indeterminate substrate (*askhêmosunê*),[11] he affirms that the hidden Father attains his fullness through a series of immaterial propagations, and that matter comes into being parasitically in the wake of defect and rupture in this fullness. Under the conditions of psychic and physical existence, the spirit takes on the penumbral qualities of matter, but that is not to say that matter and spirit are one in nature or origin. It is also true that the Father himself transcends all predication, but inscrutability is not indeterminacy, and to say of the Godhead that it is *askhêmatistos*, or wanting in determinate form, is to forget that the Monogenes, the only-begotten Logos, is the eternal *prosôpon* or countenance of the Father.[12] That which is visible cannot be truly bodiless, though the body of the Son is visible only to the noeric or intellectual faculty (*Excerpt* 10.6). Compared with his the body of an angel, which appears to us no body at all, is ponderous. Since it is an axiom to Theodotus that there can be no countenance of the *askhêmatistos* (*Excerpt* 11.2), it follows that this epithet cannot be applied to the Father whose *prosôpon* is the Son. It may be that the Father possesses a body even subtler than the Son's, but one that is not to be characterized, as matter is, by the mere privation of form and quality. Far from requiring any material substrate, the Father himself is the substrate of all being, as the Fourth Evangelist intimates when he speaks of the Son's abiding in his bosom.[13] That which surpasses all is therefore prior to all: there can be no evolution of the greater from the less.

4. Against the docetic view that Christ assumed only the phantom of a body, he avers that his passion was real and salutary: 'Sending back the ray of power of power that descended upon him, the Saviour extinguished death, while the mortal

[11] Hippolytus, *Refutation* 5.17.18–19, citing Romans 1.26–7.

[12] *Excerpts* 12.1; cf. Clement, Paedagogus 1.57 and discussion below.

[13] *Excerpts* 7.3, quoting John 1.18 and distinguishing the *monogenes* in heaven from the earthly apparition of Jesus.

body rose again, casting away its passions.' (*Excerpt* 61.7). He even declares, to the indignation of Clement, that the father sympathises with the affliction of the Son (*Excerpt* 30).[14] This vehemence is unmatched by any catholic writer of the second century after Ignatius of Antioch. Theodotus, no doubt differs from Ignatius, in his failure to affirm the identity of the man Jesus and the incarnate Christ, for it would appear that he regards Jesus as the instrument of Christ – a child or *teknon* rather than the Son – and that the death of the earthly man becomes possible only when his heavenly coadjutor deserts him.[15] But this disjunction permits him to affirm without subterfuge or reservation the facts that Marcion was supposed to have denied, in the teeth of four canonical witnesses, who give circumstantial evidence of suffering on the cross.

5. Against the Gnostic myth which represents the human frame as a replica of the heavenly *anthrôpos*, he identifies both the image and the likeness with elements subtler than the body. Fragment 21 reports that the Valentinians, glossing the Biblical statement that humanity was created 'in the image of God, both male and female', argued that the female is the weak moiety of the psychic race, the called in contradistinction to the elect, and that the extraction of Adam's rib to form Eve prefigures the disjunction of these two peoples. Whether this discrimination of sexes is property or a concomitant of the image we do not learn here, but it would seem in any case that it precedes embodiment. So much is clear from Fragment 50, where Theodotus surmises that the image resides in the earthly soul, while the likeness is a resemblance to the Demiurge, imparted by an infusion of the Spirit. Both spirit and soul, at the nadir of creation, exhibit properties akin to the corporeal, but the body itself is not the vehicle either of the image or of the likeness. Theodotus does not endorse the reasoning of Irenaeus, that body must participate in the likeness because without body there is no man.

How can one take down these dykes without letting in the flood? Speaking for the church that traced its origin to Mark the evangelist, Clement protests that Theodotus has already breached the strongest dyke by failing to maintain that 'the Word is one and the same, god in God, who is said to be in the bosom of the Father, a single god indefeasible and indivisible' (*Excerpt* 8). Here he upholds the sameness of Christ in all his manifestations against Theodotus, who argued that the son is the temporal image of the Word who abides in sameness from the beginning (*Excerpt* 19). Commenting on the tenet that the Christ who is born of wisdom is adopted as the elect of the *plêrôma*, he accuses his interlocutors of mishearing the title 'firstborn of creation' at Colossians 1.15, which meant for Paul that the risen Christ is the 'head and root' of the church that draws new life from him (*Excerpt* 33). While he does not deny that the one Christ suffers, Clement urges that only

---

14 At *Excerpts* 45.2–46, the suffering is initially an accidental property of the incorporeal, and body is then created to accommodate it in the lower world because one cannot make an *ousia* of the passions.

15 *Excerpt* 61.6. At 61.8 Theodotus appears to hold that the psychic rise again in the embodied state, while the spiritual or pneumatic receive soul as a garment.

those who have lost all sense of the Father's glory can suppose that he participates in the afflictions of the Son (*Excerpt* 30). At the same time, chaste exegesis need not preclude the marriage of cognate images, even where these differed initially in tenor: in *Excerpt 2* the elect seed is declared to be the mustard seed and the leaven of Christ's parables, which now represent not the germination of preaching in the soul or in the church, but a heavenly remnant which makes one of nations hitherto dispersed.

Clement may here be interpreting the apostrophe to the twelve tribes at the beginning the Epistle of James or the statement in the anonymous Epistle to Diognetus that the church is the soul of the world (*Diognetus* 6.1). Chance concurrences between Theodotus and Clement are not so easily detected, but it is in the deep structure of intellectual systems, not in the details, that we seek proofs of consanguinity. The five points offered here in illustration of this principle show that Clement was a critic who was not ashamed to learn from his predecessor, paying tacit homage even in disagreement to the latter's power of quickening thought in others, and arriving at conclusions which, so far as our evidence goes, did not occur to such fellow-Churchmen as Irenaeus and Tertullian, who aimed only at the discomfiture of falsehood.

Origen and the Church of Alexandria

The same can be said of Origen, who, according to the *Church History* of Eusebius, was Clement's pupil before succeeding him as head of the catechetical school in Alexandria. Most scholars now doubt this testimony, as Origen's extant writings, though voluminous, say nothing of a apprenticeship to Clement; many also question the existence of a Catechetical School, while few perhaps have any clear notion what it would have been had it existed.[16] It is also known that Origen read the pagan philosophers under a certain Ammonius.[17] Too much has been made of the fact that Plotinus, a pagan twenty years his junior, had a teacher of the same name, for the only evidence that this was the same Ammonius, is that he too taught an Origen, who can scarcely have been the Christian theologian unless the latter put himself to school at the age of fifty.[18] Confusion of the two has produced many hybrid lives of the Christian; following Eusebius and the thick corpus of Origen's writings that remains to us, we can say with confidence that he consulted a Christian

[16] On the alleged succession see Eusebius, *Church History* 6.6. On the pliable evidence from ancient sources regarding the Catechetical School see Van den Hoek (1997).

[17] Eusebius, *Church History* 6.19.4, citing Porphyry; see further Edwards (1993).

[18] Porphyry, *Life of Plotinus* 3. McGuckin (2004), 4 assumes without question that the Ammonius who taught Origen was the teacher of Plotinus, but seems to perceive that the Origen who studied with Plotinus under Ammonius Saccas was not the same person as his Christian namesake.

Hebrew in Alexandria,[19] and that before he left this city he had completed his *First Principles* and commenced his remarkable *Commentary on John*.[20] Driven forth by the jealousy of his bishop (if Eusebius can be trusted, though he also grants that his hero was ineligible for clerical office), Origen was made a presbyter in Palestinian Caesarea, where, despite the invalidity of his orders, he acquired great fame as a homilist and a champion of the Episcopal church against heresy.[21] Evidence of his having been dubbed a heretic in his turn by a contemporary synod, either in Rome or in Alexandria, is late and jejune; another chapter will be required to trace the soiling of his reputation in the three centuries after his death in 254.

Setting the compass of orthodoxy for his own times, Origen prefaced his treatise on *First Principles* with a summary of the indefeasible truths that the Church had received from the apostles. First of these is the unity of God (1, proem 4), but hard upon it come the divinity of the Son and the Holy Spirit – each, like the Father, possessing his own eternal and discrete hypostasis (*loc. cit.*; cf. 1.22 and 1.3.4). The human creature, in contrast to God, is perishable and prone to transgression. The sin which has proved mortal to the body brings moral death to the soul, though the latter remains indissoluble and free to choose good or evil both before and after its severance from the flesh (1, proem 5). Of its nature the common faith says nothing more than that it is created (*loc. cit*), and that it cannot redeem itself. It is through the united ministry of the three – through the mercy of the Father,[22] the oblation of the Son[23] and the sanctification of the Spirit[24] – that wrath is averted and innocence restored.

Like Clement, Origen held these tenets in conscious enmity to the Valentinians, to whom he ascribed a confusion of matter and spirit, a contempt for all creation outside the Godhead and a deterministic theory of salvation.

1. Clement is no monarchian. Seven centuries later, his dictum that the Son is not the *prophorikos logos* caused an irascible polymath to tax him with dividing Christ.[25] Yet the extant passage most akin to the one adduced by Photius merely admonishes simple readers that to call the Son the *logos* of the Father is not to say that he is merely a function of epiphenomenon of the divine, as common

---

[19] On his studies in Hebrew see Eusebius, *Church History* 6.16.1; on the Hebrew master (who appears to have been a Christian) see First Principles 1.3.5 and 4.3.14.

[20] Eusebius, *Church History* 6.24.1 records that the first five books of the Commentary were completed in Alexandria. On the genesis of the work see Nautin (1977), 377ff.

[21] Eusebius, *Church History* 6.19.16–17. Cadiou (1935), 99 observes that his ordination was doubly invalid because he lacked the authorisation of his bishop, and was also believed, by report at least, a voluntary eunuch (Eusebius, *Church History* 6.3.).

[22] On the philanthropy of the Father see *Homilies on Ezekiel* 6. 1.

[23] Conceived at *Commentary on John* 6.274–5 and *Homilies on Exodus* 6.9 as a ransom to the devil.

[24] Who dwells only in the elect, according to a passage (*First Principles* 1.3.5) which was thought by his detractors to imply the subordination of Son and Spirit to the Father.

[25] On Photius and Clement see Edwards (2000) and previous chapter.

speech is a function or epiphenomenon of the human.[26] On the contrary, the Son is a power or *dunamis* in his own right (*Stromateis* 7.9.1 amongst others), and one who, as Clement asseverates, died on the Cross for his testimony. Origen feels the necessity of this caveat in the first book of his *Commentary on John*, although in canvassing the rejected view he does not employ the term *prophorikos logos*, no doubt because he was conscious of predecessors who, without falling into monarchianism, has used this locution to characterize the hypostatic phase of Sonship in contradistinction to the phase of latency.[27] For him, as for Clement, there is no procession from the *logos endiathetos*, no succession of states in the being of the Son;[28] he distinguishes none the less between the character of the Son in his relation to the Father and his character in relation to the world. He is Wisdom in the first relation, Logos in the second, but for Origen these are designations of the same hypostasis.[29] In the more episodic system of Theodotus, for whom every name betokens a new entity and every plane of being has its own denizens, the Monogenes or only-begotten stands at the head of a line of saviours. Yet both agree that the terms supplied by the scriptures are not simply interchangeable, that a logical parataxis is implied and even some gradation in plenitude of being.

2. Clement entertains no doctrine of transmigration; Origen concedes that such a doctrine might be authorized by Jewish tradition and certain provisions of the Mosaic code, were it not that the church has pronounced it heresy. Both, on the other hand, concur with Theodotus in ascribing to Christ a double manifestation in the lower realm, first as the audible, then as the visible Word. While it is not clear that either postulates direct communication of truth to the Greek philosophers, both maintain that, even before the birth of Christ, the prophets of Israel made disciples of the other nations. For Origen, the legible word of scripture is the enfleshment of the Logos, who is the true though latent subject of every word in it;[30] it is through the historical incarnation, in which the Word assumes the threefold composite of body, soul and spirit, that the scripture is discovered to be a triple cord, and the outward sense becomes no longer a veil but a prism to the soul and spirit of the text.[31] Theodotus, who likewise spoke of prophecy as the advent of the Word in flesh, identified not three levels of exegesis but three vehicles of instruction – the mystical, the cryptic and the naked, the last of which is imparted only to initiates.[32]

---

26 On the post-Nicene spectacles of Photius see Markschies (2000), 85.

27 See *Commentary on John* 1.24.151; Edwards (2000), Orbe (1991).

28 Casey (1934), 22 observes that *logos en tautotêti* (*Excerpts* 8.1, 19.1) is Clement's equivalent for *logos endiathetos*.

29 For references, chiefly from *Commentary on John* 1, see Tzamailikos (2006), 52–62.

30 See Clement, *Prophetic Excerpts* 23 on god's assumption of humanity in the prophets before the nativity of the saviour; Origen *Philokalia* 5.4.

31 See especially *First Principles* 4.2.4 and discussion of allegory in the next chapter of this book.

32 *Excerpts* 66, as above. As De Lubac (1949), 176–7, observes, this dictum implies a high valuation of the literal sense of certain sayings.

Occultation thus gives way to disclosure in the first preaching of the gospel; Origen holds that the process can be recapitulated in his own day by the reader who strives to hear the Saviour's voice in every text.

3. Though Clement and Origen both affirm that the nature of God cannot be known by our mortal faculties, neither pronounces it *askhêmatistos*, and Clement seems to imitate Theodotus in styling the incarnate Christ the *prosôpon* of the Father. Both uphold the eternity of the Godhead and the contingency of matter. In contrast to Theodotus, they regard it as the creation of an omnipotent deity, not as the precipitate of an involuntary ferment in the Godhead.[33] On the other hand, they are at one with the Valentinians, not only against the Naassenes, but against the majority of the apologists in the second century, who had not determined clearly whether matter should be regarded as the first creature of God or the coeternal substrate of creation. Theophilus of Antioch, perhaps the first to state without ambiguity that the matter from which the heavens and earth are fashioned is itself God's handiwork, also retains the doctrine of a procession of the hypostatic Logos from a hitherto monadic Godhead. If the principle of alterity – that is to say, the possibility that something other than God may exist – does not reside in a meter independent of God, it must originate in God himself. It is not clear whether Clement admits this bifurcation in God, and it is certainly denied in the Latin excerpts made by which are now the chief remains of his *Hypotyposes*.[34] Origen explicitly affirms the supervenience of matter and denies the evolution of two from one in the Godhead, thus upholding only one of the complementary tenets that Theophilus shared with his Valentinian contemporaries. We cannot argue here, as we might in points 1 and 2 above, that Origen is the beneficiary of a Valentinian innovation; we can observe, however, that in choosing what to follow or amend in his Valentinian precursor, he is choosing what to follow or amend in earlier manifestoes of the episcopal church.

4. It would be superfluous to multiply proofs that Clement and Origen believed in the passion of Christ, and futile to maintain that they would not have perceived its efficacy without assistance from the Valentinians. Nevertheless, a tincture of Valentinian thought may be evident in their teaching that salvation was effected homeopathically, through the Saviour's condescension to the infirmities of his elect. Clement cannot argue, like Theodotus, that Christ came to redeem the works of the female (*Excerpts* 68, 79, 80), because he himself maintains the converse – imagines that the Father endured a kind of feminization when he produced a Son amenable to suffering.[35] Origen holds that the purpose of Christ's becoming flesh was to teach us to look beyond the flesh, and if he really supposed, as later

---

33 Theodotus in fact employs the term *askhêmatistos* to describe the luminous psychic stuff from which the world was fashioned at *Excerpts* 47.4. Gross matter is the condensation of this, but he does not say, with the Naassenes, that its rarefaction is spirit.

34 See esp. Fr. 3, p. 210 Stählin and Früchtel.

35 *The Rich Man's Salvation* 37.2: what is ineffable in him is the Father, that which shares in our suffering, is the mother.

witnesses tell us, that he assumed an aerial body to reconcile the powers who rule that element,[36] he was forcing the logic of universalism to a position that only Theodotus had occupied before him. We look in vain in their Christian forerunners – even in Irenaeus, whose traffic with Gnostic thought we have explored in the previous chapter – for any notion of the feminization of God or of the sublimation of faith through an ascent from what is manifest in the Saviour to what is hidden. Origen's suggestion that the Father voluntarily yields to grief in his contemplation of the sin of his creatures would have been more palatable in his own time to Theodotus than to disciples of Irenaeus;[37] though to modern minds it proves that he saw nothing feigned or perfunctory in the suffering of Christ.

5. Clement and Origen are merely the first in an unbroken chain of early Christian teachers who declare that we are properly identical with the inner man alone, and not with the fragile composite of soul and body. The creation of this universal self, the reasoning faculty which distinguishes us from brutes, is logically if not temporally anterior to the fashioning of the protoplasts Adam and Eve from the soil of Eden.[38] The likeness of God, which (as Origen notes) is promised but not conferred at Genesis 1.26, is attained through the exercise of virtue amid temptation, hazard and affliction. This is also the doctrine of Irenaeus, or a tenable interpretation of it; but whereas he goes on to deduce that the body too participates in the likeness of God, Clement and Origen hold that the invisible cannot be adequately depicted in the visible. The fabulous conception of the body as an image of the heavenly man is refuted by denying it any archetype in the higher regions, not by turning the deity into a luminous simulacrum of his creatures. For Origen, even the inner man no longer bears the image, since, in the wake of the fall, it has been eclipsed by the image of the devil.[39] To Irenaeus this would have been an unpalatable conceit, as it implies a catastrophic loss of perfection, not a remediable aberration in the design of God; it is, however, only a sober variant of Theodotus' annotation to the question of Christ, 'Whose head is on this coin?'.[40] According to this parable, the true coin of the realm is the faithful soul that bears the image of its Saviour, while the impression of another mint is visible in the folly of the lost.

Prosôpon and Persona

We learn nothing in the *Excerpts* of the history and origin of Theodotus. Since the title assigns him to the oriental branch of the Valentinian school, while the text gives no indication that he adhered to any school of his own, there is no

---

[36] Jerome, *Letter to Avitus* 12, the Greek version of which (from Justinian's Letter to Mennas) is inserted by Koetschau at *First Principles* 4.3.13.

[37] See *Excerpt* 30 and Origen, *Homilies on Ezekiel* 6.1, both cited above.

[38] See further Bammel (1994).

[39] See *Homily on Genesis* 1 and discussion in the next chapter of this book.

[40] *Excerpts* 86.1; cf. Clement, *Prophetic Excerpts* 24.

bar to our taking him for the same man whom Hippolytus[41] calls Theodotus of Byzantium. Writing at the end of the second century, this dyspeptic Churchman has little more to say of the Theodotians than that they treated the heavenly Christ and the earthly Jesus as distinct coadjutors, twinned but not united in his brief ministry of salvation (*Refutation* 7.35). This could be an etiolated version of the doctrine that is more faithfully transmitted in Clement's *Excerpts*; for Hippolytus, a western author, Theodotus is of less interest in himself than as a symbol of one extreme to which false Christologies lead their patrons. The other is represented by Noetus, who acknowledged no distinction of divine persons, and therefore put the Father on the Cross (*Refutation* 9.10.11–12). Hippolytus accused his own primate, Callistus of Rome,[42] of veering between these poles, because his Christ was not a perfect man who was also a perfect God but a domino, half flesh and half spirit. The Son is the fleshy domicile and spirit the heavenly sojourner who is not a discrete hypostasis but the Godhead under a temporary guise.[43] The details of the theory remain elusive, as Hippolytus found in it only what he was looking for, a tissue of blasphemy and contradiction:

> That which is seen, that which is man – this is the Son, but the spirit to which the Son plays host is the Father. 'I shall not,' he says, 'affirm two gods, the Father and Son, but one.[44] For the Father, born of himself, assumed flesh and divinized it by union with himself and made one thing, so that the Father and Son are

[41] I accept here that Hippolytus is the author of the writing commonly known as the *Refutation of all Heresies*, the first book of which long passed as the work of Origen under the title Philosophoumena. Books 4–10, discovered in 1853, were also at first ascribed to Origen by some scholars, but external testimonies to the factious conduct of Hippolytus, together with the evidence that he penned a work which bore a strong resemblance to the tenth book of the *Refutation*, have persuaded the majority of scholars that the author was the Hippolytus to whom we ascribe the first commentaries on the Book of Daniel and the Song of Songs. It can be argued that the same man was the author of a tract against Noetus and another newly-discovered work, the *Apostolic Tradition*; as Nautin and Cerrato have shown, however, it is difficult to credit a single man with this motley corpus, which is not entirely consistent in its teachings. Brent (1995a) treats the *Refutation* as the work of a disciple.

[42] The breach between Callistus and Hippolytus gave the latter the reputation of an antipope (Prudentius, *Peristephanon* 11.19), and this is the view espoused by Döllinger (1876). Yet, while he deplores the character, the conduct and the teachings of Callistus, he does not contest his primacy, and he may therefore be more plausibly regarded as a bishop of lesser standing, who was resisting the conversion of a limited into an absolute monarchy (Brent, 1995b). Though ancient sources (most of them Greek) award him the see of Portus at the harbour of Rome, it cannot be shown that such a see existed in the third century.

[43] Gerber (2001), 230–31 explains that, whereas the Father and Christ are one for Praxeas and Noetus, Callistus regards the Father and his Logos as one *prosôpon* and the Son as the one *prosôpon* which results from the assumption of the flesh into this divine amalgam.

[44] At *Refutation* 9.12.17, Callistus invokes John 14.10, 'do you not believe that I am in the Father and the Father in me?'.

> called a single God. And it is impossible that this, being one *prosôpon*, should be two, and that the Father should suffer together[45] with the Son.' For he does not wish to say that the Father suffered and was one *prosôpon*, thinking in this way, mindless[46] and fickle man that he is, to be guiltless of blasphemy against the Father (Hippolytus, *Refutation* 9.12.18–19).

It is patently impossible that the Son should be identical with the Father if they are two halves of a composite. Both positions, however, are attributed to Callistus here, the first without equivocation, the second with an imputation of subterfuge, which proves it to be more than a polemical fabrication. The teaching of Callistus, then, appears to be not that Father and Son are identical, but rather that they are contraries which unite to constitute a single agent. 'Son' would be the appellative of the man in whom the Father dwells, not bodily, but by the operation of his spirit, this spirit itself being merely a function, not a discrete hypostasis.[47] Christ is thus dynamically one, though essentially a dyad – a position no more absurd than the Platonic and Christian commonplace that man is a composite of soul and body. The distinction between the two persons in the Godhead is not effaced by the watchword 'one prosôpon', even if the rejoinder 'two prosôpa' was devised to protect the distinction. Confusion between two senses of *prosôpon* is endemic in early Christian controversy, for it may signify either the inward self – the 'person', as we might say – or the disclosure of that person to the world – the 'personality', in one sense of the English term. An instance of the second use is Clement's description of Christ in his *Paedagogus* as the *prosôpon* of the Father.[48] Here *prosôpon* can be rendered "countenance", and serves as a technical paraphrase for the words of Jesus 'he who has seen me has seen the Father' (John 14.9) – which is to say that there is no other manifestation of the Father by comparison with which his manifestation in the human form of Christ could be judged inferior or delusive. Likewise the 'two prosôpa' of Hippolytus are not two distinct epiphanies: the

45 This seems to be intended as a rejoinder to Sabellius, whose teachings Callistus is said to have proscribed (*Refutation* 9.12.15). But although Hippolytus represents Sabellius and Theodotus as antipodal figures (*Refutation* 9.12.198), Theodotus also taught that the Father suffers with the Son, and Arius, as we shall note below, had a different understanding of Sabellius.

46 Greek *anoêtos*, a sneer at the bishop's patronage of Noetus. I have elected not to make use of the tract entitled Against Noetus, which is attributed by some scholars to Hippolytus, but generally with the caveat that it has suffered interpolation. Nautin (1947) maintains that it is an integral work of the early third century, but differing so profoundly in style, construction and pneumatology from the *Refutation* that we cannot attribute both to a single author. See Nautin (1949), 220–25 for a defence of the ascription of the work *Against Noetus* to one Josippus, whom he believes to be the author of a piece *On Hades*, otherwise attributed to Hippolytus.

47 See Heine (1998).

48 *Paedagogus* 1.57.2, elucidating Genesis 32.30.

existence of the two becomes evident only when the second becomes incarnate, and it is through his visible garb that the one who remains invisible becomes known to his creatures for the first time.

Hippolytus, we may note, holds that the Son came forth as the second person only for the purpose of creation; he fails to add the customary rider that we ought not to speak of a period of repose *before* the procession, since without the revolutions of the spheres there is no measurement of time.[49] The tenet that a state of repose is prior, logically if not chronologically, to the emergence of the Son was still advanced as a norm of orthodox thought a generation later by the antipope Novatian,[50] though he is careful to observe that where there is no time there can be no strict succession of states, and resorts to such ambiguous phrases that he might mean not that the Son was first within the Father and then came forth, but rather that even when he is coming forth he remains within.[51] No author who posited this phase of latency would describe it as a state in which the Godhead is one *prosôpon*, since the sole use of this term before the fourth century was to illustrate the work of God in the created order, without regard to the properties or ends that might be ascribed to him independently of his works. This need not imply that the persons constitute an 'economic Trinity' which is not coterminous with the 'immanent Trinity' that constitutes the Godhead; the case is simply that writers of this era were less concerned with metaphysics than with the doctrines of creation and redemption. It is the in the delineation of these works that ambiguity arises, since the motto 'one *prosôpon*' may either signify either that the Father is known to us through the incarnate Christ, or else that 'Father', 'Son' and 'Spirit' are names that differ only in connotation and not in reference. The first is orthodoxy to all, the second a heresy to those who are now deemed catholic.

It does not follow that Callistus and Hippolytus could have been reconciled by adopting a univocal application of the term *prosôpon*. Callistus holds that the Father became incarnate, and that the Son had no hypostasis of his own before this event. In God there is no person but the Father, while the coexistence in the embodied Christ of two agents who are not identical almost justifies the tendentious assimilation of this teaching to that of Theodotus. The quarrel between Callistus and Hippolytus is thus not baseless; it is a real dispute envenomed by an unperceived forking of the Christian tongue.

---

49 It seems to me highly improbable that Hippolytus declared the Son to be *homoousios* or consubstantial with the Father, though we meet this locution in a text attributed to him by Richard (1964), 141. The commentary on the Song of Songs which Richard has edited seems to me to betray the influence of Origen.

50 See Novatian, *On the Trinity* 31. In defence of the tradition that Hippolytus was in later life an adherent of Novatian, see Wordsworth (1890), 158–80, and *ibid.*, 62–168 for a detailed commentary on Hippolytus, *Refutation* 9, which gathers parallel texts from Novatian, Tertullian and other contemporaries.

51 On the alleged subordinationism of Novatian see DeSimone (1970), 91–113.

Tertullian

However he expressed his belief, Callistus thought the Father coextensive with the Godhead, regarding the Spirit merely as a devolved power of this Godhead and the Son as its seat on earth. If this is a monarchian view, it is not to be confused with that of Sabellius, who held that the Son was the product of division in a Godhead which was initially monadic.[52] Different again is the patripassian doctrine that the Father became the Son to perform his ministry of salvation. An orotund proponent of this third position, Melito of Sardis, was remembered not as a heretic but as an apologist in the catholic cause; we cannot now determine whether this was the prevalent doctrine in Asia Minor around 170, or whether some disagreed but were prepared to stomach any food that a Gnostic could not swallow.[53] As for Callistus, he was the acknowledged bishop of Rome, and it has been urged that he was simply upholding the creed of his predecessors. In fact their beliefs and those of the Roman populace are unattested, except that Irenaeus, around 180, claims the bishop of Rome as his ally, together with every previous tenant of the see since the days of Peter. It is clear that they showed no countenance to Gnostic teaching, but equally clear that Justin Martyr and Tatian, neither of whom was a monarchian, passed for good Christians while they resided in the capital. It is possible that Callistus was an innovator in doctrine, as he appears to have been in penitential discipline and his handling of the canons of ordination.[54] On the other hand Tertullian of Carthage, who denounces one contemporary pontiff for his laxity and another for his indifference to a new prophetic movement, never taxes Rome with errors in theology. His silence is informative, not only because he was a contemporary of Hippolytus, but because he armed the western church with formularies which were to be repeated for centuries without change.

Among the most incandescent of his works is an ebullition against one Praxeas, whose existence has been doubted on the grounds that his name is supposed to mean 'busy-body'. Of this we find no evidence in dictionaries; on the other hand, the existence of Noetus, whose name indubitably means 'intellectual', has never been denied. We are less sure of the doctrine of Tertullian's adversary than of his name, but he owes his infamy to Tertullian's jibe that he 'crucified the Father' (*Against Praxeas* 1). That is to say, that under the ensign of monarchianism, he taught that God the Son was God the Father in human guise, a proposition anathematized by the monarchians of Rome. Tertullian replies that the Son is called God, not because he is the Father, but because he issues from the substance of the Father. His term for an exemplar of divine substance is persona, which appears to denote for him, as the word persona does in modern English usage, that which characterizes an

---

[52] See the letter of Arius to Alexander at Athanasius, *On the Synods* 16.

[53] See Melito, *On the Pasch* 8–9; Hübner (1999). Although he upheld the Asiatic rather than the Roman date for Easter, Melito is invariably cited in antiquity as a champion of the catholic tradition: see Eusebius, *Church History* 4.13.8.

[54] See *Refutation* 9.12.20–26 with Döllinger (1876).

agent in relation to other agents. At time the particularity of each is so much in evidence that Tertullian seems to be speaking of one God and two subordinate divinities, as when he depicts the Father to a king and the other two persons as his viceroys (*Praxeas* 3.3). This preserves the *monarchia* whether we mean by this the unity of origin or the sovereignty of the Father; on the other hand, it fails to secure the integrity of the Godhead, to account for the fact that God is one, not three. In contrast to this tritheistic simile, the comparison of the Father to the sun and the other persons to different portions of its radiance reduces the three to one, since it implies that the Son and Spirit are not substantial, but epiphenomenal to the substance. By likening the Father to a root, the Son to a stem and the Spirit to a flower (*Praxeas* 8.6–7), Tertullian gives them parity without making them coeval. He does not in fact appear to think the three persons coeternal with the one substance, for, although he opines that the Fatherhood is eternal and that one cannot be an eternal Father without an eternal Son, he concedes that before the Son came forth as the Father's *sermo* or speech for the creation of the world, he had no existence but as the latent reason (*ratio*) of the Godhead.[55] Tertullian adopts the Valentinian term *probolê* to describe the procession of the Son, with the rider that this did not entail an alienation or expansion of divine substance (*Praxeas* 8.1). Thus he upholds the impassibility of God, but has no term which connotes begetting unaccompanied by passion; he certainly affirms three eternals, not so certainly an eternal three.

'Three persons in one substance' is a fair distillation of Tertullian's teaching, and the immutable formula of the western church to the present day. But this was to hand posterity a scorpion, for while Tertullian's word for what is three in God, *persona*, corresponds in sense and scope to the Greek *prosôpon*,[56] his word for what is one in God, *substantia*, has the same etymology as the Greek *hypostasis*, which was not put to the same use in theology. For Tertullian the *substantia* is that by virtue of which the Father, the Son and the Spirit are God, both severally and in communion: all three of one substance, each subsisting in the individuality that constitutes his persona. The origin of the latter term is not explained, except for a passing allusion to a cryptic phrase, 'the spirit of his person', which occurs in the Greek and Latin versions of Lamentations 4.20.[57] Since Tertullian diligently

---

[55] *Praxeas* 5.3.; cf. *Against Hermogenes 3.*

[56] Both can signify 'mask', but this is a derived usage in Greek, and the original one in Latin. This is not, however, the sense that governs its usage in Tertullian, as Nédoncelle (1948) and Grillmeier (1975), 124–8 demonstrate. Attempts to plot a development in his nomenclature, like that of Moingt (1967), 615 rely upon unverified chronologies of his writing. It is also possible that the usage of *prosôpon* and *persona* as dogmatic terms has its origin in such texts as Psalm 9.4, where *prosôpon* could be taken to denote an economic manifestation of God: cf. Hippolytus, *On the Psalms* 15 in Nautin (1953), 79 and see further Driver and Hodgson (1924), 410–20.

[57] *Praxeas* 14.10, citing an accurate Latin rendering of an inaccurate Greek rendering from the Hebrew (Septuagint).

shows off his training in the forensic arts, it is likely enough that his use of this and other terms was shaped by legal practice; it is not, however, easy to agree with Harnack's thesis that he conceives the three *personae* as joint possessors of the *substantia*, in the same way as three men with rights in law may jointly possess the same estate.[58] The substance is possessed as an attribute, not as a chattel; we might call it the stuff of the Godhead,[59] with the proviso that Tertullian holds as strongly as his contemporaries that matter is the creation of God and hence no part of his eternal being. It is true that he once declares God to be a corpus or body (*Against Praxeas* 7.8); in the same passage, however, he reduces this assertion to a tautology by defining body as anything that really exists, and Augustine testifies that this is a usage known to Latin.[60] Thus we cannot infer that he joined the Stoics in holding the Godhead to be a refined species of matter; he himself states the opposite when he characterizes the substance of the Godhead as 'spirit, a term which he, in common with other guardians of the rule of faith, regarded as the antonym to 'matter', when this term denotes the substrate of creation.

It follows that Tertullian cannot contemplate any physical division or abscission in the Godhead. It is for want of a more apposite term that he speaks of the Son as a portion of divine substance (*Praxeas* 26.6), just as, for want of an apposite term, he veers to the extreme by styling the Word an operation of the Spirit (*Praxeas* 26.4). When he is determined to be precise he affirms that the persons differ not in *status* or inward constitution but in *gradus*, or succession; not by division but by distinction, not in substance but in form. In these antitheses, each term circumscribes the other, and neither can be adequately glossed by looking up its regular use in Latin, let alone by appeal to the philosophical sense of its Greek equivalent. It has been proposed, for example, that *persona* and *substantia* correspond to the first *ousia* and second *ousia* of Aristotle, the first term designating the particular and the second the form or species which is exemplified in the particular.[61] But the substance of the Godhead has a concreteness in Tertullian which Aristotle

[58] For his own palinode see Harnack (1931), 576–77n. See also Nédoncelle (1948), 297–8. Osborn (1997), 138 rightly observes that a clear dichotomy between philosophic and legal usage cannot be drawn in the work of an author who was, after all, a polymath trained in forensic manoeuvres, even if not for practice at the bar.

[59] Stead (1963), 58–62 maintains that substantia certainly denotes the stuff of particulars (*Praxeas* 16.4), the stuff of all things (*Against Hermogenes* 9.1), and a thing composed of a certain stuff (*Praxeas* 8.5). More debatable evidence can be offered for the senses 'existence' (*Against the Valentinians* 15.1) and 'nature' (*Against the Nations* 2.4.6).

[60] Letter 166. Passages which ascribe corporeality to the soul include *Against Hermogenes* 35.2, *Against Marcion* 5.15.8, but soul and flesh in Christ are clearly distinct at *On the Flesh of Christ* 13. See further Daniélou (1974), 345–8.

[61] Against Evans (1948), 40–42, Stead (1963), 54–6 notes that the *Categories* were not widely quoted in the western Church in the age of Tertullian, and that even where homologies between his terms and those of Aristotle are detectable, it is possible that Latin intermediaries (still extant) have been consulted rather than the original works.

denies to his second *ousia*, and in any case *ousia* would be more aptly represented in Latin by essential. By the late fourth century, *substantia* in the nomenclature of western Christian tends to match *ousia* in eastern parlance, but we have no evidence that Greek Christians of the second century employed the noun *ousia* to denote what is one in God. The search for a philosophical antecedent to *substantia* has obscured its biblical provenance, which could have been deduced from the following passage:

> If those invisible things, whatever they are, possess in God's sight their own corpus and their own form, whereby they are visible to God alone, how much more shall that which is sent forth from the substance of the Father not be without substance! What the substance of the Word (*sermo*) is, then, that I call his person, and for that I claim the name of Son; when I acknowledge the Son, I contend that he is second from the Father[62] (*Against Praxeas* 7.9).

This reasoning seems to imperil the distinction between *substantia* and *persona*. To understand what it means to say that the substance of the Son is his person, it may be fruitful to consider what we mean in English when we speak of a 'person of substance' or conversely when we complain that an idea is 'without substance'. It is not the constitutive substance that is denoted by such phrases, but the substantiality of the thing constituted. The substance of the Father is pre-eminently substantial, and so is anything that proceeds from it; by virtue of his procession the Son receives not only his share in the Father's substance, but a peculiar substantiality, a capacity for subsisting in his own right. It is thus the same act, the Father's generation of the Son, that differentiates the two substantialities and establishes community of substance. The more substantial the parent, the more substantial the offspring: it is because the Father's substance is inexhaustible, because he can impart substantiality to another with no depletion of his own, that three divine persons can subsist without impairing the unity of God.

How does Tertullian justify his premise that the Son is from the substance of the Father? That he offers no such justification implies that it is for him already a commonplace, though it is not directly taken from the scriptures. A clue if afforded by a near-contemporary writing, Origen's commentary on Hebrews, a morsel of which is preserved in the apology written on Origen's behalf by Pamphilus of Caesarea. The text is Hebrews 1.3, where the Son is said to be the impression of the Father's hypostasis – that is to say, the visible manifestation of the unseen reality. Origen's annotation – extant, like the rest of the *Apology*, only in Latin – explains that Hebrews of the Son as an effulgence of the Father in terms that, like the description of Wisdom as an exhalation of the power of God at Wisdom

[62] Cf. Eusebius, *Gospel Preparation* 5.30.3: 'second god after the Father'. In both instances, the causal primacy of the Father is asserted to forestall any notion of two independent deities; the locution need not imply the subordination of the Son (though both may be held, on other evince, to have maintained this).

7.25, are designed to accommodate an ineffable mystery to our understanding. Through this device:

> We may understand in part that Christ, who is Wisdom, is equally comparable to that exhalation which proceeds from some bodily substance: he himself too issues, like some exhalation, "from the power of God himself." [Wisdom 7.25]. Thus Wisdom also, proceeding from that power, is generated from the very substance of God; and thus, it is none the less also compared [also at Wisdom 7.25] to a bodily emanation and described as a pure and blameless 'emanation of the glory of the Almighty' (Pamphilus, *Apology* 99, p. 318 Röwekamp).

The Greek prototype for *substantia* must be hypostasis, not *ousia*, not only because hypostasis is the word supplied by the biblical passage, but because Origen elsewhere denies that the Son is from the *ousia* of the Father.[63] The formula 'from the substance of the Father', though not biblical, is at least of biblical provenance: current in both the Greek and the Latin spheres of Christian thought at the beginning of the fourth century, it was published again as the watchword of orthodoxy by the Council of Antioch late in 324 or early in 325, only to be supplanted at Nicaea by 'from the *ousia* (or essence) of the Father' as a preface to the insertion of a new phylactery, the *homoousion*. Tertullian's 'of one substance' would appear to be a derivative of the same formula; we hear of no corresponding affirmation of one hypostasis in Greek until the fourth century, by which time, like one *prosôpon*, it savoured of heresy. Our evidence from the third century, however, indicates that both locutions, one *prosôpon* and one *hypostasis*, could have been maintained in a sense acceptable to most catholics of this epoch and without offence to any later canon of orthodoxy.

Conclusion

Tertullian and Hippolytus belong to the generation after Irenaeus, in which the episcopal church enjoyed a clear ascendancy in talent, and perhaps in numbers also. Neither, however, felt that this preponderance justified any relaxation in pastoral vigilance – least of all in Rome, where both maintained that the bishop himself had betrayed his charges to the wolf. Neither drops his voice for an instant; neither can admit that another's teachings can be half-true or partly false. .The war-cry of Hippolytus is 'two *prosôpa*', that of Tertullian *unius substantiae*, 'of one substance'. Since however, the cognate nouns *hypostasis* and *substantia* were not used coterminously with respect to God, and since there was always an acceptable sense in which one could affirm that God the Father had no *prosôpon* but the Son, it was always possible for a catholic to challenge these slogans or to misconstrue them; the consequence was that, after these weapons had been handled by one

[63] See *CommJoh* 20.157, with Ayres (2004), 24 and following chapter.

disputant after another in the course of the next two centuries, they threatened to cut in half the populace that they had once defined.

Clement was a contemporary of these two western figures, Origen his junior and by some reports his pupil. Both were teachers of such high repute that, whether or not a catechetical school had been established, it is hard to doubt that they will have been entrusted with the instruction of catechumens. They were not, however, merely custodians of a given norm: their aim was to build up knowledge on the foundation of piety, not to thicken the boundaries of the episcopal communion, though they believed this to be both virginal and catholic. Their gleanings in philosophy lie outside the scope of the present study, but all scholars agree that both looked unremittingly for instances of harmony between pagan and Christian thought, and that Origen, when he migrated to Caesarea, required his pupils to master the philosophies of all the schools before they advanced to theological ratiocination. At the same time – and this is admitted even by scholars who hold that the result was a mongrel creed, not the faith of Jesus – they espoused philosophy only as an ancillary or a propaedeutic, not as a complementary source of truth. And so it was with Valentinianism: it was a stream to be panned, though only a fool or a heretic would bathe there. We shall see in the following chapter how Origen's reputation was to fare in an age when even the sifted gold of heretics was contraband.

Chapter 4
Origen and Orthodoxy

There is always a revolution in the course of any protracted evolution. One element in the system may outgrow the others to mar its equilibrium, or, if all grow at the same rate, a point is reach where further growth cannot be sustained without metamorphosis. A church cannot survive unless it accommodates disputation, and it is in the interest of every government to propagate knowledge, yet the effects can hardly fail to be inimical to the unity of one and the authority of the other. It was a student of the Fathers who declared that 'to change is to grow', and the maxim is eminently reversible; Newman's continuation, 'to have changed often is to be perfect' is less likely to commend itself to those who acknowledge the role of chance and catastrophe in the formation of living organisms or the body politic. In the history of Christian doctrine, the first catastrophe, in the sense of a sharp reversal of consensus, was occasioned by the discovery that champions of the Episcopal Church had entertained tenets which other champions stigmatized as Gnostic. To partisans in the controversy that followed the death of Origen, it appeared that one was bound to choose between polytheism and strict subordination of God the Son to God the Father, and that anyone who believed the body of Christ to have been governed by a human soul was in danger of making the Word a different agent from the man Jesus. Both the manhood of Christ and his divinity were more strongly affirmed by Origen than by any theologian before him, but he could make disciples of the majority only when traditional sanctions against the preaching of two gods or two sons had been obviated. In the interim he had suffered so much obloquy from defenders of these sanctions that, when his doctrines were vindicated, they were not recognised as his.

In all his public disputations, Origen was the mouthpiece of the bishops and submitted his reasoning to their approbation. It was only to be expected that the soundness of his own teachings would be judged in each new generation according to the episcopal consensus of the day. His critics and the apologists who answered them invariably maintained the same standard of truth and differed only in their estimate of his conformity to that standard, so that a catechism of orthodoxy for almost any period in the next three centuries could have been derived from a contemporary syllabus of charges against his name. The first record of such charges is the *Apology for Origen* undertaken by his admirer Pamphilus of Caesarea and completed in the same city by Eusebius. Although it survives now only in the Latin of Rufinus, it is clearly a document of the pre-Nicene era, and comparison with Rufinus' own *Apology for Origen* gives no handle to any suspicion of forgery or adulteration. Two centuries of corporate reflection on the nature of God, the gestation of the Trinity and the destiny of the human soul are digested in the Pamphilus' summary of the indictment and his own manoeuvres on behalf of Origen. It was easy for him to show that Origenism, as his adversaries conceived it, was a tissue of calumnies and misconstructions; he could not foresee that the ark in which his adversaries sailed would be capsized by a revolution in Christian thought within a few years of his death in 309. We shall see in the following chapter that only vessels built from timbers forbidden to the age of Pamphilus were spared by the oncoming tide.

Pamphilus and the Critics of Origen

The contours of monotheism

The first charge[1] is that Origen was a ditheist, ranking the Son beside the Father as an unbegotten or independent principle. Had this been his position, the New Testament and the apologists would unite to convict him of taking away the foundation of the Gospel. Christ himself had declared 'there is one who is good, the Father', while Paul, to expose the futility of offerings made to idols, proclaims that 'there be gods many and lords many, but to us One God, the Father, of whom are all things and we in him' (1Corinthians 8.7). He goes on indeed to assert that there is one Lord, Jesus Christ,[2] but it was possible for evangelists like Tatian and Minucius Felix to leave Christ out of the argument: they had still to make the world hear what it had refused to learn from Israel, that it is blasphemy to neglect the author of heavens and earth and ludicrous to pay our devoirs instead to the fragile workmanship of our own hands. The verse most often cited by the Christian on trial in martyrologies is Acts 4.24: 'Lord, thou art God, which hast made heaven and earth and the sea and all that in them is'.[3]

Even where Christ is also proclaimed, as in Justin or Athenagoras, the defence of monotheism requires not only that he be worshipped in second place, as the plenipotentiary or offspring of the Father, but that there should be some beginning to his existence as a distinct *hypostasis* or second person of the Godhead.[4] Plato is repeatedly praised for acknowledging one Father and Creator of the universe;[5] philosophers who admit many gods, or imagine that the sovereignty of the one God is curtailed by some power not of his own creation, are no better than the common folk who present their hecatombs to fallen angels. Homer's maxim – 'the

[1] Pamphilus, *Apology* 88, p. 314 Röwekampf.

[2] For the shifts whereby a doctrine of the Trinity was elicited from this text see Bray (1999), 76–7.

[3] See index to Musurillo (1972).

[4] Justin, *1Apol* 10 and *2Apol* 5.3, where the Son's generation appears to be instrumental to the creation of the world. At Athenagoras, *Embassy* 10, the Son is said to be generated though not one of the things subject to *genesis* in the sense of temporal becoming.

[5] Daniélou (1973), 107–28.

rule of many is not good; let one rule' – had been applied by Aristotle to the universe,[6] and Christian propagandists in the time of Pamphilus urged that where no one god is omnipotent, the world will be torn apart by their competing claims to mastery.[7] If there is one ubiquitous shibboleth of orthodoxy which sufficed, then as now, to discriminate those authors whom we call catholic from the Gnostics, it was the truism 'Hear, O Israel, the Lord our God is one' (Deuteronomy 6.4).

By this epoch it had become apparent that even the Platonists had joined Basilides, Valentinus and Marcion in ascribing the origin of the present world to a demiurge of inferior capacity, thus abridging the temporal sovereignty of the Good.[8] In our New Testament Paul, the Fourth Evangelist and their followers say on more than one occasion that the visible world was made through Christ, the image of the invisible Father (Colossians 1.15; cf. Hebrews 1.2–3), but nowhere do we hear that he himself is the architect rather than the instrument of creation. We do, however, hear that he is even now the bearer of the name above all names (Philippians 2.9), that he is exalted above the angels (Hebrews 1.7–8), that every knee on heaven and earth is destined to bow to him (Philippians 2.10; 1Corinthians 15.24–7), that the new creation will be summed up or recapitulated in him (Ephesians 1.10), if only that he may relinquish it to the Father on the last day (1Corinthians 15.28). Can he be less than God, or other than God, and worthy of such reverence? The apostolic era evades this question by uncoupling the Biblical names of the Creator, apportioning *theos* ('God', the equivalent of Elohim) to the Father alone, and *kurios* ('Lord', the equivalent of Adonai) to both the Father and the exalted Son.[9] The status of the Son before incarnation – in the ages when the Father was represented by his Logos, according to the Fourth Evangelist – may not have concerned his worshippers until they began to feel that it was not consonant with his dignity to call him less than 'god'. In Ignatius of Antioch the wary locution 'our god' distinguishes him from the Father,[10] but the logic of monotheism would not countenance the postulation of two gods – not even, for that matter, of a 'second god' or 'another god', for both these formulae seem to have been improvised as *argumenta ad hominem* in Origen's refutations of heretical or pagan adversaries.[11] They were

---

6 *Metaphysics* 1076a, quoting *Iliad* 2.204.

7 Lactantius, *Divine Institutes* 1.3.18–19; Constantine, *Oration to the Saints* 3; Euasebius, *Tricennial Oration* 6; Athanasius, *Against the Nations* 36–8.

8 See Numenius, Fr. 17 Des Places, *Chaldaean Oracles* Fr. 7 Des Places, Alcinous, *Didascalia* 10, with Dillon (1986), 227–9.

9 Cerfaux (1954), 137–88 concludes that the title Adonai carries an augury of the kingdom in prophetic use, and remains pre-eminently a title of God the Father in New Testament writings though it can be devolved upon the Son as the manifestation of his glory and wisdom.

10 *Smyrnaeans* 11.1 is an exception. Hurtado (2003), 238–9 suggests that Ignatius mimics salutations commonly paid to the Emperor, and argues that the Son remains 'subordinate' to the Father.

11 Edwards (2006). See *Against Celsus* 5.39, 6.61, 7.57 and *Dialogue with Heraclides* 2.22–5.

never dogmatic tools, for him or for any other Christian, since, when strictly construed, they contravene the axioms of the faith.

But to call Christ 'god', with the caveat that the term 'god' can have only one referent, would seem to entail his identity with the Father. Even if it were possible for 'God' to be the proper appellation of two subjects, the two would have to be equipollent and coeternal or one would not deserve the name. So at least some proponents of the rule of faith were obliged to maintain as an antidote to Gnostic myths of intumescence and rupture in the Godhead. Irenaeus appears to be committed by his reasoning, if not by his own confession, to a Trinity of three coeval persons; Clement, as we have seen, cannot be proved to have held any theory of evolution in the Logos, and is reported to have made him coeternal with the Father when interpreting the prologue to the Fourth Gospel for believers. Tertullian[12] and Hippolytus, on the other hand – always writing as polemicists and never as mere expositors – both adhere to the older teaching that it is only the immanent reason of the Father that can be said to be eternal, and that this was projected as a distinct hypostasis for the purpose of creation. Both, that is, would rather deny eternity to the Second Person than admit two gods.

Origen rejected three positions, each of which was espoused in his time by at least one figure whom a knowledgeable contemporary could have taken as a touchstone of sound doctrine:

1. The patripassian thesis is that 'Son' is not the name of a hypostasis, but the cognomen which the Father assumed when he took the way of Calvary. The apologist Bishop Melito of Sardis is the author of the one surviving work which asserts that God died on the Cross.[13] While Origen's own treatise *On the Pasch* may be designed to rebut the 'Quartodeciman' calculation of Easter which Melito also defended,[14] there is no extant work of his that impugns the Christology of the patripassians, perhaps because, in his own part of the world, it was already obsolete. There can be no doubt, however, that, as a proponent of three hypostases in the Godhead, he would have condemned the position adumbrated by his older contemporary Tertullian of Carthage in his torrid work *Against Praxeas*. Otherwise unknown today, Praxeas was so esteemed in Rome that he was able to dissuade its bishop, Zephyrinus, from recognizing the Montanists, or exponents of the 'new prophecy' of wich Tertullian was himself enamoured. Origen, though he was not afraid to deprecate a papal error, did not endorse the new prophecy, and may not have held Tertullian's view that the death of the Son is less paradoxical than that of the Father. Tertullian would appear to have subscribed to the common

12 *Against Praxeas* 5; cf *Against Hermogenes* 19.4, where he argues that matter cannot be anterior to the Wisdom which was 'born and established' for the creation of the world. Evans (1948), 213–4 opines, however, that the juxtaposition of *ratio* and *sermo* in the first case need not imply that there are tow chronological phases in the existence of the Logos.

13 *Paschal Homily* 74; cf. *ibid.*, 8–9 on the Father's assumption of Sonship. See Hübner (1999), 20–32 on the relation between Melito and the monarchians of the west.

14 For a circumspect discussion see Büchinger (2005), 152–8.

assumption of his time, that the Second Person is more amenable than the First to the constraints of finitude; but if he did, he was fighting heresy with arguments that would one day be reckoned equally heretical. By the standard of orthodoxy as it was later defined, one could say that the majority of ecclesiastical writers in the third century knew that patripassianism was an error, but not why.

2. The modalist or monarchian position – if we follow the modern usage of these terms, which is not quite coterminous with that of the early church – is equally unwilling either to crucify the Father or to admit to distinction of persons in the Godhead. In the teaching of a representative specimen, Bishop Callistus of Rome, the noun 'Spirit' denotes an attribute, inflexion or dynamic manifestation of the Father, which enables him to be present in the man Jesus without incurring any change or diminution in his own nature. Origen was acquainted with monarchians who deduced from the title Logos that The Son is nothing more than the revealed thought of the Father, as epiphenomenal to his substance as a string of human syllables to the one who utters them. There are many scholars today who opine that appellatives such as 'Wisdom', 'Spirit' and even 'Word' are merely reifications of divine agency; in holding that in fact they designate subjects of the name 'God' distinct from the Father, Origen may have been conscious of defying the bishop of Rome, and there is testimony from ancient times of his having been condemned by a Roman council. But so much that is said of him in the centuries after his death is mere invective that no theory as to his understanding of the 'rule of faith' can be erected on such foundations.

3. The majority of apologists before Origen, as we have noted, regarded the efferent or spoken word as a late projection of the immanent reason or wisdom of God. Philo of Alexandria, the Jewish philosopher, drew a similar inference from Genesis 1.3., where the material creation is the product of God's first utterance. To Hippolytus and Tertullian, as we have seen, this was the catholic doctrine, even if it entailed the application of the name God to one who did not possess eternity as an attribute of individuation. To contemporaries of Pamphilus who accepted the near-consensus of the apologists as a test of catholicity, it might seem that to make the Son's hypostasis eternal is to destroy all precedence within the Godhead, and hence to deny that the Second Person is the offspring of the First.

Such a reader might catch an intimation of heresy in the following passage:

> Consider whether one who assigns a beginning to the Word of God or the Holy Spirit is not in fact hurling his blasphemy at the ingenerate Father himself, since he denies that the has always been a Father and been the progenitor of the Word and possessed his Wisdom in all previous times and ages (*Apology* 56, 282–4 Röwekamp).

Origen never fails, in all the texts adduced by Pamphilus, to asseverate that the Son owes his existence to the Father; yet to maintain their coeternity is to imply that the generation of the Son is no contingency, that the Father could not have done otherwise, and that he owes his eternal Fatherhood to the Son no less than the Son depends on the Father for his Sonship. In his vindication of Origen, Pamphilus cites an otherwise unattested passage from his commentary on the epistle to the Hebrews. In this the proximity of the Son to the Father is accentuated, not to efface the order of priority in the Godhead (for that too is still delineated clearly enough), but in order to explain how Christ, as Son of God and therefore another being than the Father, could perform works that no candid mind would suppose to lie within the capacities of a human agent. Commenting on the image of Christ as a 'ray of the Father's effulgence' in his text, he compares the representation of wisdom as an *aporroia* or emanation of God at Wisdom 7.25. Assuming that the referent of both passages is God the Son, he concludes that his relation to the Father is analogous to that between an ointment and the vapour that it exudes. This metaphor, prompted by the term *aporroia*, is augmented in the quotation by a term that is neither biblical nor attested elsewhere in the extant works of Origen:

> It behoves us to be aware that the Holy Scripture makes a way for itself by certain means through particular statements which are ineffable, mysterious and abstruse, using the name 'vapour' to convey and suggest to humans a subtle meaning. It takes this name from the corporeal realm so that we can in some measure understand that[15] Christ who is Wisdom, by analogy to the vapour which exhales from some bodily substance, proceeds on his own account like a sort of vapour from the power of God himself. Thus Wisdom, proceeding from this power, is generated from the very substance[16] of God; thus none the less, according to the likeness of a corporeal exhalation, it is called a pure exhalation of the glory of theAlmighty", and a unblemished one at that (*Apology* 99, p. 318 Röwekamp).

Richard Hanson has argued that the epithet *homoousios* is an interpolation designed to forestall the suspicion of heterodoxy.[17] Yet it hardly serves that purpose, as he concedes, for it indicates only that the Son and the Father are of the same ousia, which may mean that they share one nature, one identity or simply one sum of attributes, but does not imply, according to the usage of Origen's time, that one of the consubstantial entities owes its origin to the other. Since the word *homoousios* was not an orthodox talisman before the Nicene Council of 325, the interpolation

---

[15] Reading *quoniam* with Rowekamp, who provides no *apparatus criticus*. Here the Migne text PG 17.581, has *quomodo*, 'how', as also at 580C, so that Pamphilus undertakes in the latter passage not to show *that* Origen taught the consubstantiality of Father and Son, but how. This is the reading followed by Hanson (1972), and which Edwards (1998), 659 and 663 believes to be necessary to the sense of Pamphilus' argument.

[16] The Greek is clearly *hypostasis*, both because the text of Hebrews 1.3 supplies this term, and because Origen denies that the Son is of the Father's ousia, see Origen, *Commentary on John* 20.157.

[17] Hanson (1972); cf. Edwards (1998).

cannot be laid at the door of Pamphilus or Eusebius. But if the culprit is Rufinus – in whose day the word did indeed connote dependence, when it was used of the Son's relation to the Father[18] – we can only wonder why he chose to meddle with a text that already sufficed to exonerate Origen, and why he ignored his own handiwork when arguing, in a personal *Apology for Origen*, that the latter would have subscribed to the Nicene formula. It is not his custom to use the term *homoousios* in season and out of season; of his own accord, indeed, he never uses it, not even to demonstrate his own orthodoxy or in his exposition of the apostles' creed.

In the absence of any plausible motive for adulteration, we may assume that we have the passage as Origen wrote it, and that the adjective *homoousios* owes its presence here not to editorial subterfuge, but to his readiness to innovate when quotidian usage failed him. Origen is conscious of his own hardihood in applying to God a term hitherto used only of corporeal entities; on the other hand, no other word expressed so strongly that community of nature between the Father and the Son that he affirms both here and in his other writings. The question, then, is not why he employed it but why Pamphilus chose to annex this final paragraph to an excerpt that was already long enough to support his case. As I argue elsewhere,[19] the difficulties recede if we suppose that the word *homoousios* could not be neglected in any defence of Origen before the Nicene Council because it was part of the evidence brought against him – that is to say, until the episcopal consensus made it an index of good churchmanship, it was apt to be construed as an endorsement of monarchianism, Valentinianism or some other position commonly denounced by guardians of the "rule of faith".

So much became apparent in 268, when eighty bishops met to expel their overweening colleague Paul of Samosata from the see of Antioch.[20] Although this was a the first assize to depose a bishop, only the scantiest record survived of it even in antiquity; when, in the mid-fourth century, it transpired that the proceedings had included the condemnation of the word *homoousios*, champions of the Nicene Creed of 325 were surprised but not disarmed. Hilary of Poitiers urged that the council had rejected it in the sense given to it by Paul, who had interpreted 'one substance' to mean one entity (*On the Synods* 86): the error of the fallen prelate, he argued, was to allow only one hypostasis in God, and hence to conclude, for fear of putting God the Father on the Cross, that the incarnate Christ was a man and nothing more. Athanasius, on the other hand, surmised that it was Paul who turned a false construction of the term *homoousios* on his judges: those who affirm two consubstantial persons in the Godhead (so he imagines Paul to have argued) must suppose that, like two consubstantial entities in the sensible world, they merit this description because they are fragments of the same homogeneous stuff (*On the Synods* 45). From this is would follow that father and Son are co-ordinate beings, and neither of them ingenerate. Paul's psilanthropism

---

18 See discussion in next chapter.

19 Edwards (1998).

20 See Hanson (1988), 195 with Edwards (1998), 661 n.12.

– his belief that Christ was simply a man – is attested in the synod's letter to Rome and Alexandria, which Eusebius transcribed in his *Church History*.[21] Athanasius and Hilary offer only their own conjectures, but they would not have felt obliged to explain away the embargo on the term *homoousios* had they been able to deny it, and their endeavours may therefore be taken as proof that the term was indeed condemned in 268.

Readers of the heresiologists knew that the term was in frequent use among Gnostics. Around 320 the Alexandrian presbyter Arius held it up as a bugbear when his bishop Alexander required him forced to justify his own confession of three hypostases, all distinct in nature (Sozomen, *Church History* 1.15). If, he rejoined, you deny that the Second Person is created out of nothing, you must either divide the monad, like Sabellius, or make him an emanation of the Father, like Valentinus, or conceive him as a *homoousion meros*, consubstantial part of the Godhead, which is to be a Manichaean. By this date, the synthesis of Christian and Zoroastrian teachings devised by Mani in 241 had won adherents throughout the empire, and had incurred the hostility of legislators even before the accession of a Christian Emperor. In its principal myth[22] the divine is represented as an extended realm of light, which has been forced into battle with the neighbouring darkness and, being worsted, has left a portion of its substance in captivity. Some particles of this light perform a daily pilgrimage as heavenly lights, while others must be redeemed by the elect, who, to ensure that their diet contains the greatest quantity of light, subsist entirely on vegetables. Trusting rightly that this crude notion of God will be unpalatable to his correspondent, Arius hints that he can escape it only by granting that the Son is not of one substance with the Father. Although his Alexandrian superior, Alexander, is alleged to have forced the term *homoousion* on the Nicene Council with the connivance of the western prelate Hosius of Cordova,[23] he makes no use of it in his public castigations of Arius, and goes no further than to affirm that the Son is a peerless image of the Father, rebuking Arius for his failure to concede that the two are like (or alike) in *ousia*.[24]

Athanasius, the successor of Alexander, was compelled to admit, that their saintly predecessor Dionysius of Alexandria, who was prevented only by illness from presiding at the synod that deposed Paul of Samosata, had himself been accused of heresy because he was not prepared to assert the consubstantiality of the three persons.[25] The plaintiffs laid their evidence before his namesake, Dionysius of Rome, who called him to account for his opinions. The patriarch complied by

---

21 *Church History* 7.30. For this and other documents see Loofs (1924), 323–39.

22 See Augustine, *Against the Letter Called Fundamental*.

23 Philostorgius, *Church History* 17, the work of a man who never tells the truth without a good reason.

24 Socrates, *Church History* 1.6; on the Origenistic tone of the letter see Simonetti (1965), 116–20. On the absence of the *homoousios*, see *ibid.*, 125n.76.

25 The evidence comes chiefly from Athanasius, *On the Opinion of Dionysius*; for commentary see Abramowski (1992).

affirming everything but the *homoousios*: Father and Son were one in kind, related as the sun to its light, as the shipwright to his vessel, as the monad to the dyad – in short, as any two entities, one of which owes its being to the other. Creation out of nothing is precluded, as Athanasius observed, and so is the absolute identity of the two. Between these poles of error, it seems that both Dionysii were willing to entertain any conceit which would illustrate the Son's natural dependence on the Father, the Roman pontiff seems to have been no more inclined to exact a confession of the *homoousion* than the Alexandrian patriarch to vouchsafe one.[26] When Pamphilus took up his pen on behalf of Origen, then, the *homoousion* was not yet a phylactery for the orthodox (whoever the orthodox were); it was a strange and ambiguous neologism which required an emollient gloss.

The gloss was all the more necessary in Origen's case because a captious reader could easily find in him the source of every heresy that Arius threw the teeth of Alexander. For example, he had spoken of God as a monad (*First Principles* 1.4.6), though he was not the first[27] and Arius too used 'monad' and 'dyad' as sobriquets for the Father and the Son, at least in verse.[28] Again, he was accused of entertaining the Valentinian theory that Christ was an emanation of the Godhead – a charge to be weighed in the following section of this chapter. And he had stated in his *First Principles* that the sun and moon are animated creatures, whose souls, more virtuous than ours, have accepted servitude as ministers of light to the lower cosmos. Even one flirtation with the term *homoousios*, therefore, would expose him to the suspicion of denying the oneness of God, of making his substance material and fissible, or at least of making the Second Hypostasis both coeval and co-ordinate in his origin with the Father. This was to make his scriptural title 'Son' a capricious accolade; worse still, it entailed two independent principles of being, and hence two gods.

Origen and the Valentinians

The second accusation[29] is that Origen regarded the Second Hypostasis as a projection, or – to borrow the Valentinian term – prolation from the Father, a position that requires no elucidation in this dossier, since to Pamphilus, as to Origen's detractors, it is self-evident that any projection of the Father's substance would entail both passibility and diminution of being in one whom faith and metaphysics alike declared to be incapable of change. The impeachment is easily answered by an excerpt from the First Principles: if Origen states expressly, in this thesaurus of heterodoxies, that the Son is not a prolation as some have falsely supposed, that this term connotes an act like that which a man or a beast performs in sowing his progeny, that by contrast the Father of all begets by fiat, so that

26 Abramowski (1992).

27 See Athenagoras, *Embassy* 6.2.

28 See Stead (1964), 18 and (1978), 30, with Athanasius, *On the Synods* 16.

29 *Apology* 102–8, pp. 320–24 Röwekamp.

his offspring needs no substrate but his omnipotent will – if he says all this, then plainly he is not a Valentinian, and the critics are put to flight.

But if we inquire, not whether the charge is true but how it arose, we shall have no difficulty in discovering its grounds. We have noticed that, in seeking metaphors to characterize the Son's procession from the Father, Origen borrows the noun *aporroia* or emanation from the Book of Wisdom, attributed to Solomon. But the authority of this book, which lacked a Hebrew prototype and was not universally deemed canonical, would not have sufficed in all quarters to extenuate his use of a term which, literally construed, implies that God can surrender a portion of his own substance. The gravamen of this charge, like that of the last, is thus that Origen has sullied God with the properties of matter.

In the passage adduced by Pamphilus to rebut this charge, the Second Person is said to be an immediate product of the Father's will. Elsewhere Origen notes that, whereas every creation in our world has a material substrate, no other substrate than the Father's will is required for the generation of his perfect image.[30] To Pamphilus this was evidently the catholic opinion of his time. Yet this distinction between the Son and things of the material order is weakened by two caveats in the rest of Origen's work. On the one hand, there are passages in *First Principles* where he doubts whether matter is after all an indispensable postulate of cosmogony;[31] if it is not, the Father's will is the universal substrate, and it is hard to see what peculiar distinction could attach to the generation of the Son. On the other, when he returns to Hebrews 1.3 in his *Commentary on John*, the nomenclature changes, and he contends not that the Father's will is the matter of the Son, but that the Son is the offspring of the Father's power or *dunamis* (13.25.152–3). These statements are interchangeable, as the equation of matter with *dunamis*, or potential for being, had long been a commonplace among philosophers. In the second variant, however, Origen echoes the philosophers once again in contrasting *dunamis* with *ousia*, the actuality or essence of the Father. Thus the dictum 'born of the Father's will' must carry the rider 'and not born of the Father's essence'. Those who published this inference on the eve of the Nicene Council in 325 fell under the ban of the assembled bishops,[32] and some years later Athanasius argued that to call the Son a product of the Father's will is to make him a creature like any other creature (*Against the Arians* 3.62). Orthodoxy, as Pamphilus understood this at the beginning of the fourth century, prescribed both that the Son should be born of the Father's will and that the two should possess a common nature. Neither he nor Origen tried to reconcile these positions, but when Arius discarded the second

---

30 See *Commentary on John* 20.22.182 with Harl (1987), 244–5 and Widdicombe (1994), 89. On the evidence that Origen used the word *ktisma* (creature) of the Second Person, see Lowry (1938) and Abramowski (1992), 28–30.

31 *First Principles* 4.4.7 entertains the view, which is forcefully maintained in *Philokalia* 24, that bodies consist of nothing but properties.

32 The offenders include Eusebius of Nicomedia, according to Theodoret, *Church History* 1.5.

in favour of the first, he was making asymmetrical use of Origen's reasoning, but no more so than anyone who cited him as a witness to the eternal generation of the Son. The eternal generation became a dogma, more than a hundred years after Origen first maintained it; in his own day the countervailing thesis that the Son is the progeny of the Father's will was received more favourably, but the passage of the same hundred years turned this asseveration into a heresy.

Origen and Christ

The third article[33] against Origen is that, anticipating Paul of Samosata, he denied the incarnation[34] and saw in Christ no more than a man inspired by God. The charge was never repeated, its provenance is not explained, and as Pamphilus observes,[35] it sits uneasily with the complaint that he exaggerates the dignity of the Son. It is easily confuted by two excerpts from Origen's commentary on the epistle to the Galatians, so emphatic in their assertion of Christ's divinity that they annihilate his manhood, at least in his first encounter with Paul.[36] Perhaps the ground of impeachment can be discovered in these passages. It is a hermeneutic principle for Origen that the scriptures sometimes speak of Christ as a man, sometimes as God, sometimes as both. For example at John 8.40 – 'you seek to kill me, a man who has told you the truth' – the Saviour, punishing ignorance with ignorance, describes himself as his persecutors see him (*Commentary on John* 19.2.6). Less candid readers might deduce from such expositions that Origen himself thought Christ no greater than he professed to be; further evidence could be culled from his treatise *On Prayer* where he discountenances the offering of the same worship to the Son as to the Father on the grounds that he differs in *ousia*, or essence, and in his *hupokeimenon*, or material substrate (*On Prayer* 15.1). It is clear that the second term at least pertains only to his manhood, and that Origen's objection rests on a literal construction of the commandment which forbids the adoration of visible gods. The term *ousia* may signify the hypostasis of the Son, in contradistinction to that of the Father, or the creaturely existence that he assumed in becoming human; since he never, except by analogy, grants a common *ousia* to the Father and the Son, it may even imply that they differ in essence (though not in *phusis* or nature[37]) as persons of the Trinity. But even if this last conjecture is set aside, the assumption of manhood entails that the Son is no fit subject for prayers of adoration, though he may, like other saints, receive those of intercession and thanks (*On Prayer* 11.2–4).

---

33 *Apology* 108, p. 324 Röwekamp.

34 See Lang (2000), 77.

35 *Apology* 87, p. 112 Röwekamp.

36 *Ibid.*, pp. 324–8 Röwekamp, an otherwise unknown annotation to Galatians 1.1.

37 At *Commentary on John* 2.10.76 the Son is *phusei* (by nature) the only-begotten.

What orisons were commonly offered to Christ in Origen's time we cannot say, but it would no doubt have been possible to argue than, as Athanasnius argued a century later, that to be God is to be worthy of adoration, and that therefore one cannot refuse this to Christ without curtailing his divinity.[38] The episcopal letter announcing the deposition of Paul of Samosata records that one of his crimes had been to substitute his own name in hymns to Christ (Eusebius, *Church History* 7.30.10). Profane as the second half of this action was, the other half is almost vindicated in the practice of the western churches, for the commonest form in Roman Catholic and Protestant liturgies is not to apostrophize the Son directly but to commend prayers to the Father through the Son.

It might be more plausible to represent Origen, not as a forerunner to Paul of Samosata, but as the successor to the Ebionites, who did not (as is commonly said today) deny the celestial origin of Christ, but divided the Saviour into two agents, Jesus and Christ, the first a prophet born in the usual course of nature, the second a divine chaperone, who accompanied him throughout his ministry.[39] There are passages in Origen which suggest such an intimate union of God and man in the Saviour as to render the two natures indiscernible;[40] on the other hand, his fissiparous exegesis befits a subject who is not so much God incarnate in man as God and man in synergy. Ebionites and Samosatenes (or Paulicians) were not carefully distinguished in early Christian polemics, and if the allegation here is that Origen separates the man Jesus from the Logos, rather than that he finds no place for the Godhead in his Christology, the third charge is a preliminary study to the fifth, which is that Origen preached two Christs.

In answering this,[41] his apologist hints that it may have been deduced from an innocuous remark in Origen's *Commentary on Isaiah*, where he notes that *christos* 'anointed' was an epithet before it was a name, and that in this rudimentary sense there are as many christs in scripture as there are saints (*Apology* 116). As Origen goes on to differentiate the one Christ from the many anointed, this philological observation cannot support the case against him. But Pamphilus goes on to admit that the criticism may have been inspired by a far less tractable difficulty – the significance that Origen attached throughout his writings to the presence of a human soul in Christ (*Apology* 122). He was not the first to insist upon this tenet, for Tertullian had already adduced those passages in which Christ confesses trouble of soul or infirmity of purpose in his refutation of Apelles (*On the Flesh of Christ* 9–11). The latter taught that the soul and flesh of the Saviour were identical, and that this, the composite, resided from eternity in heaven until it borrowed the womb of Mary as a conduit to this world. Tertullian merely enumerates texts in which something is predicated of Christ's soul that could not be predicated either of

38 See *Against the Arians* 3.28.11–12, citing 2Thessalonicans 3.11.

39 See Eusebius, *Church History* 7.30.10–11; Lang (2000).

40 See for example *First Principles* 2.6.3 on the liquefaction of the humanity in the divinity; *Against Celsus* 3.41 on the *anakrasis* or mixture of human and divine.

41 *Apology* 116–22, pp. 336–40 Röwekamp.

his body or of the Word in his divine character. Origen, on the other hand, was the first to attempt an anthropology of the incarnate Word, assigning to Christ a human body, a human soul and a human spirit, each with its own capacities and its own perfections. The body was the vehicle of his teaching and his miracles, and the one element that passed from the Cross to the tomb, while the soul descended to Hades and the Spirit returned for a season to the Father (*Dialogue with Heraclides* 7). In the course of the earthly ministry, the soul was the seat of grief and trepidation; it is not the hegemonic element, either in the Saviour or in us, and its sufferings illustrate his readiness to partake of our condition. It is the spirit, or ruling element, in Christ that is peculiarly exempt from sin and weakness, by virtue of its fusion with the Logos. This fusion is no arbitrary miracle, for his is the only soul – the term here designating the whole of the inner man – that has been cemented to the Logos by the fire of love from the moment of its creation. The prescience that his bond with God confers on the spirit enables Christ to contemplate his own death, and thus to feel a commotion unknown to us (*Commentary on John* 22.18.218–28). His spirit, however, imbibes not only the prescience of the Logos, but his imperturbability, and therefore this commotion which originates in the exercise of a supernatural faculty manifests itself in the natural pathology of the soul.

These may be quaint speculations; to us at least they are not heretical, whereas the oecumenical councils of the fifth century pronounced it heretical not to affirm a human soul in Christ. It would seem, however, that after the defeat of psilanthropism in the late third century, there were many who found it hard to conceive that the human nature of Christ could remain entire, yet serve as a vehicle for the Logos. If there were not to be two Christs, and if the Logos was to descend, not merely to animate the man Jesus from above, he must perform some operation when incarnate that would otherwise have been performed by a natural human faculty. But if the Logos and the natural faculty were to coexist in Christ, would it not follow that one or the other was supernumerary? Origen's disciples were sufficiently impressed by this dilemma to treat the question of a soul in Christ as an open one, though Origen himself manifestly believed it to have been decided by the plain text of scripture. Pamphilus is content to quote the gospels, and to gather affidavits to the unity of Christ from Origen's writings. Eusebius, in copious works produced before and after the Nicene Council, takes up the matter only once, and then not to speculate on his own account, but to give the choice of heresy or submission to his adversary Marcellus of Ancyra.[42] Here, then, is another instance in which Origen can be said to have set the norm for orthodoxy in the future, but only by setting up his own work as a mark for the ecclesiastical censors of his age.

We have departed from the order of charges in Pamphilus, because the fifth proved to be almost a duplication of the third. The fourth[43] is not the duplicate but the antithesis of the third: it asserts that Origen construed the Saviour's ministry in the flesh as an allegory, acknowledging only a phantasmal incarnation. Docetism

---

42 On Against Marcellus 2.4 see Struttwolf (1999), 323–33.

43 *Apology* 113–15, pp. 328–44 Röwekamp.

(as we now call it) was a spectre that had to be exorcised anew by each generation of bishops. Ignatius had asked how martyrs could be bred among those who denied that Christ had suffered. Writing against the Gnostics or their epigones, Tertullian and Irenaeus barely distinguish those who deny a body of any kind to Christ from those who credit him with psychic or attenuated flesh. Hippolytus is the first to employ the name (*Refutation* 8.1–11), though for him it is only the appellative of an obscure sect, which appears not to deserve it more than others. It never merely meant that the Saviour was immune to carnal or spiritual temptation (as it does for some modern authors), and was never supposed, by authors now deemed catholic to be a logical corollary of the belief that Christ was God. That Christ's flesh should be palpable was the test of his being human, and, as the gospels relate that the test was applied to his risen body, it was equally wrong to treat him as an ethereal presence after the resurrection. This at least was the view of those contemporaries whom Pamphilus felt bound to answer on Origen's behalf, and it does not seem to have troubled them that Paul speaks only of rising in the body, not in flesh.[44]

Of course it was easily demonstrated that Origen accords a body of flesh to Christ before the resurrection. In contrast to Clement, he never doubts that the Saviour required the same physical sustenance as the saved, and in the passage adduced by Pamphilus[45] he notes that it was his eating that set Christ apart from the Baptist. He proceeds, in the same discussion, to cite the circumcision as proof of the solidity of Christ's body, the emission of blood and water on the Cross as evidence of its passibility, and the troubles of his soul as a sign that the inner man perceived what the outer man suffered. Even if, as a recent editor indicates,[46] the context of this passage has been disguised, there are other references in Origen to the shedding of blood and psychic tribulation, where his argument undoubtedly requires both to be real. Once again, it remains for us to ascertain not whether the charge was just but how it arose.

Our clue is the supplementary libel that Origen handled all historical passages in the sacred text as allegories. Although this is appended to the statement of the fourth charge (*Apology* 112–13), no exculpation is offered until Pamphilus takes it up as again as the sixth item in the indictment.[47] He proves, from Origen's commentary on the epistle to Philemon, that he recommended literal obedience to the majority of the laws enjoined on Israel under the covenant of Sinai, and rebuked the weak faith of those who thought the narratives of the Old Testament too incredible to be received as history (*Apology* 125). Again it need not trouble us that the commentary on Philemon is unattested elsewhere,[48] for in a celebrated passage of the *First Principles*, where the three levels of exegesis are anatomized as the body, soul and spirit of the scriptures, the body is no more dispensable

44 See Chapters 1 and 2 for a fuller discussion of these topics.

45 *Apology* 113, of uncertain provenance.

46 Röwekamp (2005), 144 surmises that it comes from the treatise *On the Resurrection*.

47 *Apology* 120–27, pp. 340–46 Röwekamp.

48 See further Heine (2000) and Röwekamp (2005), 342n.

than that of Christ himself (4.2.4) The literal sense is to be discarded only when it is incongruous or immoral; Origen's practice in homilies and commentaries is to work his way to the higher sense through the scrutiny of the *lexis* or patent meaning of the text, every jot and tittle of which he believes to be an utterance of the spirit and an expression of the omnipresent Word.

The presupposition of all exegesis in Origen is his analogy between the invisible presence of God in Christ and the occultation of a spiritual meaning in the text.[49] If critics failed to perceive that his aim was to elevate but not to overwrite the plain word of scripture, that may be because tropology in earlier Christian writers is almost always inimical to the literal reading. Barnabas, Justin Martyr and Theophilus of Antioch looked beneath the surface only when need arose, where the specious reading of some law, event or prophecy in the Old Testament would favour the Jew or alienate the philosopher. They did not maintain, like Philo of Alexandria, that he would honour the spirit of the law must obey the letter; they believed whatever purported to be historical unless it was manifestly incoherent or absurd, but offered no apologetic or hortatory application of such passages except where they foreshadowed the earthly ministry of Christ. Origen's goal, however, was to deduce from every phrase some truth or precept that would edify his Christian contemporaries; this enterprise required him, not only to sublimate the literal sense of texts that were plainly didactic or confessedly obscure, but to unearth the hidden parable in perfectly lucid narratives which would otherwise convey historical truth but no instruction. Those who could not decipher the resulting palimpsest assumed that the natural sense had simply been expunged. The more assiduously he pursued his method, the more it seemed to his detractors that he doubted all historical records, even those attesting the incarnation of the Saviour in body, soul and spirit. Pamphilus fails to observe that it is the threefold incarnation of the Word, accredited as a fact of history, that promotes and corroborates Origen's threefold reading of the scriptures; he contents himself with a proof that his master did not in all cases spurn the literal sense.[50]

Origen and the Resurrection

The seventh charge[51] is that Origen denies the resurrection of the body, or (as Pamphilus hints in a post-script) that he affirmed the resurrection of the body but not the flesh. He is acquitted first by an excerpt from his treatise in two books *On the Resurrection*, where he protests that since the body shares the afflictions of the soul it is equally worthy of its reward; then by a chaste catena of observations on the Apocalypse and the First Epistle of Paul to the Corinthians; and finally by a passage in which Origen corrects an injudiciously literal reading of the verse

[49] On the anagogic journey from the literal sense to the recognition of Christ in the text see now King (2005).

[50] See Edwards (2002), 134–5 on *HomLev* 5.2.

[51] *Apology* 128–50, pp. 328–57 Röwekamp.

'his tabernacle is in the sun'.[52] Assuming, as his interlocutors do, that Christ is the subject of this dictum, Origen argues that his tabernacle, or body on earth, is the church, and that the term sun denotes not the visible luminary but Christ himself, the sun of righteousness. Since it would seem more calculated to weaken than to reinforce the proof that Origen taught the resurrection of the body, it is probable that this passage, like the one declaring the Son to be *homoousios* with the Father, had initially been cited against him, not in his defence. The citation in the *Apology*, then, is palliative: it is not the resurrection of Christ but his subsequent itinerary that is allegorized, and the argument presupposes some perpetuation of bodily existence after death.

The argument that body and soul deserve the same recompense for the same affliction comes from a dialogue, and was pressed into service by detractors of Origen who believed that it did not represent his own view. Remnants of dialogue survived in a polemical composition by Methodius of Olympia, a contemporary of Pamphilus who was held in high estimation by posterity. Yet even his work perished, and the received text of it today is a hybrid of Syriac translation and Greek epitome.[53] In this redaction the mouthpiece of false teaching is called Origen, though we cannot say whether the name was given to him by Methodius, Origen or an annotator. This interlocutor argues:

1. that the coats of skins which God contrived for Adam and Eve are Biblical symbols of the flesh which attires the fallen soul;
2. that the man of whom Paul says 'I was alive before the law' is the heavenly prototype whom God created before he fashioned his earthly tenement;
3. that while the soul survives death, the body is not renewed;
4. that the bodies of those who rise in glory will be spherical;
5. that after death the soul retains only the incorporeal form or *morphê* of the abandoned body.

These charges, as they stand, are not coherent, and the third is leveled not at Origen but at 'Origenists'. The first charge is brought against Origen by a number of ancient witnesses, though it cannot be verified from his extant writings;[54] the complaint is not, as it might be in modern scholarship, that he tempers an anthropomorphism by allegory, but rather that he seeks the literal counterpart of the skins in mere corporeality, not in the mortality and corruption entailed by sin. The second charge is corroborated in part by Origen's reading of the two accounts of the making of humanity in Genesis, which he takes, with his characteristic

52 *Apology* 147, citing Psalm 18 (19).5.

53 Reconstructed in N.P. Bonwetsch, *Methodius: Werke* (Leipzig 1917).

54 See now Heidl (2005), 152–4 on *LevHom* 6.2. But, while he demonstrates that Origen found the episode susceptible to an allegorical construction, it does not follow that he denies the historicity of the event which is ostensibly reported at Genesis 3.21.

'literalism',[55] to signify first the creation of the inner man and next the fashioning of his carnal envelope (*Genesis Homilies* 1). The pretext for the fourth charge[56] is to be found in Origen's statement that the spherical form is an element in the perfection of heavenly bodies (*On Prayer* 31.3); the fifth would be just if 'form' were not understood to exclude corporeality and materiality, both of which are expressly said to be Origen to be indispensable conditions of individuation, in the next life as in this (*First Principles* 1.6.4; *Against Celsus* 5.18–21).

One thing is evident: Origen's dialogue on the resurrection was too subtle, too wary and yet too candid a work to serve the purpose of any litigant in the posthumous trial of his orthodoxy. Both sides held, as an unexamined axiom, that either one must affirm that flesh and blood will be recreated to form a new tenement for the soul or one must deny the resurrection of the body. The prosecution argues, 'He does not espouse *our* doctrine, and hence can hold *no* doctrine of the resurrection.' The defence rejoins, 'He clearly holds *some* doctrine of the resurrection, and hence you have no reason to doubt that he espouses yours'. Origen, for his part, being better versed in Paul than either his friends or his accusers, was aware that he had not grasped either horn of this dilemma. Flesh is Paul's name for that we inherit from Adam, a nature that, on account of his sin, is mortal and prone to error. The flesh is that which boasts of its subjection to the law, mistaking circumcision for obedience; but it is worthy of commendation only when it becomes not merely the slave of the law but its ark, when the law that Moses received on tablets of stone is inscribed anew on hearts of flesh (2Corinthians 3.3; cf. Jeremiah 31.33). Until this regeneration is accomplished, flesh is the enemy of spirit (Galatians 5.17); that it cannot be accomplished in this world is the consequence of our being bound to 'this body of death' (Romans 7.24). In this life, then, the body is the sphere of flesh; in the nest it will rise again, not as a psychic but as a spiritual body, which is to say that its vital principle will be spirit and not soul. 'Flesh and blood', on the other hand, 'cannot enter the kingdom of heaven' (1Corinthians 15.50); even in this life to be moved by God is 'not to confer with flesh and blood' (Galatians 1.16), and to 'know Christ after the flesh' (2Corinthians 5.16) is to remain in one's intellectual and spiritual nonage. Whether this means that the body in the afterlife will be of another texture than the gross envelope that we now wear, the apostle does not say, but it is certain that he proclaims the resurrection of the body, not the flesh, and that he never attributes flesh to the risen Christ. In his exposition of Biblical passages, Origen is careful not to discover more than his witnesses chose to say. His conjecture that different mansions will be allotted to souls is warranted by Paul's dictum that every body has its own predestined glory, by his assurance that the bodies of the saints will be conformed to the glory of Christ, and by the enigmatic prophecy of the Apoclaypse that the bodies of the reprobate will be cast into the sea.[57]

---

[55] Crouzel (1989), 258–9.

[56] Cf. Chadwick (1947), 43.

[57] *Apology* 134–9, citing 1Corinthians 15.41, Phillipians 3.21, Revelations 201.3, and alluding, in the conjecture that souls receive diverse *habitacula*, to John 14.2.

From this supererogatory defence of Origen's biblical anthropology, we can infer that leading Churchmen of the third century had not escaped the position of Irenaeus in his controversy with the Valentinians. They were so afraid of attenuating the hope of resurrection – so apprehensive, perhaps, that if the body that we now wear were not assured of immortality, it would not be surrendered readily to martyrdom[58] – that they failed to stand by the letter of the New Testament. They proclaimed as orthodoxy what Paul denied, and scented heresy in their own contemporaries who adhered to his distinction between the flesh and the body. Pamphilus allows us to assume that, if Origen taught a resurrection of any kind, he taught what all catholics believed; to make Origen an advocate of a resurrection in flesh and blood, however, would be to misconstrue his own teaching and to contradict that of Paul.

The seventh indictment includes the charge that Origen held no doctrine of retribution after death. It is false as it stands, and Pamphilus can marshal a series of passages in which the future torment of the wicked are described with great vivacity and conviction. There is nothing in these testimonies, however, to prove that anyone suffers eternally, no intimation that a sinner can be so obdurate as to outlive the possibility of repentance or to forfeit the love of God. On the contrary, Origen says in his treatise *On Prayer* (to which Pamphilus merely alludes without quotation) that even the most abandoned sinner, so long as he possesses life, will also have enough liberty of will to return to God (*On Prayer* 27.15). In his *First Principles*, a fiery purgation is promised to every soul when it quits the gross body, except for the few that have expiated all their sins in the present world. The punishment is sustained until all the vicious passions and carnal weaknesses of the soul have been cauterised, and, as the difference between the imperfection of one and that of another is only a matter of degree, there would appear to be no bar to the eventual salvation of every sinner. In his own lifetime Origen was obliged to deny that he expected the salvation of the devil; it is a symptom of reticence rather than of ignorance that this charge should be overlooked in the *Apology*, for it figures in the polemics of the fourth century and fell under the anathema of the Fifth Oecumenical Council in 553.

One could argue that these questions remain undertermined to the present day. The word used of the suffering of the damned in the Greek New Testament is aionios, and, although this is almost invariably rendered as *aeternus* in Latin, a Greek would know that it often denoted a finite period.[59] There were thinkers after Origen, some still in good repute, who did not consider it heretical to pray for the redemption of every soul, or even for the restoration of the devil.[60] It can be maintained that universalism and the belief in the fixed duration of penal suffering after death, have never been condemned by an oecumenical council, except where they were coupled with other tenets that were patently heretical, such as

58 On the (alleged) complaisance of the Gnostics see Frend (1954).

59 On Origen's usage see Crouzel (1978), 320–21.

60 See Gregory of Nyssa, *Catechetical Oration* 26, with Farrar (1892).

those that Pamphilus has to address in his refutation of the next two charges. But if Pamphilus does not take this position, and prefers instead to maintain, or to insinuate by silence, that there is no end to the punishment of the reprobate in Origen, we may be sure that he was tempering the opinions of his master to the episcopal consensus of his day.

The ninth accusation, that Origen held false views on the constitution of the soul, is too discreetly worded in the Apology to convey any palpable heresy. Pamphilus can meet it simply by quoting Origen's own assertion of his right to speculate on matters that the church has not determined. In the time of Pamphilus, Christians were not of one mind in rejecting the doctrine of the soul's pre-existence, provided that this took only the attenuated form of positing separate creations for soul and body, so that each exists independently of the other before their union. Even in the fourth century, Macarius and Augustine[61] entertained this proposition; if it was never universal, it was never universally proscribed unless it was annexed to some pessimistic myth, which proclaimed that the true abode of the soul is not this world, and that its sojourn here is either the penalty or the immediate consequence of transgression.[62] It is widely believed today, on the authority of witnesses in the fourth and subsequent centuries, that Origen adopted this scenario from Gnostic or Platonic sources, tracing the descent of the soul not to any divine provision but to its own fatigue or satiety in the contemplation of God. As this imputation is not supported by his extant works, it is possible that the silence of Pamphilus indicates in this case that there was no charge to be answered. Some contamination of Origen's views with those of Philo may be suspected, as the latter undeniably taught that souls can succumb to fatigue in heaven;[63] if that is so, the calumny is more likely to have originated in Alexandria than in Caesarea.

That it is a calumny, or at best an exaggerated truth, has been apparent to every scholar in recent years who has attempted to disengage the words of Origen from the posthumous invectives which embroider the margins of our printed texts. It is these interpolations that are repeatedly held up to illustrate 'Origen's' conceit that fallen souls are assigned to grosser or lighter envelopes in proportion to their apostasy, so that those have cooled the most acquire the bodies of demons, the lukewarm the bodies of angels, and the middling sinner becomes a human soul.[64] This scheme is at odds with Origen's known opinions, as it implies that the bodies of demons are denser than ours, whereas he assigns them tenuous bodies suited to airy domiciles.[65] Nor does it seem consistent that the best and least should be

---

61 See Jerome, Letter 131.7 for Augustine's hesitations.

62 Scott (1991), 147 argues that this is true of the sun and moon in origin; but the uncleanness that is imputed to them at *First Principles* seems rather to be the consequence than the cause of their mundane servitude, which they undertake voluntarily for the sake of other creatures.

63 See for example Philo, *Who is the Heir of Divine Things* 240.

64 On this see now Edwards (2008b), 32–7.

65 This point is made eristically by Augustine at *City of God* 11.23.

sentenced to perpetual imprisonment, while the bodies of those in the intermediate class should be so fragile that do not always survive the hour of birth. The one complete redaction of *First Principles* is the Latin translation, and here we learn nothing of any descent from heaven, though satiety and lassitude are proposed as causes of the soul's fall from innocence in this life. Paradise for Origen is a place on earth (*First Principles* 2.11.6), and in the longest work of his that survives entire in Greek, the sin of Adam[66] and Eve results in an occlusion of the senses, not in any change in the texture or location of the body (*Against Celsus* 7.37). While he holds that a meritorious soul can become an angel, he does not suggest that angels can ever sink to our condition, except perhaps by some peculiar dispensation.[67] That souls descend to bodies from the hand of God is certainly his doctrine; that they descend through sin or hebetude may be a legitimate inference from passing observations in his *Commentary on John*,[68] but we cannot be sure that this inference is intended, or that Origen would have stood throughout his life by every position that he canvasses in this exercise. In our current state of knowledge, we cannot say what real or putative anomalies in Origen's thought would have been addressed in a less elliptical answer to the ninth charge.

The final charge, that Origen maintained the transmigration of the soul from body, is clearly baseless: he did not believe that one soul could inhabit two human bodies, let alone those of a human and an animal. He argues in his *Commentary on Romans* that, if the doctrine is invoked to account for our present woes as chastisements for the sins of previous lives, it must assume that all the soul's previous hosts were human, since an animal cannot sin.[69] The theory that one human soul can animate a succession of bodies is canvassed in his commentaries on Matthew and John, where he has to explain how some took John the Baptist as a reincarnation of an earlier prophet; this, he decides, may be a notion for Jews, but not for Christians.[70] Two speculations in *First Principles* might have prompted an injudicious reader to credit Origen with a theory of transmigration. At 1.8.4 he proposes that the stoning of beasts for sodomy under the code of Leviticus 20.16 might indicate that animals have rational souls, were it not that the church has anathematized this doctrine. And at, in considering the fate of an incorrigible delinquent, he surmises that there are some who have grown so dull of wit and conscience that they have no more power of repentance than a beast (*First Principles* 1.8.4). He is speaking metaphorically, but so was Porphyry, one of the most eminent philosophers of the third century, when he argued that in Plato's account of the soul's vicissitudes, different species of beast represent not physical

66 Here Adam is taken for a historical character. On the juxtaposition in Origen's writings of Adam the protoplast and Adam the universal man see Bammel (1989).

67 See *CommJoh* 1.31 (34) and 1.31 (25) on the hypothesis that the Baptist was an angel.

68 On *Commentary on John* 20.142 and 20.182 see Edwards (2008a), 352–3.

69 *CommRom* 6.8.1.21 on Romans 7.9, vol. 2, pp. 502–3 Bammel. On his denial of transmigration see Kruger (1996), 117–26.

70 *Commentary on John* 1.11 and 6.14, with reference to John 1.21.

metamorphoses but moral peregrinations.[71] In one abode the soul may exhibit the vices of a particular brute, in its next abode the weakness of another, but for all that it remains a human soul. It is possible that Porphyry, Origen's junior by some fifty years, was drawing upon an older source that was also known to Origen, and that in this source, as in Porphyry, the emblematic treatment of migration into animals coexisted with a literal belief in the passage of souls from one human being to another.[72] A reader who was acquainted with this precedent might therefore have been beguiled by his learning, rather than by malice, into taking Origen's speculation as only half a metaphor. The truth, none the less, is that Origen and his calumniators hold the same standard of orthodoxy regarding the pagan doctrine of transmigration. Neither for him nor for them does the rejection of this tenet make it impossible to affirm the pre-existence of the soul.

Concluding Reflections

In modern historiography, an Origenist is likely to be a proponent of one of three opinions, all (it is thought) sufficiently untypical of the catholic tradition to deserve this appellation. He may hold that there is no resurrection except for the soul – a position incontrovertibly heretical, but not espoused by Origen. He may believe that any sacred text will be susceptible of an allegorical reading; but so did almost all fourth-century authors who were not later regarded as heretics, for the figurative reading was denounced only when it extruded the literal sense. Finally, he may assume that the Son is a lesser being than the Father; but even if the Bible does not teach this, we have seen in the present chapter that it was taught in Origen's time by a broad consensus of churchmen, some of whom suspected him of according too much equality to the Son.

Modern study of Origen is apt to dwell on elements of his thought that were singled out for praise or calumny in the three centuries after his death. Quiet innovations which were received without offence or controversy in ancient times are also likely to elude the modern reader. To take one instance, the tenet that humanity has retained the image of God in its fallen state, and that all that Adam lost was the likeness, is now commonly regarded as the bequest of Irenaeus to the eastern church, which therefore has a saint to set against Augustine's doctrine that the will has been rendered impotent by the weakening or defacement of the image. Origen, who is deemed to be a man of the east, is now more often applauded than condemned for his warm conviction that no punishment can be justly inflicted on those who possess no liberty of choice. His inference that divine torment after death is not only retributive but salutary, with its implication that all will at last be saved,

---

[71] See his *On the Powers of the Soul*, extracted from Stobaeus as cited as Porphyry, Frs 251–5 Smith.

[72] See Fr. 300 Smith, with Augustine, *City of God* 10.30, 12.27 and 13.19. On the reliability of Augustine's evidence see Edwards (2000), xxxii n. 83.

is among the heresies anathematized at the Second Council of Constantinople. For all that, it is not clear that his universalism would have offended the Greeks had it not been thought to entail that the devil himself will at last repent.[73] This was the position imputed to him in his lifetime, and the letter in which he disavows it is produced by Jerome as an example of his duplicity. Here, as elsewhere, the more palatable tenet is assumed in modern scholarship to be characteristic of an entire tradition, while the heresy (if such it is) is ascribed to him alone.

But, while he was not the first Christian to maintain that only a free act can be justly punished, Origen performs an original synthesis of two inherited doctrines when he argues that free will is accorded to those who have been created in the image of God in order that they may realise the likeness (*First Principles* 3.6.1). Irenaeus draws the contrast only in his fifth book against the heretics, where he states that both the body and soul of Adam were created in the image, that the likeness which God is fashioning in us includes both body and soul, and that it was forfeited when Adam sinned, and that after the death and resurrection of Christ it has been restored to those who by their own choice are numbered with the elect (5.6.1). Whether the likeness granted to the saints surpasses that which Adam received, and whether it is vouchsafed at the very moment of conversion or perfected through continuing obedience, are questions that will not cease to be debated. Elsewhere in Irenaeus image and likeness are inseparable,[74] and in one place we are given to understand that together they constitute the end that God designed for his creatures rather than an endowment that was lost (4.38.3). There appears to be no passage in his works which affirms that the image alone was granted to Adam, without even the promise or possibility of the likeness; but it is certainly assumed that neither the image nor the likeness was destined to be revealed in its fullness before the incarnation of the Word (5.16.1). It is because the incorporeal God was resolved from the beginning to assume a human body that the corporeal form of Adam can be said to have been fashioned in his image and to participate in the perfection of the likeness.

---

[73] Jerome, *Defence against the Writings of Rufinus* 2.18. At 2.19 Jerome reports that in a dialogue with the Valentinian Candidus, Origen denied that the devil is naturally incapable of contrition, and that Candidus accused him in return of holding the diabolic nature to be capable of redemption, Rufinus, *On the Adulteration of Origen's Books*, denies flatly that he countenanced the salvation of the devil, and, as Crouzel (1973) observes, there is no passage in the extant works of Origen which affirms this. Nevertheless, John Scotus Eriugena purports to quote such a passage (without malevolence) at *Periphuseon* V. (*Patrologia Latina* 122), 930c, which is identical with *First Principles*, except for the addition of the noun *diabolus* where the Rufinian text speaks merely of the *novissimus inimicus* who will be overcome, not by reconciliation (cf. 1Corinthians 15.26). Even without this increment, the passage is applied to the salvation of the devil by, for example, Görgemanns and Karpp (1993), 657n.

[74] At *AH* 3.18.1 we read that the state of 'being in the image and likeness' was forfeited by Adam, which, if his usage is consistent, he must, since he no longer possessed one element he no longer had the pair.

There were Gnostics, as we have seen, who represented Adam's body as a poor copy of the androgynous physiognomy which shone down on the world created by the archons. Clement of Alexandria opines, with Irenaeus, that both image and likeness were fully exhibited only in the incarnate Christ, but with the new corollary that the likeness was withheld from Adam, because it was God's intent that it should be consummated in each saint by obedience and endeavour.[75] Origen's distinction is to have shown that it was not the parsimony of the Creator but his benevolence that dictated this economy:

> For this is the opinion of Moses before all others when he describes the original creation of humans, saying: *And God said 'Let us make man in our image and likeness'* {Gen 1.26}. Then he goes on to say: *and God made man; the image of God he made him, male and female he made them and pronounced his blessing upon them* [Gen 1.28]. The fact, then, that he says in the image of God he made him, saying nothing of the likeness, can only mean that he received the dignity of the image in his original condition, but the perfection of the likeness is reserved for him at the consummation. The purpose is evidently that he may acquire it for himself by exerting his own zeal in the imitation of God. In this way, the possibility of the likeness having been vouchsafed to him through the dignity of the image, he may at last consummate the perfection in himself through the performance of works (*First Principles* 3.6.1).

Volumes which promote schematic contrasts between eastern and western Christendom frequently allow us to suppose that all Greek authors after Irenaeus embraced this view that the image resides in every man and woman, while the likeness remains to be perfected by the Holy Spirit. In fact, this notion falls into desuetude among Greeks of the catholic tradition in the fourth century. Gregory of Nyssa has no use for the distinction, perhaps because his defence of the equality of the three persons in the Trinity requires him to make as little as he can of the orthodox commonplace that Christ is the image of God. Cyril of Alexandria denies that either term connotes more than the other, while his gadfly Theodoret dedicates one of his longest questions on Genesis to the meaning of the term 'image' with only parenthetic mention of the likeness. These authors survived where Irenaeus perished, though his contrast between the indelible image and the squandered

---

[75] At *Paedagogus* I.98.2–3, Christ is the image and likeness of God in fullness, but we receive only the image with the power to attain the likeness. At *Stromateis* V.94.5 the logos is the image of God, and the human mind an image of the image. The image is manifested in well-doing (*Strom.* II.102.2) and in the fathering of live progeny (*Paed.* II.82.2; cf. II.78.2 and *Protrepticus* 98.3). It resides properly in the soul (*Strom.* VII.64.6); as the world is an icon of its archetype for the Platonists (V.93.4), so the church in the world is an icon of the heavenly communion(IV.66.1). The image in humanity is one (VII.86.2) and is never entirely lost (VII.71.6); only in the Gnostic, however, is it fully assimilated to Christ the 'second cause' (VII.16.6).

likeness proved more durable than his works. Revived by John of Damascus in his treatise *On the Orthodox Faith*, this rediscovered heirloom is today held up by many as the ancient and canonical teaching of the eastern church.[76]

It has no claim, however, to be either the sole or the universal teaching of the Greek fathers, even in circles where the image and the likeness were distinguished. Origen's name may have fallen into disrepute, but his doctrine that Adam received the image alone and not the likeness was republished in a homily falsely attributed to Gregory of Nyssa.[77] Among his heirs in the west we may perhaps reckon Augustine, who concurred with Irenaeus in distinguishing the image from the likeness and in holding that Adam did not come perfect from the hand of God. But these to him were two discrete positions. The image and likeness, he holds, reside in the outer man so far as he exercises his vital faculties, and in the inner man so far as he exhibits *sapientia* or wisdom (*83 Diverse Questions* 51). The spirit, inasmuch as it is that element which resembles God in substance, is more properly regarded as the image, and more properly still as that which is made according to the image, since the true image is Christ the Word.[78] The likeness is displayed by the other elements of humanity, not by any approximation to the properties of God but by the manifestation of excellence in their own kind. The likeness is thus a shadow or ancillary to the image, not, as in Irenaeus, the destined consummation of the image. The acquisition of both, however, depends on the advance of the creature from *ratio*, or reason, to *sapientia*, from a state in which one is formally cognizant of the principles that define the good to a state in which one's conduct is infallibly directed by those principles (*On Free Will* 5.72). If we consider only that both image and likeness are granted in part to Adam, and both susceptible of growth or diminution, we may say that this is one of a number of theories prefigured in Irenaeus; if we note that one gift is conferred and a better withheld, we may conclude that Augustine is of the school of Origen.

Behind Origen stands Clement, and behind Clement, as we saw in the previous chapter, stand Theodotus and his fellow-Valentinians. They are apt to represent the image, not as a propaedeutic to the likeness but as a poor substitute; at *Stromateis* IV.30.1 Clement declines to endorse their dictum that the left-hand is for those who bear the image and the right for the elect who bear the likeness. The first Alexandrian spokesmen of the Episcopal Church reclaimed the likeness for all, but as a possibility rather than as a prelapsarian gift. At the same time – in contrast to Clement, no less than to Irenaeus and John Damascene – Origen holds that the image is lost, and that the soul in which it once resided bears instead the image of

76 *On the Orthodox Faith* 2.12 and 3.1; cf. Russell (2004), 299.

77 See PG 44.273. On this and on the fusion of the same motif with Plato, *Theaetetus* 176b–c in Diadochus of Phoitke (*Homily on Perfection* 78), see Russell (2004), 210 and 246–7.

78 Christ remains in all minds as the regulative principle of the understanding, not as an object of knowledge (*On the Teacher*); when he becomes incarnate the soul discerns 'without her in humility the one whom had proudly abandoned within' (*On Free Will* 3.30).

the devil.[79] It lies outside the scope of the present book to determine whether he believed that every soul is in origin a naked intellect and that its fall is a descent into the body. If he held this view, it was balanced by another, according to which the parents of the human race were embodied denizens of the earthly paradise, whose eyes were at first the doors of pure intelligence, until their vision of God was sealed by the opening of the senses. Athanasius also held that sin entails a fall from intellectual to sensual contemplation; Augustine, in an early work, declares that in our pride we have forsaken the God within us, only to find him in humanity outside us (*On Free Will* 3.30). Augustine cannot entertain any notion of a fall before embodiment, and, while he holds that the image was disfigured in Adam's progeny, he does not speak of its being obliterated or supplanted. Nevertheless, the pattern for him, as for Origen, is that something is given, something withheld and something lost; thus it appears that the child of a great tradition could give seminal form to a tenet that became a diagnostic of orthodoxy in the west.

---

79 *Homily on Genesis* 1.13, pl. 17.12 Baehrens.

Chapter 5
The Nicene Council and its Aftermath

The fifty-year paroxysm which was formerly known as the 'Arian controversy' is now perceived to have been a mêlée rather than a duel – or, if we take the irascibility of the contestants as a measure of their sincerity, a collective 'search for the Christian doctrine of God'.[1] The seekers include Eusebius, the Homoiousians and the Origenists, none of whom would now be classed as Arians in the work of a competent scholar; the quarry, on the other hand, still; falls to Athanasius and the there Cappadocian Fathers, whose 'pro-Nicene' or 'neo-Nicene' formulations were canonised in 381 at the Second Oecumenical Council and made binding on the Roman world by the legislation of Theodosius I and his successors. In the modern accounts, the historian Eusebius is a conservative[2] who saw nothing but party spirit in every new refinement of orthodoxy; homoiousians are the midwives to a stillborn compromise, which even a brief insufflation from Athanasius failed to animate. Origenists are harder to identify, as no-one is wholly untouched by the thought of Origen and no-one merely admires him without reservation or apology. In the present chapter it will be argued that Eusebius is in fact one of the architects of the homoousian victory, since he raises the Son to the dignity of the Father; that it was not the homoousians but the misnamed homoiousians who were first seen as proponents of a metaphysical, rather than merely economic, parity between these two divine persons; and that the obloquy which Origen suffered in the late fourth century was a kind of vindication, in that his critics of the third century deserved it more than he did, and those premises of his teaching which they impugned most strongly had now become the main timbers of orthodoxy.

The Nicene Watershed

For over 1,500 years the presupposition of systematic theology has been a doctrine of the Trinity which states that there are three divine persons, the Father, the Son and the Holy Spirit, each of whom is properly and fully identical both with the being called God and with that substance or nature which we call the Godhead. It is both a logical and an ecclesiastical deduction from these tenets that the Godhead is identical with God – to speak philosophically, that the essence of God is identical with his existence – but the church does not accept that the identity of each person with the Godhead entails that the persons are identical with one

[1] Hanson (1988); on the diversity of parties see Ayres (2004).

[2] On his representative character see D. Williams (1998).

another. Nor is it acceptable to argue that each is God individually while all three are generically identical with the Godhead, for that would be, not only to divorce God from his essence, but to treat this essence as though it were a category or species exemplified by three particulars, as the human species is exemplified by particular humans. That would be to postulate three gods, whereas the axiom of good Churchmanship is that, while the Father is God and the Son is God and the Holy Spirit is God, there are none the less not three gods but One.

It is also held as an indefeasible premises that no one of the three is greater or less than either of the other two, though it is admitted that the Son and the Spirit depend upon the Father for their existence and that in the divine economy it is they who are sent by the Father and the Son who saves the world by his obedience. To infer that this obedience bespeaks his inferiority to the Father is the heresy of 'subordinationism';[3] to suggest that because the Son and the Spirit depend upon the father they are posterior to him in time is Arianism; to circumvent the difficulties of the orthodox doctrine by treating the persons merely as designations of the same divine subject in distinct epiphanies is 'modalism', 'monarchianism' or 'Sabellianism'. The names are a coalition of ancient and modern; the teaching is supposed to be that of the creeds established in the patristic era, though in fact it is clearly adumbrated only in a Latin declamation, falsely ascribed to Athanasius, which has never been recited in eastern liturgies and has now fallen into desuetude in the west.[4] A modern theologian who is challenged to state its provenance is likely to answer either that it can be derived from scriptural testimonies – a claim that now appears fanciful to most professional students of the New Testament[5] – or that the nucleus of it is found in the creed that was promulgated in 325 at the Council of Nicaea and refined by the Second Oecumenical Council of 381.[6] The majority of scholars now engaged in writing the history of doctrine in the first five centuries of the Christian era would agree that this is too sanguine a reading even of the text that is somewhat questionably traced to Constantinople in 381, let alone of the 'Symbol' that the real Athanasius taught the Church to regard as an immovable standard of orthodoxy some years after Constantine procured it in 325 from a fatigued but cacophonous mob of ecclesiastics. The symbol of 325, like many that followed it in the fourth century, seems initially to have been intended more as a protocol to conclude a meeting than as an adamantine canon of belief.

It would not have been formulated but for the heresy of Arius, an Alexandrian presbyter who maintained that that the Son was created 'out of nothing' by the

---

3 See for example Zachhuber (2001), 68 against the view that the object of the Council of Nicaea was to proscribe the subordination of the Son.

4 Generally held, after Morin (1932), to be first attested in Caesarius of Arles, though Brewer (1909) finds the rudiments in Ambrose.

5 See Wiles (1976), 1–18; Barrett (1982), 19–36.

6 On the chequered evidence see Kelly (1972), 296–331. It is clear, as Kelly observes, that the Nicene formula of 325 was subject to variation, so that a new creed may have emerged in 381 without design.

Father's will,[7] and that any other teaching – any teaching, for example, which implied a division of the Father's substance or an eternal and hence involuntary procreation – would be to rob the Father of those attributes which make him God. Such divine attributes as the Son possessed he believed to pertain to him not by nature but by participation in the immutable Godhead of the Father; since he affirmed three persons or hypostases, we must presume that he held the Spirit, like the Son, to be 'a creature but not as one of the creatures', a perfect ectype of the wisdom and goodness which inhere primordially in the Father as the 'one true God'.[8] In contrast to the Father, the lesser hypostases have a beginning and derive their immortality from him, though the Son at least does not originate in time. In his encyclical condemning Arius, his Bishop, Alexander of Alexandria, asserted that as the Father was always Father he must always have had a Son, that his birth is anticipated in the Psalmist's testimony, 'My heart has disgorged a goodly word' (Psalm 44/45.2).[9] Origen had endorsed the first proposition but declined to join the 'monarchian' in inferring from the second that the Son is merely a function of the Father.[10] The most illustrious prelate in the time of Arius, Bishop Eusebius of Nicomedia, would perhaps have contested both.[11] Once Arius had appealed to him, the peace of the Church was not to be restored without a council. The resulting formulary upholds Alexander against Eusebius and Arius on all the points that were then in debate, but leaves unresolved many questions that were to agitate the church in the next few decades. The wording, as we receive it from Athanasius, who purports to be reproducing a letter by the great historian Eusebius of Caesarea, runs as follows:[12]

> We believe in one God, Father, Almighty, Maker of all things visible and invisible;
> And in one Lord Jesus Christ, the Son of God, born of the Father only-begotten (*monogenes*), that is, from the essence (*ousia*) of the Father,
> God from God, light from light, true God from true God,[13]

---

7 Stead (1998), 676–7 observes that this was a prophylactic against an interpretation of the formula 'from the Father' which implied diminution of the latter's substance.

8 See letter to Alexander at Athanasius, *On the Synods* 16.

9 See Socrates *Church History* 1.6.16.

10 See *Commentary on John* 1.125, p. 25 Preuschen, with Orbe (1991).

11 See his letter to Paulinus at Theodoret, *Church History* 1.6, where he repeatedly denies that the Son is from the *ousia* of the Father.

12 Following the text and punctuation of Kelly (1972), 215–16, with the addition of the word 'created' in the penultimate line. The original sources are: Athanasius, *On the Decrees of Nicaea* (appendix); Socrates, *Church History* 1.8; Theodoret, *Church History* 1.12. Theodoret does not report the word *ktistos*, and there is more matter in the closing sentences of his transcript from Eusebius' commentary than we find in Socrates.

13 Applying John 17.3 to the Father and John 5.20 to the Son. The syntax in the second case is ambiguous. Westcott (1886), 196–7 takes the Father to be the subject though he argues that the verse attest a belief in the triune character of the Godhead.

Born not made, consubstantial (*homoousion*) with the Father,
Through whom all came to be, things in heaven and things on earth;
The one who descended on account of us human beings and our salvation
And was enfleshed and made human, suffered and rose again on the third day,
Went back up to heaven, and is coming to judge the living and the dead.

And in the Holy Spirit.
But those who say 'there was when he was not',[14]
and 'before being born he was not',
and that he came to be from things that are not,[15]
or declaring the Son of God to be of another *ousia* or *hypostasis*,
or created[16] or changeable or variable –
These the holy catholic and apostolic church anthematizes.

It would appear that both Eusebii signed the creed, although Eusebius of Nicomedia was deposed for his refusal to sign the anathemas.[17] Alexander of Alexandria's name appears first among the Greek signatories, after that of the westerner Hosius of Cordova, who presided at the council.[18] Another signatory in the surviving lists, Marcellus of Ancyra,[19] was the bishop of the see which had been the prospective venue for the proceedings until, for reasons still obscure, it was translated to Nicaea.[20] Since Theognis of Nicaea was one of the few to share in the mortification of Eusebius of Nicomedia (Socrates, *Church History* 1.8), the choice of a site for the council cannot be seen as a vote of confidence in its bishop, and Marcellus himself was subsequently exiled because he was thought to have refused to acknowledge three hypostases before the Nativity. So long as historiography of this period was governed by the polemics of Athanasius, who was exiled in 339

---

14 Attributed to Arius by Alexander of Alexander in Socrates, *Church History* 1.16.15. While, as Hall (1991), 122 remarks, this saying is not attested in the meager remains of Arius, it would be characteristic of him to use a formula that gave precedence to the Father, but not priority in time.

15 Cf. Arius' letter to Eusebius at Theodoret, Church History 1.5, and the letter of the council to Alexander at Socrates, *ibid.*, 1.9.3.

16 See below on the questionable provenance of this term.

17 So Sozomen, *Church History* 1.21, following Athanasius, *On the Decrees of the Nicene Synod* 2–3, against Socrates, *Church History* 1.8, who reports that Eusebius was deposed for his refusal to sign the creed. For the (characteristically) ludicrous report that he signed a homoiousian creed see Philostorgius, *Church History* 1.9; for comment on these passages, and on the tradition that he was alleged to have entertained parties hostile to the catholic church, see Gwynn (2007), 117–18.

18 Gelzer (1995), LX, 4, 61.

19 So Gelzer (1995), LXII, 30 (though here one version has Marcus rather than Marcellus) and 63. See, however, Parvis (2006), 91.

20 See Logan (1992), 428–36.

and formed an alliance with Marcellus, it was common to represent both men as victims of an 'Arian reaction', a concerted design to re-consecrate all that had been condemned as heresy at Nicaea.[21] Now that the controversies of the fourth century are no longer painted only in black and white, it may be instructive to ask how many of the views that Athanasius has taught us to regard as 'Arian' or 'anti-Nicene' could have been described in the same terms by his elders when they assembled at Nicaea in 325.

1. In the eyes of the world, an Arian is one who assimilates the origin of the Son to that of creatures by asserting that he (or the Word) is 'out of nothing'. In a letter to Eusebius of Nicomedia, Arius complains that he is suffering persecution on account of a saying that has no aim but to guarantee the immutability of the Father's substance.[22] His reward was to see the phrase anathematized at the council of Nicaea. No other theologian is known to have held this tenet, though Eusebius of Caesarea speaks against it after the Council as an unwarranted speculation.[23] It can therefore be applied without misgiving as a diagnostic of Arian sympathies, though it is probable that on this definition the Arians at Nicaea would have formed a party of one.

2. To Marcellus and Athanasius one is an Arian if one holds that the Word, in so far as he is the Word and not yet man, is a *ktisma* or creature of the Father. This position requires some legerdemain on the part of Athanasius since, in contrast to Marcellus,[24] he opines that Christ is speaking under the name of Wisdom at Proverbs 8.22, where the Greek of the Septuagint is, 'The Lord created me in [or 'for'] the beginning of his ways' (Proverbs 8.22). If the sense 'in the beginning' is accepted, the creation of Wisdom antedates that of the world. To forestall the inference that the second hypostasis is a creature, one may argue, with Marcellus, that the text is too arcane to support a dogma,[25] or, with Gregory of Nyssa, that this wisdom is not the power that we call the Word (*Against Eunomius* 8.22). Another stratagem, also proposed by Gregory of Nyssa (*Against Eunomius* 2.10), is to appeal from the Septuagint to other versions, perhaps more faithful to the Hebrew, where the reading is not 'created' but possessed. Athanasius took the fourth way of surmising that, although it is indeed the Word who speaks here, but only of his creation for the beginning, that is to say the fashioning of his human body in preparation for his ministry on earth (*Against the Arians* 2.78). That some were prepared to try more than one expedient is a sign that they were less concerned to arrive at the best construction of the passage than to evade the false construction put upon it by those who argued that the Word came to be from nothing, or in time.

---

[21] Cogently rebutted by Elliott (1992), but still accepted without misgiving by Burgess (2000), 150.

[22] Epiphanius, *Panarion* 69.7; Theodoret, *Church History* 1.5.

[23] See his letter at Socrates, *Church History* 1.8.53; *Ecclesiastical Theology* 1.9.6.

[24] Eusebius, *Against Marcellus* 1.4.28 cites a remonstrance against the use of Proverbs 8.23 by Asterius, though Eusebius himself sees here a criticism of Origen.

[25] *Against Marcellus* 1.4.28. Cf. Gregory of Nyssa, *Against Eunomius* 1.22.

It was possible, none the less, to give the words 'in the beginning' their natural sense and to maintain that they are spoken by the Word, without concluding that he originated in time or that he was of some other substance than the Father's. For Origen, the creation is that which perfectly represents the design of God in contradistinction to the things of the world, which are doomed to imperfection because they are formed from some other substrate than his will; he therefore sees no paradox in speaking of a creature that is eternally distinct from the Father and one in nature with him.[26] To Marcellus the eternal generation of the Word and his creation before the ages are the head and tail of the same chimaera; to his critics any doctrine of pre-existence appeared more catholic than his own belief that the Son is begotten as a discrete hypostasis only when the man Jesus is born in Bethlehem, so that his birth and the creation of his flesh constitute a single episode in the course of recorded history.[27] Eusebius of Caesarea interprets Proverbs 8.22 as the utterance of a distinct *hypostasis* before the ages; he refrains from affirming either that this hypostasis and the first are coeternal or that he came into being later than the Father. In the scriptures he found no answer to the question of Isaiah 53.8, 'His generation who can declare?', but thought it certain that he was not produced by any subtraction from the Father's substance or from any material but the Father's will (*Gospel Demonstration* 4.3).

Thus one can suppose, with Athanasius, that the Word is begotten eternally and his body created in time;[28] or with Marcellus, that his creation coincides with his nativity to mark an epoch in the course of history; or with Eusebius that he is born in time and created before the ages, though either term might be substituted for the other. Against the last position Athanasius pressed two arguments one from the scriptures and one from the creed of 325. The scriptures, he argues, speak of our creating sons who are properly begotten, never of our begetting what is properly created; when, therefore, creation and begetting are affirmed of a single agent, we must assume that the term 'creation' is used with licence (*Against the Arians* 2.4 and 2.48). This is a fair deduction, and the appeal to the creed would be sounder still if the last anathema did indeed exclude from the church all those who hold that the Son is changeable, mutable or creaturely. It has been observed, however, that Eusebius, whose citation of this document Athanasius purports to be transcribing, shows no awareness in the accompanying letter, or in his treatises of the next decade, that the term 'creaturely' has been condemned by anyone but Marcellus.[29] Cyril of Alexandria was later to quote the same creed in its entirety, except for

26 See Widdicombe (1994), 89 and discussion in previous chapter.

27 See Robertson (2007), 111–17.

28 As Anatolios (1999), 116–25 demonstrates, Athanasius believes that the Father's power would be diminished if he failed to beget an equal, but not if he refrained from the creation of beings inferior to himself.

29 At *Ecclesiastical Theology* 1.10.5, he urges that no term sued of the Son is to be taken in its quotidian sense, and that, just as he is not a son like other sons of God, so he is a creature of another kind than those things that are created out of nothing.

the proscription of the word 'creaturely', in his Third Letter to Nestorius.[30] It has therefore been suspected that Athanasius has reproduced an augmented version of the original Creed.[31]

3. To judge by another anathema, an Arian is one who holds that 'before he was born he was not'. This is a negation of the apocryphal dictum, 'blessed is he who was not before he was born', which was attributed to Solomon by Lactantius and Irenaeus.[32] In discovering these words to be unbiblical, the church did not deem them unorthodox; the embargoed saying, on the other hand, admits of more than one paraphrase, not all invidious. That the Son did not exist before he was born would be a trivial corollary of belief in his eternal generation, and it was evidently not this view that fell under the interdict of the Council. The doctrine that he did not exist before he was born of Mary is heretical, but was imputed to Marcellus,[33] not to Arius; we should not for that reason assume that it is not the position, or one of the positions, to which the anathema refers. When Arius used this phrase, he meant that although the Son was generated before all ages, he was not eternal because 'there was once' when the Father existed alone. This doctrine excludes a phase of latency, in which the Father's Word or Wisdom is a dynamic function, not yet propagated in the form of a second hypostasis. Athanasius too would have wished to disown this commonplace of the second century, but not at the cost of positing the existence of the Father without his Son.

We cannot say, in the wake of his condemnation, how many members of the council held the same doctrine as Marcellus or were prepared to entertain it. Eusebius, in his account of the session, relates that the Emperor Constantine intervened to explain the consubstantiality of Father and Son by the old conceit that the Son existed in potential before he emerged as a distinct hypostasis.[34] This is wholly at odds with any theology which, like that of Eusebius, spoke of the Word as a creation of the Father.[35] We have thus no cause to doubt his candid narrative, but the conduct of Eusebius after the council shows that an Emperor had the power

---

30 Cyril, *Third Letter to Nestorius* 3; cf. Basil, *Letter* 140 and the Armenian version of the Nicene Creed at Thomson and Howard-Johnston (1999); 126. Bindley (1899), 52 observes that Thodoret's etxt of the letter of Eusebius (Church History 1.12.8) contains no anathema on the word *ktiston*.

31 Wiles (1993). Note that the predicate *ktisma* is already anathematized at the Council of Antioch in 324/5: Abramaowski (1992b), 11.

32 Irenaeus, *Apostolic Teaching* 43 'blessed is he who was before he became man'; Lactantius, *Divine Institures* 4.8 'blessed is he who was before he was born'. Both allege Jeremiah as the author though only Jeremiah 1.5 in the extant book resembles this quotation.

33 See for example Eusebius, *Ecclesiastical Theology* 1.18.

34 Theodoret, *Church History* 1.12.17, not paralleled in the transcript of the same letter by Socrates.

35 See his objection to the title *logos endiathetos* at *Ecclesiastical Theology* 1. 17.7. At Constantine, *Oration to the Saints* 6 this locution signifies the embedded rationality of the created order. At *Oration* 9 he does not say how the Father produced the Son.

at most to introduce a few syllables into the creed. There was no authority which could guarantee that the same words would convey the same sense to a gathering of over two hundred prelates.

It ought, perhaps, to surprise us that both Arius and his critics adopt 'begetting' as a term for the inception of the Son's existence as a hypostasis.[36] In the Gospels of Mark and John, the title 'Son' accrues to him only at the beginning of his ministry, and signifies not consubstantiality with the Father but the Father's choice of him as plenipotentiary.[37] In the Gospels of Luke and Matthew it is his birth from Mary without a human consort that reveals God to be his Father, though in Luke it seems that he also deserves the appellative 'Son of God' as the second Adam.[38] In his character before conception, he is described by Paul as the firstborn of creation (Colossians 1.15), and by John as the Word coeval with all that is made (John 1.1–4). In neither of these passages is there a whisper of eternal generation, and the expression is first attested in Plotinus, a Greek philosopher of the third century.[39] In Greek philosophy there was no ubiquitous distinction between the terms *genesis* and *gennêsis*, though some Platonists decreed that if the latter were used of the world it would imply a beginning in time, whereas the former was compatible with eternal dependence on an eternal cause. In Christian thought there is evidence of a similar demarcation as early as the second century, when Athenagoras states that the Son, though not *genêton*, is the *gennêma* or offspring of the Father (*Embassy* 10). Here both terms allow the priority of the Father in time and dignity, but the word *gennêma* implies that the Son originates from the substance and not merely from the will of his progenitor. The Council of Nicaea stipulates both that the Son is of the Father's substance and that he never emerged from a previous state of latency, as Athenagoras still supposed; but almost half a century was to elapse after 325 before apologists for the council propounded a strict distinction between the *genêton*, which is brought into being in time by the will of God, and the true *gennêton*, who, as the issue of an eternal superabundance in the Father, can himself be no less than God.

4. From the creed and from the letters of the heresiarch, an Arian can be characterized as one who denies that the Son is *homoousios* with the Father. The adjective is not defined in the creed, but the juxtaposition of the clause 'true God from true God' and the proleptic phrase 'from the *ousia* of the Father' suggest that it ought to denote a true sharing of the Father's nature and not merely, as Eusebius of Caesarea pretends, a communication by the Father of those attributes which set

---

36 Begetting, creation and foundation (but not making) appear as synonyms in his letter to Alexander at Athanasius, *On Synods* 16.

37 Mark 1.1 and 1.11; John 1.34.

38 Matthew 1.18 and 3.17; Luke 1.35 and 3.38.

39 At *Enneads* 6.8.20.27 we read: '[the first principle] is one with its making and, so to speak, its eternal generation'. At Enneads 5.1.6.39 Plotinus declares that 'that which is perfect generates unceasingly and [generates that which is] eternal, though what it generates is less than itself'.

him apart from his creatures. Yet no interpretation of the term could be enforced so long as the creed did not define it, and for the next thirty years even Athanasius seldom invokes it when he argues for the divinity of the Son. When its meaning was not so impoverished as to render it useless, it could be so misconstrued as to challenge the axioms of faith. To Arius it conveyed a Manichaean notion of God as an extended light which could multiply itself by alienation or division of its substance (Athanasius, *Synods* 16), and there is no doubt that in his time the term was most often used of entities derived from a common substrate or of amalgams which owed their uniform texture to the homogenization of two unlike materials.[40] There were some who knew, or professed to know, that the word had been anathematized in 268 by the council which evicted Paul of Samosata from the see of Antioch.[41] Its defenders were driven to the unlikely hypothesis that Paul himself had employed it in a Sabellian sense, to mean that the Son and the Father were one and the same (Hilary, *Synods* 86); or else, it was urged, the council was rejecting Paul's invidious construction of the term, according to which both Father and Son possessed only a supervenient identity as precipitates of a hitherto undifferentiated Godhead (Athanasius, *Synods* 45). It came to be known that the eminent Dionysius, pupil of Origen, Bishop of Alexandria and rudder of the church under persecution, had been so reluctant to countenance the term that members of his own flock had denounced to his namesake Dionysius of Rome. It was not so clear that the latter regarded the term as a talisman of orthodoxy, and it was not necessary for either to confess the *homoousion* before they could reach an accord. Origen was no witness to the currency of the word in his time, for he introduced tentatively in one passage of his *Commentary on Hebrews*, and not to say that the Son is *homoousios* with the Father, but that the relation between the two can be compared, with the usual caveats, to the relation between an ointment and its vapour.[42] Even in Alexandria, then, it appears to have been Bishop Alexander who first enforced the confession of the *homoousion*; if we believe one ancient satirist,[43] he cherished it only because he was aware that it was term to which Arius could not subscribe.

5. 'Subordinationism' is almost a synonym for 'Arianism' in modern historiography, but in the Church of the first five centuries it was not a recognised category of error.[44] Before the Nicene council the affirmation of equality between persons of the Godhead could be regarded as a dangerous compromise with

---

40 See Iamblichus, *On the Mysteries* 3.21.150.9, with Williams (2000), 222n.44.

41 Announced in a letter by George of Laodicea c. 353: see Epiphanius, *Panarion* 73.12.8.

42 See Edwards (1998), upholding the authenticity of the citation in Pamphilus against Hanson (1977), but agreeing that the term is not applied strictly to the Son, but by analogy with the relation between a vapour and its source.

43 Philostorgius, *Church History* 1.7. The method of Philostorgius, in his history of the Council, is simply to invert the prevailing narrative.

44 See, for example, Edwards (2006).

the polytheism of the ambient culture; more pernicious still, and by no means superannuated, were the Gnostic myths in which the Creator is overthrown by an heir whom he sires in ignorance, or the exegesis of Genesis 1.3 according to which the Father prays to the Son for light. If one holds not only that the other two persons depend for their existence on the Father, but that the unity of the Godhead resides in his primacy as cause, one is almost bound to conclude that in some sense he is greater than the Son. Even to Athanasius this is the natural exegesis of Christ's own confession at John 14.28.[45]

Some modern authorities argue that an Arian can be detected by his willingness to confess a *deuteros theos*, or second god. This locution is in fact very rare, occurring two or three times in the apologetic writing of Origen, once in that of Eusebius of Caesarea.[46] In controversy between ecclesiastical figures, the proclamation of second god would be felt to violate the fundamental truth that God is one. This proposition thus appears only as a logical consequence which a polemicist will derive from the work of his adversary, or attempt to forestall in the statement of his own doctrine. Those who strongly affirmed that Christ was 'second' were apt to deny that he is god in precisely the same sense as the father; those who maintained that 'God' cannot be an equivocal term avoided ditheism by declining to number the bearers of this predicate. Conciliatory resolutions throughout the fourth century suggest that there was not so much fear of subordinating the Son to the Father as of positing two independent deities: for advocates of the Nicene *homoousion*, the preposition was not the least important term in the formula 'God from God'.

6. The council pronounced an anathema on those who hold that the Son is 'from any other *ousia* or *hypostasis*'. The assertion in the creed itself that the Son is from the *ousia* of the Father is an innovation, determining the sense of the word *monogenes*, which might otherwise be legitimately understood to mean 'one of a kind' or 'of one kind', rather than 'only-begotten'.[47] It would have been embarrassment to Eusebius of Nicomedia, the protector of Arius before the council, who (in a letter that cannot be confidently dated) denies expressly that the Son is 'from the *ousia* of the Father'. That the Son is 'from the hypostasis' on the other hand, was, as we have seen, the doctrine of Tertullian and Origen, and the proof-text for the latter is Hebrews 1.3, where the Son is called an 'impression of the *hypostasis* of the Father'. Although it might be thought that this verse defines the Father's nature in contradistinction to that of the Son, Origen himself affirms three hypostases. The second and third of these derive their being and their divinity from

---

45 *Against the Arians* 1.58, with the inference that the Father and Son are therefore members of the same category, and with the caveat that the Father has precedence in the order of generation, not in dignity or power.

46 See below, with Edwards (2006). For Origen see *Against Celsus* 5.39 and 6.61, with 7.57, though in the last case nothing more is affirmed than that the son takes second place in Christian worship. Cf. Justin, *1Apology* 13.3–4, with the admonition of Gregory of Nyssa that this does not entail inferiority in power or nature, Against Eunomius 1.197–204.

47 See Skarsaune (1987).

the Father, and the Son at least is of the same nature and consubstantial with him by analogy to material objects of the common world; at the same time, he holds that the will of the Father is the substrate of the Son and denies that he proceeds directly from the *ousia* of the Father. The Council of Nicaea does not say more than that the *hypostasis* of the Father is the cause of the Son's existence, and does not decide whether the Son possesses or constitutes a distinct hypostasis; to render the Greek as though it forbade one to hold that the Son is '*of* another hypostasis' is to make heretics of almost every supporter of the council but Athanasius. On the other hand, the assertion of three *ousiai* in the Godhead was condemned at a preliminary session in Antioch,[48] and would be inconsistent both with the *homoousion* and with the gloss on the term *monogenes*. A grammar is prescribed in the creed for only one of the nouns in this anathema; to assume that they are synonyms is as tendentious as to maintain that the council of 325 was consciously advancing a doctrine of one *ousia* in three hypostases.

Since hitherto the tenet that the Son was from the *hypostasis* of the Father had implied only that the Father is the cause of his existence, the first half of the anathema did not incriminate Arius or the Eusebii. It is rather a prophylactic reassurance that the consubstantiality between Father and Son does not entail two gods or deprive the Father of his priority in the order of causation. It is when hypostasis is yoked with *ousia*, and when this term is so defined as to make the Son's origin analogous to emanation or natural reproduction, that the rearguard of the older tradition is forced into inconsistency, defiance, or equivocation one step short of subterfuge.

7. It has been put about since the time of Athanasius that, since immutability is a divine prerogative, Arians maintain that the Word is changeable, seeking evidence of his frailty in the tears, the ignorance and the trepidation that were observed from time to time in his human ministry. In writings securely attributed to Arius himself, we do not find any explanation of these phenomena, and the Word is nowhere alleged to be changeable, but is said on the contrary to be preserved from change by the Father's will (Athanasius, *Synods* 16). It was Alexander of Alexandria who inferred that, if he owes his constancy to another agent he must be changeable by nature; but even if this is its logical corollary, the position ascribed to Arius implies that the one who became incarnate was already proof against change, so and hence that his tribulation as man cannot be traced to any infirmity in the nature that belonged to him as the Word (Socrates, *Church History* 1.6). Another thinker who might have been accused of importing change into the Godhead was Marcellus, for if the God who was one becomes three when he takes on flesh, we can scarcely deny him some liability to vicissitude.[49] But of course it

---

48 On the proceedings see Chadwick (1958). On the affirmation that the Son is from the hypostasis of the Father, see Williams (2000), 276 and 301n. On the allusion to Hebrews 1.3 in the Greek prototype see Abramowski (1992b), 1–5.

49 Note that Alexander, in the same letter, thinks it pertinent to insist that the incarnation entails no change.

is improbable that an anathema of 325 was aimed at a man who was not deposed for some years and whose name appears in every extant catalogue of signatories. Nor, though Dionysius of Alexandria had pictured God as a monad who expands to become a dyad, is it likely that Alexander of Alexandria would have sanctioned even a tacit aspersion on his predecessor.[50] The target, no doubt, is Arius after all – though not the man himself, but the figure of Alexandrian caricature.

Eusebius and Nicaea

If an Arian, then, is to be defined as one who contradicts the Nicene Creed or is subject to one of its anathemas, Eusebius of Nicomedia can be assigned to this class because he would not concede that the Son is from the *ousia* of the Father. Eusebius of Caesarea, on the other hand, was not convicted of any theological error after a preliminary hearing to Nicaea, held in Antioch, where he was rash enough to contend that there is more than one *ousia* in the Godhead.[51] After the Nicene Council he no longer maintained this, nor (since he was addressing fellow-churchmen rather than pagans) did he revive the inaccurate sobriquet 'second God', which he had countenanced – once only – in his apologetic writings.[52] He continued to urge that the Word is not *autotheos* by himself, that he is properly said to exist not eternally but before the ages, and that Solomon described him as a creature, though not in a sense that precludes his being the Father's offspring. In a public letter written in the immediate aftermath of the Nicene Council, he attributes a different sense to the word *homoousios* than the one intended by the Alexandrians; yet the fact that he suffered no recrimination suggests that his glosses fell within the accepted latitude of belief, and Athanasius quotes this text to prove that he subscribed to the Council's resolutions not that he misread them. It is true that he regarded Athanasius as a meddler with the peace of the church (*Life of Constantine* 4.81), but so did the majority at a number of tribunals in which Eusebius played no conspicuous role.[53] Marcellus was his bugbear after the Council, but Marcellus, by the time of his death, had been pronounced a heretic in both halves of the Empire. In accordance with the Nicene canon against the translation of bishops, he declined the see of Antioch;[54] on the other hand, he is never aware in his writings against Marcellus that he is courting the anathemas of a synod which he commends, in

---

50 See Abramowski (1992a) and Chapter 3.

51 Chadwick (1958).

52 *Gospel Demonstration* 5.3.30. I am at a loss to follow the reasoning of Barnes (2001), 34–5, who takes *deuteros theos* as an Arian shibboleth, and deduces purports to illustrate Eusebius' fondness for it before the Nicene Council with a series of citations, none of which contains the word *theos*.

53 On the trials of Athanasius see Arnold (1991); Barnes (1993), Gwynn (2007).

54 Eusebius, *Life of Constantine* 3.60. On the ineffectuality of this canon see Socrates, *Church History* 7.38 and Bright (1882), 47–51.

one of his latest works, as the first oecumenical gathering of bishops. In the older historiography of this period he was characterized as an Arian, and Marcellus as the victim of an Arian reaction; recent commentators have found their own niche for Marcellus, but distinguish the theology of Eusebius from that of such 'pro-Nicenes' as Athanasius.[55] This form of words is certainly less polemical, but to say, of the one subscriber to the Nicene Creed whose commentary has come down to us, that he understood the mind of the council less well than a man too young to sign it is to read history in reverse.

Eusebius had been dead for two years when the Dedication Council of Antioch in 341 proscribed the belief that Christ was a creature like other creatures,[56] and in any case neither he nor Arius taught this. He was long dead when the church at large discovered that it was heresy to deny a human mind to Christ, and in any case, there is little to show that his views differed greatly from those of Athanasius or that either had been much exercised by the question. It is unfortunate that scholars, having ascertained enough to temper, dissipate or excuse the heresies once alleged against him, have been content to say that he represents a less innovative faction within the catholic church, and have not asked what contribution he may have made that that fructification of the homoousian faith which theologians label 'orthodox' and historians 'neo-Nicene'. As this is personified in Athanasius, it teaches that the Son is coeternal with the Father, that the two are divine in the same sense, and that the birth of the second hypostasis is not the means to any temporal end, but the unquenchable effusion of that love which constitutes the true and eternal being of God. All these propositions Eusebius would have regarded warily as accretions to the scriptural deposit; yet he can cull texts from the scriptures with both hands in support of the homoousian axiom that the Son is of equal dignity to the Father and ought to receive the same devotions from the Church.

A passage from Eusebius' *Demonstration of the Gospel* is often quoted, aptly enough,[57] as evidence that he did not believe the Son to be of the same nature as the Father:

> He seems to be in this way the image of God, once again ineffably and inexplicably to us, being a sort of living image of the God who lives, subsisting of himself immaterially, incorporeally and free from all admixture with the contrary; but again not at all like an image among us, which would have a different substrate with respect to its essence and a different form. On the contrary he is entirely form and in very essence likened to the father, and it is in that way that he is the most living aroma of the father, once again ineffably and inexplicably to us (*Gospel Demonstration* 5.1.21).

[55] See Ayres (2004). Eusebius is still characterized as an Arian in Cameron and Hall (1999), 3ff.

[56] See Kelly (1972), 262–74.

[57] See for example Hanson (1988), 52.

It had been a philosophical commonplace since Aristotle that, where the archetype and the copy of different stuffs, there is no *logos tês ousias* in common, no one determination of the essence.[58] But this work was published before the Nicene Council, as a synopsis of all that can be defined with regard to the Son from the evidence of the scriptures. One of its aims, along with the conversion of the Greeks and the confutation of the Jews, was to silence the bickering of heretics, but at the time of writing the author is unlikely to have been aware that the consubstantiality of persons could be held as a Christian dogma. Origen had indeed affirmed a community of nature,[59] but his star, as we saw, was waning; we have also seen that in the late third century an assertion of equality between the Son and the Father seemed to many irreconcilable with the unity of God. In Chapter 3 we noted that the formula 'one *prosôpon*' was adopted as an antidote to ditheism by Roman Christians catholic enough to win the approval of their bishop; we added that, if this meant only that Father and Son were jointly and fully revealed in the incarnation, it was unexceptionable in any epoch of Christian thought. Those who opposed it, representing what we now call the catholic tradition, could have understood it to signify either (a) that 'Father' and 'Son' are different names for a single subject, or (b) that the Father alone is God and the Son his created instrument on earth.[60] Eusebius, holding (a) that the Son is a being distinct from the Father, and (b) that the distinction is not merely temporal but sempiternal, holds at the same time (c) that each is god, albeit with some gradation of divinity. To avert the ditheistic interpretation of (c), he conceives of the relation between the Father and the Son as a pattern for the incarnation: Christ's aphorism, 'he who has seen me has seen the Father' (John 14.9), is as true of the Word in heaven as on earth.

Origen had compared the Father and Son to two figures, one infinite in magnitude, the other resembling it in every detail but proportioned to our capacities (*First Principles* 1.2.7). This picture, in which the difference eclipses the likeness, seems at first to have been intended to distinguish thc pcrsons in their eternal character; within a few lines, however, it becomes evident that Origen is speaking of the self-disclosure of God in the word made flesh. In another notorious passage (*On Prayer* 15.1) we meet the same equivocation: the Son, he opines, should not receive the same prayer of adoration as the Father because he is not the Father's like in *ousia* or in *hupokeimenon*, in substance or in substrate. The notion of an incorporeal substrate is odd enough to suggest that Origen is alluding here to the flesh in which the risen Christ ascended to the Father; yet, while he may have held that Christ the man is not worthy of worship in his own right, it is barely conceivable that the believed the divinity of the Son himself to have been impaired by the assumption of the flesh. If the Son is not entitled to all that the

---

58 Aristotle, *Categories* 1a1–12. As Zachhuber (1999), 46 observes, the relation between an image and its archetype was regarded in antiquity as the standard case of likeness in name between unlike in *logos tês ousias*.

59 *Commentary on John* 2.76, p. 68 Preuschen.

60 The patripassian and Noetian heresies, distinguished in Chapter 3.

Father receives, it is therefore because he is always the image, not the prototype, even in his divine character: the import of this passage is not so much that the glory of Christ was lessened by his incarnation as that the Word stands timelessly in a relation to the Father which explains at once his servitude on earth and his subordination in the liturgy.

If the Son does not approximate more closely to the divinity of the Father in Eusebius than in Origen, he approximates more closely to his dignity. There may not be intrinsic parity, but there is parity of esteem. 'When the statue and its king are honoured, the honour is one and not two, for there are not two kings' (*Gospel Demonstration* 5.4.10). And again: 'Rightly the gospel (John 1.1–3) calls him god, because through the aforesaid words also the Word who is now spoken of as god was pronounced to be the wisdom and the offspring of God, his priest and anointed king and lord and god and image of God' (5.5.2). And finally: 'The Word of God, having received lordship and sovereignty from the Father in second place, as his true and only Son, will himself rightly and reverently be termed a second Lord' (5.5.7). The appellative *deuteros kurios*, 'second lord' (for which *deuteros theos*, 'second god' is an alternative at 5.3.30, an appositional variant at 5, proem 23) is not employed here to connote inferiority but a perfect communication to the Son of the Father's attributes, which makes him in power and function all that the Father is to his creatures and thus entitles him to equality of nomenclature.[61] The 'second god' is another God, or God writ double.

The epithet diminishes Christ if we speak, as the Bible never does, of the second hypostasis as he is in himself before revelation as the Word. Athanasius pushes the argument beyond the horizon set to it by Eusebius when he urges that, if we rightly pay to the Son the devoirs that we pay to God the Father, that is because we have found he is by nature all that the Father was known to be:

> In the Son the Godhead of the Father is contemplated. This one will be able to comprehend more readily from the example of the Emperor's image. For in the image is the form and shape of the Emperor, and in the Emperor is the form that is in the image. For there is in the image a peerless likeness[62] of the king. Thus the one who beholds the image sees the Emperor in it, and conversely the one who sees the Emperor perceives that he is the one in the image. And because there is no discrepancy in the likeness, the image could say to the one who wants to see the Emperor after the image, 'I and the Emperor are one' (*Against the Arians* 3.5).

Here he elides what is noted by Eusebius, that the image and the orginal are not one in *ousia*; both agree, however, in holding the unity of the Godhead to be pre-eminently a unity of honour. When he examines biblical texts Athanasius is generally rebutting deductions made by his adversaries; in arguing from the liturgy

---

[61] For an inventory of passages in which the Son is deuteros to the Father, see Grillmeier (1975), 171. He too finds only one case of *deuteros theos*.

[62] Cf. Alexander of Alexandria at Theodoret, *Church History* 1.4.47.

to the divinity of Christ he can take the offensive. Paul of Samosata is said to have tried the converse argument a century before by erasing Christ's name from the hymns of Antioch. Eusebius, who saw in Paul the rudiments of Marcellus' heresy,[63] took the opposite course, not even dwelling, as later opponents of the *homoousion* did, on the fact that Christ comes second in all devotions to the Trinity. Reasoning that, as image and prototype merit the same devotion they are alike in honour and constitute one Godhead, he became a harbinger of the homoousian doctrine against the tenor of his own theology.

In the technical language of philosophy, Eusebius is content to posit an axiological unity, while Athanasius argues that an axiological unity must be the index of an ontological unity.[64] In the following chapter, we shall find that the same antithesis can be drawn between the Christology of those who held, with Theodore, that the unity of God and Word and Jesus the man is sufficiently established by our worshipping the two together, and those who averred, with Cyril, that the man can be worshipped only if he and the Word are not merely conjoined, but one and the same.

Homoiousians and Homoousians

For many churchmen of the mid-fourth century, the authority of the Council of 325 was at once confirmed and eclipsed by that of the Dedication Council held in 341 at Antioch. As it met two years after the deposition of Athanasius, he was not a party to any of the confession associated with this meeting; when he first takes notice of it, however, he does not accuse its delegates of hostility to his own person of infidelity to the Nicene Creed. Its membership was not coextensive with that of the Nicene Council, but only a few can be shown to have been remonstraters at that gathering. Since the etiquette of every great synod held between 325 and 381 included the promulgation of a creed, we cannot be sure that any of the five confessions associated with this event was designed to supersede the Nicene formula. The second of those recorded by Athanasius was officially disseminated as a resolution of the Council, and concurs in most respects with the Nicene Creed, except that, in place of the *homoousion*, it affirms that the Son exhibits an 'incomparable' likeness to the Father. It anathematizes the notion that the Son is any other, but stops short of the unconditional interdict on the word *ktiston* that Athanasius and Marcellus would have imposed. While the bishops protested that their office forbade them to borrow their opinions from a mere presbyter like Arius, it can be argued that they took more pains than the Nicene Council to banish the errors attributed to Marcellus, whose orthodoxy was at this time under scrutiny in Rome. The temporary acquittal of Marcellus in the west may have sharpened the vigilance of his critics, and in 351 his putative disciple, Photinus of Sirmium, was

63 See *Ecclesiastical Theology* 1.14.2, 1.20.43, 3.6.4.

64 Alexander of Alexandria also asserts equality of honour at Theodoret, *Church History* 1.4.52.

deposed by a synod held in his native see. The decrees of this assembly suggest that orthodoxy was understood at this time as a navigation between the pagan assertion of two gods and the Sabellian blending of the three hypostases in one person. Homoousians could be accused of either, and for this reason the assertion of the Son's consummate likeness to the Father was still considered the safest canon of orthodoxy. It seemed to Athanasius that the gate which had been locked against Arius in 325 was now standing open: he began to inveigh against the Council of 341, maintained that it had been secretly orchestrated by the same cabal that had forced him into exile, and became an indefatigable champion of the Nicene *homoousion*.[65] But a rival to this arose in the phrase *homoios kat' ousian*, which, after a brief experiment in compromise, Athanasius found a less adequate talisman than the *homoousion*. For all that, it is possible that he and a majority of recent commentators have misjudged his rejected allies, and that a fusion of homoousian nomenclature with homoiousian sentiment resulted in an augmentation, rather than a dilution, of Nicene teaching on the divinity of Christ.

The doctrine commonly known as homoiousian was propounded in the 350s by George of Laodicea, and Basil of Ancyra, who had inherited the see of Marcellus but not the same eccentricities in doctrine. The word *homoiousios* was not their own variant of *homoios kat'ousian*, which means 'like (or alike in essence', but a neologism coined by their opponents, which, because it can mean only 'of like essence', seemed irreconcilable with the Nicene teaching that the first and second persons share one essence. The aim of George and Basil was in fact not so much to compromise as to purify the Nicene formulation. Favoured though it was by the disgraced Athanasius and his western allies, the *homoousion* was the one ingredient of the Nicene Creed of 325 which had not been ratified in any subsequent formulary; worse still, according to archives known to Basil, it had been condemned in 268 by a venerable council of eighty bishops held in Antioch. To defy this council was to side with Paul of Samosata,[66] and its reasons for proscribing the *homoousion* did not seem to require much scrutiny, for if the epithet was applied to God in its usual acceptation, it would connote some parting of the Father's substance in order to produce the Son. The phrase *homoios kat'ousian*, by contrast, proclaimed a community of essence between the two persons without these dangerous connotations, and with the salutary proviso that the two are not the same, since nothing is ever said to be *homoios* with itself (Epiphanius, *Panarion* 73.15.6). To speak of the second person as a creature – an immaterial one, of course, without the blemishes that mar our viscous and fallen creaturehood – is to say that the Father did not experience any passion or division in producing him (Epiphanius, *Panarion* 73.17.1); to speak of the Father's begetting him, on the other hand, is to say that he possesses all the attributes of the one to whom he owes his being, and

---

[65] See Gwynn (2006), 200–209 on the scales which fell on the eyes of Athanasius as he looked back to this council after a decade.

[66] Who is coupled with Marcellus by Basil of Ancyra at Epiphasnius, *Panarion* 73.12.2.

thus stands in the same relation to him as a perfect son to the natural father whose image and likeness he bears.

This position is a compromise only insofar as it marries two traditions of nomenclature. It does not accord to the Son a lower dignity than is implied by the *homoousion*; it does not suggest that he is half divine, or that his essence is merely similar to that of the Father but not identical. The likeness to the Father which constitutes the Son's divinity is the complement to the likeness of humanity which he assumes in his incarnation (Epiphanius, *Panarion* 73.9), and it was obvious to professing catholics of this epoch that the man whom the Word became or assumed was like us insofar as he took our nature, not merely insofar as he took a nature resembling ours. It is not in power alone but in his own being that Christ is divine (*Panarion* 73.16.8), and, although the term 'creation' is not proscribed, his origin is more properly described as a begetting (*Panarion* 73.5.7). Despite the polemical origin of the locution *homoios kat' ousian*, homoousians briefly hoped to make common cause with its patrons against those parties which had abandoned the word *ousia* altogether.[67] But homoousians and homoiousians suffered shipwreck together in 357, when the council of Sirmium declared that every compound of *ousia* was unbiblical and heretical when used in association with the Godhead. This decree was ratified in 359 at Rimini and Seleucia and again in 360 at Constantinople. The return of Athanasius to his see was facilitated by the deaths of George and Basil, whose subtleties did not outlive them.

The arguments of Basil of Ancyra, on the other hand, were reviewed with uncommon subtlety and insight by the homoousian Marius Victorinus, the first Latin defender of the Nicene watchword, and the first writer in either tongue to undertake a philosophical exposition of the unity of three persons in one substance. His theory, which is protean and cannot be canvassed here at length, requires that, in divine agency as in other forms of agency, there should be a potentiality for action, and actualising of the potentiality and an activity characteristic of this actuality. The first is the Father or Being, the second the Spirit or Intellect, the third the Son or Life. Since there is no matter to inhibit the actualising of the potential or its subsequent activity, the predicates of all three will be coextensive, and the work of the Son and the Spirit will be an unfolding of the energies that were latent in the Father. A catholic parsing of the *homoousion* therefore vindicates not only the divinity and equality of the three persons but the priority of the Father, though this is not a priority that entails either temporal precedence or disparity in power. The rival theory of the homoiousians fails, according to Victorinus, on three counts, metaphysical, logical and dogmatic. A sound metaphysic, he argues, holds similarity to be a property in qualities, not in the substance; hence a similarity in substance is nonsensical (1.23). Logic, moreover, prescribes that if there were two similar substances, they could not both posses the same property of universal causation, for if there is a cause of all things, it must be one (1.25). Finally, it is a dogma of the faith that the Son is what he is by virtue of his generation from

[67] See Hilary, *On the Synods* 89–91, but contrast Athanasius, *On the Synods* 41.

the Father, but this is not preserved if we affirm a merely symmetrical relation between the two (1.29-30). The unity of divine substance, the integrity of the first principle and the asymmetry between Father and Son in the order of causation are all obscured by the homoiousian formula.

Victorinus assumes that the phrase *homoios kat'ousian* (which he regularly, and treacherously, contracts to *homoiousios*) signifies likeness or similarity of substance, not possession of the same substance. But *homoios* in Greek is a more ambivalent term than its Latin equivalent similes, and can be applied to different members of the same class rather than to members of similar classes, 'Like to like' is an adage known to Plato, which implies that members of the same kind attract one another, not that they are drawn to similar species. One might use the term *homoios* of a person who was always true to his character or consistently of the same mind; in Aristotle's *Politics* it indicates not similarity but equality of rank, and at *Iliad* 18.239 it denotes 'the same earth'. To take an example from Christian prose, when Cyril of Alexandria spoke of angels as *homoioi kata phusin*, he evidently did not intend to say that they belonged to different species, but that they shared a common nature.[68] Not 'like in nature' but 'alike in nature' would be a fair rendering of *homoios kata phusin*. This usage is anticipated in Basil of Caesarea, who, with his fellow-Cappadocians, came to be recognised in his own lifetime as a steward of Nicene orthodoxy. In one of his early letters, he asks Apollinarius, the future heresiarch,[69] to 'explain what the meaning [of the term *homoousios*] is, and how it might be predicated without offence of those who are perceived not to belong to a common overlying class or to share an underlying matter' (*Letter* 361). He himself opines that the *homoousion* states nothing which could not be conveyed with more lucidity by the affirmation of an incomparable likeness between the persons:[70]

> If one should say that the Father's essence is light, intellectual, eternal, unbegotten, one will say that this too is the essence of the Son. And it seems to me that to express this notion, the affirmation of an unparalleled (*aparallaktos*) likeness is more apposite than that of the *homoousion*.

If this passage is evidence of a 'homoiousian' leaven in Basil's thought, it affords no evidence that the term *homoios* circumscribes the divinity of the Son. It might

---

[68] Quoting *Dialogue on the Trinity* 1.394.35–7 and 6.592.24–6, Vaggione (2000), 162n.61 adds the gloss that angels 'cannot be both *homoousioi* and distinct' in the absence of matter. Cf. Origen, *First Principles* 1.6.4, where an exception is made for the Trinity.

[69] Prestige (1956) is generally held to have demonstrated the authenticity of this correspondence.

[70] Among those who believe this correspondence to mark an abrupt transition in Basil's thought see Drecoll (1999), 337. For response and bibliography see Zachhuber (2001), 78.

as well be cited as an attestation of 'Eusebianism',[71] since Basil is employing the vocabulary that any Greek would use in praising a statue for its resemblance to the original. He is enough of a Eusebian – enough of an Athanasian,[72] for that matter – to preserve the asymmetry between the persons: the Son is compared to the Father, but the Father submits to no comparisons. We have seen that the true homoiousian as Victorinus paints him, was supposed to be one who posits a reciprocal identity of attributes between persons of the Godhead; this was the complaint of Basil's enemy Eunomius, whom contemporaries dubbed an Anomoean[73] because he held that the Son and the Father were wholly dissimilar in essence. His teaching may be regarded as a hypertrophy of Alexander's principle 'always Father, Always Son'; from this he infers, to the consternation of those who had embraced the Nicene Creed in its entirety, that the Father and Son are of antithetical natures, the one essentially unbegotten, the other essentially begotten. He considered it impossible that paternal and filial predicates could be accidents to the persons, since in that which is incorporeal and eternal there can be no attribute less essential or more detachable than any other.[74] The same axiom of divine impassibility forbids him to accept the Nicene teaching that the Son is from the essence of the Father, as this implies that the essence is subject to division. The primacy of the Father is maintained, with the homoousians, against the homoiousians; divine impassibility is upheld, with homoiousian logic, against the homoousians. Each possesses half the truth, and the error of each is to hold what the other denies:

> We confess that the Son alone is born from the Father, subject to him in essence and will (for he himself confesses that he lives on account of the Father and does nothing of his own), neither *homoousios* nor *homoiousios*. For the former implies generation and division of the essence, the latter equality (*Apology* 18).[75]

Athanasius had conceded that, when the Son declares 'the Father is greater than I', this is true of him even as second person of the Trinity, though he goes on to make this a proof of their common nature, on the plea that we do not employ the terms 'greater' and 'less' except when appraising members of the same class (*Against the Arians* 1.58). Eunomius, who certainly denied that Father and Son were equipollently divine, maintained that it was the *homoiousion*, not the

71 Cf. Hanson (1988), 353.

72 Note also that *aparallaktos eikôn* is the formula by which Alexander of Alexandria means to confer the highest dignity on the Son: Theodoret, *Church History* 1.4.47. The attribution of this letter to Athanasius' predecessor appears to be undisputed.

73 The term may originate in Alexander of Alexandria's protestation that the Son is not *anomoios* to the Father: Socrates, *Church History* 1.6.16 (attributed to Athanasius by Stead).

74 See especially *Apology* 8 (p. 43 Vaggione) and 10–11 p. 47.

75 I do not deny that there is a 'typically homoiousian' principle of subordinating the Son, as Zachhuber (2001), 76 and 80 observes. Many were no doubt glad to avail themselves of the ambiguity of the 'homoiousian' formula.

homoousion, which implied this. Against him the Cappadocians too maintain it: consubstantiality, in their usage, is a predicate of each person of the Trinity in relation to the others. In litanies the name of the Son comes second, but in majesty no person is inferior to the others; they are distinguished neither by essence nor by accidents but by their mutual relations, and the Son is as much a cause of the Father's fatherhood as the father of the Son's sonship. The unity of the Godhead, in Gregory Nyssen's letter to Ablabius, resides in their common possession of the inscrutable nature which we know as their theotes or divinity; with suitable qualifications, one can argue for an analogy between the there who are God and three individuals who all exemplify the species 'man'. In Gregory Nazianzen, it is the *monarchia* of the Father that cements the unity of the three divine persons, but *monarchia* signifies sole causality, rather than hegemony or precedence in time. The same 'genarchic' unity had been ascribed to the Trinity is the reply of Apollinarius to Basil's hesitations over the Nicene *homoousion*: the common essence, explains the future heretic, is not a single genus to which they pertain or a single matter that constitutes them, but a unity of origin, just as derivation from a common ancestor is assumed in Holy Writ to confer not merely a nominal but a personal unity on the members of one household. Both Nazianzen and Apollinarius shun Nyssen's model because they do not wish to lose this cardinal implication of the Nicene *homoousion*; but all three Cappadocians are at one in their 'homoiousian' conviction that the *isotês* or equality of the persons means, not only they participate in one Godhead, but that words such as 'greater' and 'less' cannot be applied to them even in the most etiolated sense.

One consequence of a half-century of wrangling was the recovery for the catholic tradition of the apophatic or negative mode of speaking about the divine.[76] Against Eunomius this could be a weapon of defence, for if no words of ours can define the essence of God, we cannot conclude that the Father and the Son are of different essences because we have given them different predicates. At the same time, a consciousness of God's unfathomability quickens mystical devotion and assures us that in the afterlife there will be no end to the increase of beatitude or the deepening of knowledge. If it be said that this reasoning disarms all sides in the Nicene controversies, since we can no more prove that God is in essence a trinity than that he is not a trinity, appeals can be made to scripture and the traditions of the church, – although it cannot be said that either is an unequivocal witness on the side of the homoousians. An apophatic vein, as we have seen, is characteristic of Gnostic literature; since, however, different motives prompted the Cappadocians and precedents could be found in Clement of Alexandria, Philo and the Platonists of the third century, it would be rash to surmise, without evidence, that they baked their catholic bread with the dough of heresy. But in the case of Marius Vixctorinus the dough survives.

---

[76] This attracted the imputation of Valentinianism: see *Against Eunomius* 2.2.448 (*Opera* I, p. 356.21) and 2.464 (*Opera* I, p. 362.9).

The Coptic *Zostrianus* was discovered in 1945 at Nag Hammadi in Egypt. If it fairly represents the Greek archetype, deemed worthy of refutation in forty books by an eminent colleague of Plotinus, it reveals that the triad of being, life and mind is older than Porphyry.[77] Even if the original was embellished in the light of controversy, the extant copy antedates Victorinus, and suffices to prove his acquaintance with a Greek version that already contained the triad. One of his attempts to force a logical path from the One to the triad he substitutes beatitude for intellect and assumes a declamatory tone not characteristic of the whole treatise:

> This is God, this the Father, pre-existing his own beatitude in his pre-intelligence and his pre-existence, preserving his very self in unmoved motion and for that reason in want of nothing, perfect above the perfect, a tri-potent spirit in unicity (*unalitas*), perfect also above spirit. For he does not spirate, but spirit in him is all that which it is for him to be, a spirit whose spiration results in his being spirit, since he is spirit inseparable from his very self, his own space and his own denizen, abiding in himself, alone in the alone, existing everywhere and nowhere, one in simplicity while he co-unites three powers, all existence, all life and beatitude, all these being none the less one and a simple one; and the potency of life and beatitude are eminently in that which is what it is to be, namely existence. For that whereby he is and exists, the potency which is that of existence, this is also the potency of life and beatitude, itself through its very self both the idea and the logos of its own self, and possessing life and action by virtue of that non-existent existence of its own self, a co-uniting of the indivisible spirit: divinity, substantiality, beatitude, intelligentiality (*intelligentialitas*), vitality, besthood (*optimitas*) and universally all in every mode, pure ingenerate fore-being (Greek *proon*), the unicity of co-uniting without any co-uniting (*Against the Arians* 1.50).

Equally crepuscular texts are adduced from the *Zostrianus* by Tardieu:[78]

> The [whole] Spirit, perfect, simple and invisible, has become singleness in activity and Existence and activity and a simple triple-[power], an invisible spirit, an image of that which really exists (*Zostrianus* 79.16–20) … It is in every place and yet in no place that the ineffable, unnameable One (74.17) … and the power is with the Essence and Existence of being, when the water exists (17.1–3)… How [does he come into existence] as a simple one, differing from himself? Does he exist as existence, form and blessedness? How has the existence that does not exist appeared from the existing power? (3.8–13)… He exists as [lacuna] since he is in [the] mind. He is within it, not coming forth to any place because he is a single perfect, simple spirit (16.16–17).

---

77 See Porphyry, *Life of Plotinus* 16, with Tardieu (1996). For criticism of Tardieu's argument that Victorinus was indebted to this text see Majercik (2005) and Abramowski (2007).

78 Tardieu (1996). English text from Robinson (1990).

Our texts are not coextensive: the liturgical interests of the Zostrianus, for example, find no echo in Victorinus. Nor would it be impossible to cull analogues from other Gnostic writings, other works of Greek philosophy, even perhaps from Indian scriptures. Rather than postulate direct borrowing from the *Zostrianus*, we might surmise that both are derivatives of the same Greek original[79] – but even then, as Hadot observes,[80] some Gnostic intermediary must still be invoked to explain the prominence of the term 'spirit' in both these texts, since a common antecedent for this in pagan literature is barely conceivable. We ought not to be surprised that terms and concepts which had once been reckoned perilous or heretical by the episcopate should be re-baptized by a writer against the Arians in the fourth century. We have seen that when Tertullian spoke of the Son as a *prolatio* or projection of the Father, he did not conceal the Valentinian provenance of this term; Origen used its Greek antecedent *probolê*, and was posthumously accused of having adulterated the faith that he purported to be defending against the monarchians.[81] Arius, in the same letter to Alexander which denies that Christ is a *homoousion meros* of the Father, hints that anyone who denies that he is created out of nothing must be a Valentinian if he is not a Sabellian or a Manichee (Athanasius, *On Synods* 16). Valentinus, of course, was not alive to answer him, but there is evidence that Eunomius had made enemies among one group represented at Nag Hammadi:

> Hand out the word and the water of life? Cease from the evil lusts and desires and (the teachings of) the Anomoeans,[82] evil heresies that have no basis (*Concept of our Great Power*, NHC VI.4.40.4–9, trans. F. Wisse and F.E. Williams in Robinson (2000), vol. 3, 305).

There is no obstacle to construing Anomoeans as the name bestowed by catholics on those who held that Father and Son are wholly unlike in essence.[83] *The Concept of Our Great Power* could not have passed for orthodox with adherents of the

---

79 For those who follow Bechtle (1999) in dating the anonymous commentary on the Parmenides to the second century, this could be the common archetype. Hadot (1996) accepts, since the *Zostrianus* was already known to Plotinus (Porphyry, *Life of Plotinus* 16), the philosophical source will date from the 'middle Platonic' era; he continues, however, to argue that the anonymous commentary is the work of Porphyry, and hence that it cannot be an ancestor to this Gnostic text.

80 Hadot (1996), 124–5. But why should the *Zostrianus* itself not be the archetype?

81 See previous chapter.

82 This is a transliteration of the Greek *anomoion*, as 'heresy' is a transliteration of *hairesis*.

83 F. Wisse and F.E. Williams, in Robinson (2000), vol. 3, 292, state that 'the reference to the Anomoeans provides a rough terminus a quo after the middle of the fourth century'. For the invention of the term see Athanasius, *On Synods* 31 and Epiphanius, *Panarion* 76.1. On the teaching of Aeetius and Eunomius see Kopecek (1970), vol. 1, 199–298 and vol. 2, 170–94, with Vaggione (2000).

Nicene faith, and no one of this persuasion would have turned to such a work as the *Zostrianus* if he was not, like Marius Victorinus, a convert to the church from Platonism. But the diction of the fourth century reclaims the discarded idioms of the second, even in authors who did not tolerate any blending of theologies. Controversy had liberated catholics from their aversion to the word *Gnôstikos*, which Evagrius, a friend of the Cappadocians, applies to the ideal Christian without attracting censure;[84] Gregory Nyssen too will have known the pedigree of such terms as *ogdoas* and *plêrôma*,[85] on which he builds conceits that might have wakened the derision of Irenaeus. Even if one does not consummate an alliance with him, the enemy of one's enemy cannot fail to exhibit some of the characteristics of a friend.

Origen's New Clothes

We have seen in the previous chapter that it was Origen's denial of a temporal beginning to the Son and his elevation of the Son to a dignity consonant with the Father's that were thought to require excuse at the beginning of the fourth century. His admirers and his detractors agreed that absolute parity between Son and Father was incompatible with the profession of one God. Three quarters of a century later, the charge of Arianism was apt to be pressed against those who held that the Son was a creature or would not grant him every attribute of the Father except that of being un-begotten. Origen himself was not a mark for the first generation of polemicists. Marcellus deprecates his exegesis of Proverbs 8.22, but does not impugn his orthodoxy; no fear of contagion is apparent when Athanasius recruits the 'industrious Origen' as a witness to the eternity of the Son. The Cappadocians also hold him in high regard, though the *Philokalia* which Basil and Nazianzen are supposed to have compiled from his works does not excerpt any passage that subordinates Christ to the Father. But once it had become a presupposition of those who upheld the Nicene Council that its teaching was coterminous with the teaching of Athanasius, elements in Origen's thought which passed in his day as common phylacteries of monotheism were discovered to be errors pernicious to faith in the triune God. The old libels against his teaching on the resurrection had not been silenced, and may have been deliberately propagated in this era to bring discredit on his seductive exposition of texts relating to the person of the Son. Origen's name had not passed into oblivion, and a supporter of the Nicene Creed must be with him or against him. For those who upheld the Athanasian reading of the council it was necessary to prove that all subordinationism was Arianism and that if one took Origen's part in this, one was likely to find oneself a patron of heresies that had never been tolerated in churches faithful to the apostolic tradition.

---

[84] On the meaning and scope of the term see now Konstantinovsky (2008).

[85] On the 'eighth' which follows the hebdomad, see Inscriptions on the Psalms 2.4 at *Opera* V, p. 83.21. On the *plêröma* or *fulfilment* of humanity see *On the Soul* 152, p. 506 Ramelli.

One vigorous opponent of the 'Arians', Bishop Eustathius of Antioch, wrote a treatise upbraiding Origen for his exegesis of the episode in the first book of Samuel in which the Witch of Endor summons the wraith of the prophet Samuel from Hades.[86] Origen had accepted the literal meaning of the text, whereas Eustathius, with an animadversion on Origen's curious failure to apply his favourite tool of allegory in a case where faith demands it (Chapter 21), urges that any apparition of the dead must be a contrivance of the devil (Chapter 4). Wrongly assuming that allegorical readings are incompatible with the retention of the literal sense, he appears to have been the first to allege that Origen reduced the fall of Adam to a myth. In this respect his polemic foreshadows that of Epiphanius,[87] the champion of an orthodoxy which recognized no truth before Methodius or later than Nicaea. Although he reproduces page after page of Methodius; strictures on Origen (*Panarion* 64.10), Epiphanius seems not to perceive that Origen posited the attenuation rather than the summary dissolution of the body, and that in making the resultant superficies the envelope or *morphê* of the soul, he made both amenable to the same refining fire. Like Methodius, therefore, he has unwittingly vindicated the true opinion of the man whom he purports to be refuting. He shows the same want of candour when, repeating the charge that Origen's gloss on the coats of skins at Genesis 3.24 implies that the body was an afterthought in the creation of humanity, he goes on to allege that did not regard paradise as a place on earth.[88] There is no passage in the extant work of Origen which implies that materiality is a consequence of the fall, though he undoubtedly held that the sin of Adam and Eve debauched the intellect (*Against Celsus* 7.39), that the body imbibes the grossness of the will in the rebel angels, and that soul was prior to body in the creation of the first man (*Genesis Homilies* 1).

Epiphanius, though he does not revive the charge of teaching the transmigration of souls, was perhaps the first of Origen's critics to scent a heresy in the mere notion of existence before embodiment. According to his report (*Panarion* 64.4), the great heresiarch had argued that the incorporeal souls had been created to dwell eternally with God, but that each in turn, has fallen and is now undergoing is now undergoing chastisement. Later authorities[89] add that the cause of the trespass was satiety or coolness, and that each soul acquires a body of a texture corresponding to the degree of its estrangement. The human body is thus the penitentiary for those who have fallen further than the angelic powers but not so far as demons. This is the marrow of 'Origenism' in many textbooks even now, yet it is hard to reconcile it with other teachings which are frequently attested in Origen's writings – as, for example, that the demons, being denizens of the air, have a finer carapace than ours, or that the sun and moon have submitted to embodiment not to purge their

86 See 1Samuel 28 with Greer and Mitchell (2007).

87 See Dechow (1998); Clark (1992), 43–104.

88 Jerome, *Letters* 51.5; Epiphanius, *Ancoratus* 55; cf. Origen, *First Principles* 2.11.6.

89 Chiefly John Damascene and Antipater of Bostra. See the augmentations to *First Principles* 1.8 in Koetschau's edition (Leipzig: GCS 22, 1913; also Epiphanius, in Jerome, *Letters* 51.4; Jerome, *Letters* 124.9; Theophilus, in Jerome, *Letters* 98.12.

own uncleanness but to give light to an unclean world (*First Principles* 1.7.5). He certainly opined that soul becomes spirit when it is purified of sin (*ibid.*, 2.8.3), and seems to have held that the ascending soul will attain, or perhaps pass through, the angelic state (*Homilies on the Song* 20.8); he is, however, so far from maintaining that every soul is a fallen angel that he hesitates to entertain such a theory with regard to a privileged emissary of God like John the Baptist (*Commentary on John* 1.31.186–92). Where his extant works impute satiety to the soul, they may be speaking of its decay from innocence after it joins a body (*First Principles* 1.4.1). He maintained with vigour both that the soul comes into the embryo from the hand of God and that it exercises reason and moral choice in the mother's womb;[90] but the second doctrine would have seemed incontestable to all Christians of his day, while the first amounts to no more than a rejection of 'traducianist' position that the soul is imparted with the father's seed.

But hermeneutic charity would be wasted on Origen if, as Epiphanius thinks, he held a Trinitarian theology that belied the incarnation of God as man. By 373, when he wrote his charge to the monks, or *Ancoratus*, it was the common view among champions of the Nicene Creed that consubtantiality precluded all gradation of power or dignity in the Godhead. Epiphanius therefore looked with more severity on the Arians, who denied the equality of the Son and Father, than on the so-called Anthropomorphites, who ascribed a human form to God the Father, as though the whole deity were identical by nature with the man who had been miraculously assumed by the Second Person. To Origen's disciples this was idolatry: since Adam, as their master repeatedly urged, was not the image of God but the one created according to that image, there was no somersault of logic that would enable them to credit God with traits analogous to those of his sensible creation. On the other hand, while Origen had affirmed the coeternity of the Father and the Son as distinct hypostases, he had sought to preserve the unity of the Godhead by distinguishing the Father as *autotheos* (essential deity) from the Son who is *theos* or God by derivation (*Commentary on John* 2.2.16).[91] It was his lot to be attainted first for his failure to uphold and then for his failure to deny the superiority of the Father to the Son.[92]

---

90 *First Principles* 1.7.4, 3.3.5, 2.9.7, 3.3.5.4.

91 Thus at Jerome, *Letters* 51.4 he asserts that Origen denied knowledge of the Father to the Son, though the cited passage, like *First Principles* 1.1.8, means only that the Son does not perceive the Father with carnal organs. Cf. Jerome, *Against John of Jerusalem* 7, *Letters* 124. 2.

92 It lies outside the scope of the present discussion to trace the provenance of the thirteen points which constitute the heresy of the 'Origenists' in *Panarion* 63. Epiphanius does not lay them at Origen's door or corroborate any of them by citation from his works. The utmost malevolence could not derive the majority of them from Origen's extant writings, they do not recur elsewhere in the philippics of Epiphanius or his allies, and, although they were later paraphrased in a catechetical work, the *Handbook of Joseph*, they do not figure among the charges brought against Origen by Justinian or by the Second Council of Constantinople.

The most zealous of Origen's partisans, Rufinus of Aquileia, retorted that a man who espoused the term *homoousios* cannot be an Arian (*Adulteration of Origen* 1). Thus the very word that had seemed to require apology in the age of Pamphilus could now be adduced as an unequivocal mark of orthodoxy. Rufinus translated Pamphilus, together with a corpus of works by Origen, few of which have survived in Greek. By his own account he amended any passage on which a reader of the fourth century would be apt to put a heretical construction that would not have been intended in the third. Furthermore, he professed to have detected interpolations which were duly excluded from his Latin versions. In the absence of the original Greek, we cannot say how many of his author's heterodoxies may have been obscured by his arbitrary dealings with the text. He was certainly accused of dissimulation by his embittered friend, the shrewd and acerbic Jerome,[93] who, for reasons which are now not wholly recoverable, had fallen under the spell of men who matched him in neither quality. One was Epiphanius, whose letters he translated, and whose cause he espoused against Origen's champion, Bishop John of Jerusalem. The other was Theophilus, patriarch of Alexandria, who, in the hope (as we are told) of hiding his own misdemeanours, forced a group of Origenists from their monastery and Egypt, then attempted to depose their protector, Bishop John Chrysostom of Constantinople. In his letters he taxed Origen not only with lending countenance to astrology and magic but with denying the eternity of Christ's kingdom (Jerome, *Letters* 96.7–17). Tendentiously, he sees an attenuation of God's omnipotence in a text which merely asserted that any actual creation of omnipotence must be finite.[94] A further charge, that Origen forbade prayer to the Son, follows Athanasius rather than Origen in admitting only one species of prayer.[95] Rome intercepted his dealings with John Chrysostom in 402, but the intrigue served at least to ensure that Origen would enjoy no honour in his native city.[96]

In the west, Jerome too was largely content to reproduce the strictures of Epiphanius, though he may have been the first allege that Origen had posited a second fall from heaven, which would entail a new creation of the material realm as a house of punishment. If we can trust Rufinus, Jerome took for Origen's own view what the latter had presented as the absurd result of another's speculations.[97] Jerome's claim, on the other hand – partly verified by his *Commentary on Ephesians*[98] – is that, far from augmenting the blemishes in Origen's work, he distilled the best of his exegesis and spared the Greekless reader any knowledge of his doctrinal heresies. He was never the less than a scholar, and in contrast to Epiphanius and Theophilus, he knew that it was not the resurrection of the body, but the resurrection of a carnal body (*Letters* 84.5), that Origen had denied.

93 Clark (1992), 11–42 and 159–93.

94 Jerome, *Letters* 96.17; Origen, *First Principles* 2.9.1.

95 Jerome, *Letters* 96.14; Origen, *On Prayer* 15.1.

96 On the structures of the anchorite Shenute see Clark (1992), 151–9.

97 *First Principles* 3.6.3 (Rufinus); Jerome, *Letter to Avitus* 10.

98 *Patrologia Graeca* 26. 485–6 on Ephesians 1.12.

To westerners – even to westerners of untainted orthodoxy like Rufinus and Augustine – 'the creed' was not the symbol of 325, but a cognate formula, traditionally ascribed to the apostles but now known in standard histories as the Old Roman Creed, or 'R'. In 357 the bishop of Rome, Liberius, put his signature to the homoian Creed of Sirmium, which affirmed that the Son was like the Father without admitting community of substance or identity of attributes. Although it was urged by champions of Nicaea that he had succumbed to duress, we do not hear that he tried to revoke his signature when events overthrew the policy of Constantius. His suffrage helps to explain the longevity of homoian teachings in such centres as Milan, whose bishop Ambrose took the inquisitor's role at a conference held in the northern Italian city of Aquileia in 381.[99] The questions that he put to his interlocutor Palladius amount to a breviary of Arianism as it was now defined by proponents of the Nicene *homoousion*. Is the Son coeternal with the Father? Does he possess immortality on the same terms as the Father? Is he good as the Father is good, or endowed with wisdom of the same order? The answer in every case is no, and Palladius appeals to John 17.3 to prove that the Father is the one true God, contesting the prosecutor's application of the same words to the Son at John 5.20. Denying the validity of the council, he assumes the right to interrogate his accusers: why do they refuse to subordinate the Son to the father in the teeth of his own confession that 'the Father is greater than I?'. After some procrastination, Ambrose replies, in the manner of Athanasius, that the Son is inferior only in so far as he has taken flesh in voluntary obedience to the Father. As he did not have the power to deliver a judgment, the acts conclude with an adjournment; at a subsequent hearing the Nicene faith prevailed by royal decree.

It cannot be said that the charge of Arianism was factitious, as there is a precedent in the letters of the heresiarch for every position taken by Palladius. But the Nicene Creed had not set up these letters as a tariff of heterodoxy, and its own provisions are not contradicted except in the refusal of Palladius to concede the full divinity of the Son. It might be said that the Nicene article 'true God from true God' invests the Son with every attribute that scripture and logic predicate of the Father, and the reticence of Eusebius in his letter to Caesarea suggests that he found this a more intractable element than the *homoousion*. But, as we have seen, the position of Eusebius after Nicaea seems to have fallen within the accepted latitude of interpretation: he was never called to account for his belief the Son has the attributes of deity only by virtue of his dependence on the Father. The teachings were controverted in the anathemas of 325 – that the Son is changeable and 'out of nothing', that 'there was when he was not', that he is 'from another *hypostasis* or *ousia*' are not entertained by the Homoians at Aquileia. The canon applied by Ambrose, which forbids any differentiation of properties or ranking of the persons, would have been endorsed by the Alexandrian delegates at Nicaea, but had never received the oecumenical sanction of the episcopate. It may be that

[99] For the proceedings see Zelzer (1982). McLynn (1994), 124–36 maintains that Ambrose turned the tables on Palladius. On the theological disputation see Hanson (1986), 805–20.

the most conscientious parsing of the Nicene Creed would approximate to the Alexandrian reading, but it is not so clear that this is the theology which critical scholarship would now elicit from the New Testament. The eventual victory of Athanasius is attributable in no small part to the fact that he was a young man in 325 and that, after upholding the *homoousion* for a decade against a succession of weaker formularies, he survived long enough to bury all rival memories of the Nicene Council and its aftermath.

The homoian, homoiousian and homoousian doctrines were concentric if the greatest possible latitude was allowed to the word *homoios*. For a time Athanasius contemplated a peace with the homoiousians, but it was his zeal on behalf of the *homoousion* that taught the church to see Basil of Ancyra and his party as 'semi-Arians', almost as inimical to the Nicene promulgation as the 'anomeoan' Eunomius, who maintained that Father and Son were unlike in essence. For those who thought like Athanasius, there was no paraphrase of the *homoousios* that could secure the gates of the Church against blasphemy. For all that, even he could not permit every alliance to founder on a word, and he took a different view of the notorious proclamation of one hypostasis in the Godhead at the council of Sardica in 343. He was bound to defend the assembly to which he owed his own vindication in the west, but he could hardly endorse the Greek transcript of the proceedings which, by rendering *substantia* as hypostasis, had not only eschewed the vocabulary of Nicaea, but had subverted the confession of three hypostases which was regarded as a canon of orthodoxy in the east. In this case, therefore, he urges that the thought matters more than the word, and that this council had intended to denote by the term *hypostasis* all that the fathers at Nicaea had elected to convey in neologisms:[100]

> Were those whom these men reproach for affirming one hypostasis holding the opinion of Sabellius when they affirmed this, annihilating the Son and the Spirit as though the Son had no *ousia* and the Spirit no *hypostasis*? No indeed, they themselves were adamant that they meant no such thing, and were never of this opinion. In fact, in saying hypostasis, we mean the same thing by *hypostasis* and *ousia*, and we opine that it is one on account of the Son's being from the Father's essence, and on account of the identity of natures.[101] For we believe that there is one Godhead, and that the nature of this is one, and that it is not the case that the Father's nature is of one kind, the Son's alien to this and likewise that of the Holy Spirit (*Patrologia Graeca* 26.801).

[100] The *Tome to the Antiochenes* was designed to heal the schism at Antioch, where Basil favoured the homoousian neophyte Meletius, while Rome, the protector of Athanasius, urged that the true successor of Eustathius was Paulinus, a robust opponent of any creed that failed to incriminate Arius. On the consequences of this episode see Zachhuber (2000).

[101] Athanasius speaks here as one of those present at Sardica (though his title to participation was disputed by the easterners, who seceded to form their own council). He also assumes that theological reasoning at Sardica was governed by the ordinances of Nicaea, rather than (say) by those of Antioch in 341.

No contemporary of Athanasius seems to have argued for the complementarity of one *ousia* and three hypostases in the Godhead. We have seen in Chapter 3 that Latin distilled the formula *unius substantiae* (of one substance) from the principle, common to east and west, that the Son is from the hypostasis of the Father, and that the source of this in turn is Hebrews 1.3, where the Son is called an impression of the hypostasis of the Father. A distinguished exposition of the doctrine of three hypostases in one *ousia*, attributed both to Basil of Caesarea and to Gregory of Nyssa,[102] admits that there is no evidence in the scriptures for more than one *hypostasis*, and replies that it is his being from the *hypostasis* of the Father that imparts hypostatic identity to the Son.

The Cappadocian author thus maintains the *homoousion* with the caveat that the Son and the Spirit could not subsist independently of the Father. In this he concurs, of course, with all other Churchmen, with Eusebius no less than with Athanasius; only the homoiousians were alleged to think otherwise, and then not justly. This passage, however, raises the further question, whether the unity and the divinity of the three persons might have been upheld without recourse to the innovative of Nicaea. There were in fact a number of Christians who made no use of the adjective *homoousios*, or acceded to it only on demand. The case of Marius Victorinus shows that even those who espoused the Nicene term with vigour sometimes found that they could express themselves more lucidly in a different nomenclature. *Essentia* is his equivalent for *ousia*, but at times he speaks instead of a common substance originating in the Father and manifested in three distinct substances. Basil, for whom each person in the Godhead is a *tropos hyparxeos*, 'mode of existing', might have been content to affirm a unity of substance and a plurality of *hyparxeis*, were it not that the *homoousion* was already ensconced in the ground that he wished to defend.

One road that might have been taken, then, is revealed by the council of Sardica. To imagine another, we need but suppose that providence had extended the life of the Emperor Constantius or abridged that of Athanasius. No fewer than 600 prelates had met at the council of Rimini, which Constantius summoned in 359, two years (as it proved) before his sudden death. Even when the dissident minority is subtracted, twice as many signatures were appended to the homoian creed of Rimini as to the Nicene *homoousion.* This fact did not escape the Vandal conquerors of Africa when, a century later, they lent the apparatus of torture and despotism to the homoian settlement. The reconversion of Africa was inaugurated by a Byzantine victory and cemented by the marriage of a Vandal prince to the daughter of the Emperor. Humanly speaking, these events were no more inevitable than the mutiny of Julian against Constantius, the abrupt death of the latter and the return of Athanasius in the wake of his rival's murder. None of these events was inevitable, and had history taken a different course there might have been no challenge to the armistice of Rimini. Basil and Athanasius would have been

[102] [Basil] Letter 38. For bibliography on the question of authorship, and a strong case for the attribution to Gregory, see Zachhuber (2003).

obliged to use another vocabulary than that of the Nicene council; they would not have been obliged to give up or dissemble their convictions, so long as the creeds of 325 and 359 were interpreted with prudent casuistry.

Chapter 6
Apollinarius and the Chalcedonian Definition

The Council of Chalcedon, held in 451, is the latest of the oecumenical councils before the fall of the western Empire, and the last to promulgate a definition which is generally agreed to remain authoritative in churches which describe themselves as catholic. The account of its origins and deliberations that prevailed, at least among English-speaking scholars, throughout the greater part of the twentieth century is one that, if true, could have been rehearsed in the present chapter with little modification, since it perfectly exemplifies the thesis of the whole book. According to this conciliatory narrative, the Church had been divided for over a hundred years between two theologies, each of which laid salutary emphasis on one half of the dogma of the incarnation. The Antiochenes were resolved to uphold the integrity of Christ's manhood in contradistinction the divinity of the Word who assumed that manhood; the Alexandrians (loosely so called) denounced any speculation on the two natures that might compromise the unity of Christ's person in the course of his earthly ministry or thereafter. Peaceful coexistence became impossible after 428, when Cyril, the patriarch of Alexandria, made capital for his own ends of the indiscretion of his Antiochene rival, bishop Nestorius of Constantinople. In fact the deposition of Nestorius was secured at the council of Ephesus in 433 only after his persecutor had accepted an Antiochene amendment to his teaching. The dispute continued to fester none the less because no creed had yet been issued which affirmed at once the unity of the person and the duality of the natures. When partisans of the Antiochene School were overthrown with violence at a second council of Ephesus in 449, the meeting at Chalcedon was convened to correct the bias of the first Ephesian council. The document which emerged is supposed to have harmonised the unilinear formula of the two traditions, not without the assistance of another unsolicited, but useful, text which Leo, Bishop of Rome, had penned for the edification of the eastern prelates. For Catholics the intervention of Leo illustrates the dexterity of the Roman see in mating truth with catholicity; for Anglicans Chalcedon is a model for all future ecclesiastical gatherings, insofar as it proclaimed only the truths already agreed to be fundamental, without canvassing the difficult and disputable particulars which a truly catholic church will permit the faithful to examine for themselves. The typical verdict of Anglican scholarship announces the rehabilitation of almost everything that Nestorius had maintained, except his own innocence.

Yet truth is soul of charity, whether the church or the academy weighs the issue. I shall not be arguing here that it was either the aim of the Council or a result of it to undo what had been recently achieved at its oecumenical predecessor; I shall not urge that they showed more liberality than they professed when they repeated the condemnation of Nestorius and canonised the Tome of Leo only on the premise that it agreed with Cyril's canonised epistles. Recent studies have argued that the three Antiochenes whose doctrines were stigmatized at oecumenical councils – Theodore of Mopsuestia, Nestorius and Theodoret of Cyrus – were not in fact representatives of a durable tradition even in their own locality, and certainly not of any that has a claim to be oecumenical.[1] A close reader of Theodoret has concluded that those tenets which he denounced in Cyril were not those which the Council found eccentric or unpalatable, but those which it republished with acclaim.[2] Again it has been demonstrated that Cyril's conduct at the Council of Ephesus in 431, which is often deemed overbearing and precipitate, was diplomatic rather than disingenuous, and forced on him by the dilatory or equivocal manoeuvres of other parties.[3] In short, it is now the opinion of a majority among scholars who have published a book in English about these controversies during the last ten years that the Chalcedonian Council of 451 was not so much a corrective to Cyrilline teaching as a ratification of his true opinion against caricatures that had been advanced in his name. At the same time, however, I shall undertake to show that, if the council achieved any synthesis of known with neglected truths, the man whose teaching they belatedly redeemed was one who, because he had been condemned at the Second Oecumenical Council in 381, could not be named as the sponsor of any ecclesiastical dogma. My thesis in this chapter is that elements in the decree in the decree of 451 which are often said to be Antiochene because Cyril does not affirm them with conviction are at least as incompatible with the attested statements of Antiochene authors, and that their father is more likely to be a heresiarch who is second in notoriety only to Arius – Apollinarius of Laodicea.

Two Cities?

In much twentieth-century mapping of early Christian controversies, Antioch and Alexandria figure as the tropics of Christology, the equator (it is supposed) having been discovered at last in 451 at the Council of Chalcedon. It is frequently assumed that if anyone's lot was to be born in one of these centres, or even to study there under local teachers, his thoughts could hardly fail to acquire the dominant pigmentation. At the same time, where the taxonomy is supposed to be universal, it is common to speak as though every theologian, whatever his birth or affiliation, were subject to a similar fatality, so that the Gregory Nazianzen of Cappadocia and Apollinarius of Syrian Laodicea can be said to have taken different sides in

---

1 Notably Farbairn (2003). On the catholicity of Cyril see Keating (2005).

2 Clayton (2007) will be cited again below as occasion arises.

3 See especially McGuckin (2004), though Wessel (2004) perpetuates much of the old hostility to Cyril.

the quarrel because the former was a scion of the Antiochene, the latter of the Alexandrian school.[4]

The theory states that the consequence of being an Alexandrian, whether by birth or by pedagogy, was the adoption of a logos-flesh Christology,[5] according to which the body and the lower soul are the only human elements in the Saviour, while the Logos discharged the rational or hegemonic functions which in other individuals we should ascribe to the inner man. Alexandrians are apt to describe the meeting of God and man in Christ as *henosis*, or union, not as *sunapheia* or conjunction; they speak of the man whom the Word became, of the flesh that he made his own, but not of the man that he assumed. The logos-man Christology of the Antiochenes, on the other hand, is alleged to have held so fast to the presence in Christ of all three human elements – body, soul and intellect or spirit – that it took insufficient pains to secure his integrity as a person or to forestall the possibility of conflict between the Word and his creaturely will. Furthermore, whereas Alexandrians readily proclaim that the Virgin Mary was the mother of God and that God suffered on the Cross, these propositions are either contradicted in Antiochene thought or qualified to the point of atrophy. The Alexandrians, none the less, get the worst of this dichotomy in the common account, which accuses them not merely of commuting Christ's humanity but of mingling incompatibles, of translating the proper qualities of each nature to the other and thus of making the Godhead subject to our infirmities and passions. Their errors, like those of almost every Christian thinker before the Reformation, are laid at the door of Plato; the bellwether of Antiochene theology according to this scheme is Aristotle, who, for all his imperfections, had enough of the Gospel in him to know that the real lives in the particular, and not in the exsanguinated figures of abstract thought.[6]

All of these positions have been challenged in recent scholarship, yet there are works of some authority which one or more of them, and it is possible to accept the whole agglomerate while maintaining a predilection for the 'Alexandrian school'.[7] It may not be superfluous, then, to explain at the outset that the present chapter

---

4 On the inadequacy of modern accounts of the Alexandrian school see Young (1971). For the argument that Theodore and Nestorius constitute a school by themselves, at odds with the teaching of some in Antioch and most in other parts of the Roman world, see Fairbairn (2003), 5 and 28–62.

5 See especially Grillmeier (1975), 414–17. For criticism see Welch (1994).

6 It is hard to think of ancient Greek philosopher who did not exhibit the 'rationalism, ethical interest and interest in free will' that are advanced by Sellers (1940), 109 as hallmarks of Aristotelian philosophy. The mere fact that Siddals (1987) and Boulnois (2003) can represent Cyril as an Aristotelian proves the fragility of this thesis, whether or not we endorse their arguments in detail.

7 Sometimes with a qualification, as when Studer (1993), 199–210 observes that the Alexandrian school has primitive roots whereas the Antiochene school begins properly with Theodore. That is to say, it is a pedagogical succession, not the endemic tradition of any one place.

eschews these labels on the grounds that (1) the geographical nomenclature hides much and elucidates nothing; (2) even as heuristic tools of modern scholarship, these terms cannot be applied with rigour to every Christian thinker of the fourth century; (3) the bifurcation between logos-flesh and logos-man Christologies is artificial, and does not in any case fit the geographical taxonomy; and (4) whatever divided Christians in the fourth century when they spoke of the Incarnation, it was not their adherence to different pagan schools.

1. If we credit a man with a Scottish accent or a Texan walk, it is likely that we are framing some conjecture about his origins. If we say that he has a Roman nose, on the other hand, we should not be surprised or abashed to learn that he had never been in Rome. In the former case the epithet may possess a divinatory or explanatory force; in the latter it is merely adjectival. In the same way, the labels 'Alexandrian' or 'Antiochene', when used as genuine toponyms, may intimate that the person thus described was predisposed by his education or by ties of affection and kinship to reason in a certain manner or to adopt a particular axiom; if we are only recording our perception that the doctrines of some early Christian resemble those of another Christian resident in one of these great cities, we have turned a geographical description into a catalogue heading, useful in the ordering of phenomena but powerless to explain them.

It cannot be denied that there was in Antioch a pedagogic tradition which accustomed the mind to certain modes of thinking and induced it to hold as truisms certain postulates that were open to doubt elsewhere. Diodore, according to ancient testimony, was the master of Theodore, Theodore of Nestorius, and all there held a Christology which could be characterized invidiously as a doctrine of two sons.[8] There was, however, no matter on which the inhabitants of this factious city were all of one persuasion: Chrysostom preached assiduously to the laity of Antioch, but none of his declamations is held up in modern scholarship as a typical specimen of the Antiochene school. Theodoret proved his allegiance by his championship of Nestorius and Theodore after the former had been condemned at the Council of Ephesus;[9] yet in his commentaries on Paul he is often content to pare down the eloquence of Chrysostom.[10] It was in the Antiochene region that we meet the first partisans of Apollinarius, the bugbear of both Theodore and Nestorius; it was from the episcopal throne of the city, 150 years later, that the patriarch Severus issued homilies and letters denouncing the notion of 'two natures after the union' on the grounds that if it meant anything it would mean that there were two Sons.[11] Thus it was never illuminating to say of a teacher 'he holds this view *because* he is an Antiochene': education or residence in the Syrian metropolis exposed one to

---

8 On the association of the two, in life and in subsequent portraiture, see Abramowski (1992c).

9 He can still indeed be credited with a Nestorian Christology of two persons at this juncture, according to Clayton (2007), 134–66.

10 See Edwards (1999), xix.

11 See Torrance (1988), 37–58.

a variety of intellectual overtures, and it was only by choice that one became an Antiochene in the taxonomic rather than the toponymic sense.

By contrast, it is true that every teacher who rose to fame in Alexandria after 300 held a Christology that scholars would now describe as Alexandrian. Origen is amphibious, not only because he migrated from Egypt to Palestine, but because his fleeting statements on the constitution of the incarnate Christ do not fall into any consistent pattern that is authorised by our textbooks.[12] None of his compatriots in the three centuries that followed his death, however, fail to match the stereotype. It was not the Alexandrian superiors of Arius but Eustathius, Bishop of Antioch, who complained that the Logos supplanted the human soul in the Christology of Arius.[13] Athanasius found an explanation for the apparent possibility of the Logos without ascribing his infirmities to a soul, and throughout his writings flesh and body are the sole concomitants of the Word in his earthly ministry. Cyril, his heir and admirer, considered this a better protocol than the confession of two antithetical natures in Christ; the latter formulation was condemned with illegal force by Dioscorus, Cyril's nephew and successor as patriarch of Alexandria.[14] When his actions forced a schism between the Alexandrian church and the wider communion, the assertion of one composite nature in Christ became the watchword of the Egyptians, and was defended by the erudite metaphysician John Philoponus in the teeth of general councils and imperial decrees.[15] It would seem, then, that adherence to the logos-flesh Christology in Egypt was not merely a badge but a birthmark.

Yet the topographic and taxonomic senses of the term are not coextensive in modern scholarship. Some historians deny Eusebius of Caesarea any notion of a human soul in Christ, yet it was in his native city that he came into possession of Origen's library, not through any connexion with Alexandria.[16] Arius commended himself to Eusebius of Nicomedia as a fellow-pupil of Lucian, a scholar and martyr of Antioch; and, although Apollinarius is held up as the archetypal Alexandrian, he gathered no supporters there to reinforce the party that he had formed around the Syrian metropolis.[17] Eutyches, who is not so much the paradigm as the caricature of Alexandrian teaching, was an archimandrite in Constantinople, and is not known to have visited Egypt. We shall see below that even Eusebius and Apollinarius show traits which, in the binary notation of modern times, would be

---

[12] See Chapter 4.

[13] See Grillmeier (1975), 238–45. Sellers (1928) attributes to Eustathius the belief that the man (not the body) is a temple of the Word (p. 106) and a concept of the 'moral union' between the man and the Word which is Antiochene in the most pejorative sense.

[14] On his machinations at the Latrocinium, or second council of Ephesus, in 449, see Price and Gaddis (2005), vol. 1, 25–37; for the process that resulted in his deposition see *ibid.*, vol. 2, 29–116.

[15] See Lang (2001). Philoponus is not a monophysite, if this term connotes the denial of either human or divine attributes to the Word incarnate.

[16] See further Barnes (1981),

[17] See Lietzmann (1904), 1–6 on the career of Apollinarius.

deemed Antiochene rather than Alexandrian; for the present, enough has been said to show that both terms serve at best to circumscribe an author's views, but not to explain how he came to hold them.

2. It has been a consistent aim of the present study to dismantle the antithetical constructions which obscure the diversity of Christian thought in our modern patrologies. We have seen that Valentinus sowed on both sides of the hedge that we have erected between Catholicism and Gnosticism in the second century; we have seen that for the majority of churchmen in the fourth century, the controversies excited by the Council of Nicaea could not be reduced to a simple choice between a created and a homoousian Christ. In this age of theological casuistry it would be surprising if the difficulties raised by the doctrine of the incarnation were either so few or so interdependent as to admit of a neat distribution between two schools. Latin, after all, had its own traditions which were not engendered either in Antioch or in Alexandria; these traditions are reaffirmed in the Tome of Leo the Great, which, though designed to counter the hypertrophy of Alexandrian thought in Eutyches, also ratifies the condemnation of Nestorius.[18] It has been argued, from his day to ours, that Leo was an Antiochene in spite of himself, and this is another theory that must be reserved for examination. Greater than Leo in the estimation of many commentators, and geographically not so remote from Antioch, were the Cappadocian fathers; the limits of the present book will not permit full discussion of their Christology, but enough can be said in a paragraph to show that even a *prima facie* case cannot be made out for assigning all opponents of Apollinaius to the same camp.

If strenuous affirmation of the presence of a human soul in Christ were enough to make one an Antiochene, the two Cappadocian Gregories Nyssen and Nazianzen should have been given the freedom of the city of Antioch. It was Nazianzen who propounded the maxim that the soul must be assumed if it is to be saved;[19] it was Nyssen, not the teachers native to Antioch, who urged that Christ's obedience could not be meritorious if it were not an exhibition of human freedom.[20] Twentieth-century champions of the Antiochene Christology have been apt to make this its leading premiss, occasionally warping Theodore's notion of a voluntary union of God with man into a vindication of Christ's human liberty.[21] But if we restore the honour of this discovery to Gregory of Nyssa, we shall have some difficulty in reconciling the other tenets of his Christology with those of Theodore, Nestorius or Theodoret. Cyril of Alexandria himself would have had some difficulty in endorsing Gregory's statement in his letter to Theophilus that the humanity is so

18 See now Green (2008),

19 *Letters to Cledonius* 101 and 102; cf. Apollinarius Fr 76 Lietzmann.

20 See *Antirrheticus against Apollinarius* 40–41, pp. 194–9 Mueller.

21 See for example Wallace-Hadrill (1982), 123, where it seems to me that the author fails to draw a distinction between the exercise of human volition *after* the incarnation (which is certainly affirmed) and the role of human volition in *bringing about* the incarnation (which is not affirmed so clearly).

irradiated by the divinity that it at last becomes indiscernible, like a drop of oil in the ocean;[22] nor, however readily he predicates human sufferings of the Logos, would Cyril have acquiesced in the logic of Gregory's treatise *Against Eunomius*, where divine and human attributes are not simply predicated of the one *person*, but each *nature* receives the attributes of the other.[23] In Nyssen, then the extremes of the Antiochene and the Alexandrian doctrines appear to converge.

Less open to the censure of posterity, but equally inimical to any dissociation of the man Jesus from God the Word, is the 37th Oration of Gregory Nazianzen, another Cappadocian and a vehement critic of Apollinarius:[24]

> What he was he set aside; what he was not he assumed. Not that he became two things, but he deigned to be made one thing out of two. For both are God, that which assumed and that which was assumed, the two natures meeting in one thing. But not two sons; let us not give a false account of the blending.

The name Jesus, as Beeley observes,[25] is applied by Gregory to the one who creates (*Oration* 14.2) and of the one who was with God in the beginning (*Oration* 37.2, citing John 1.1). In a series of anathemas in his 101st epistle, Nazianzen defends the salutation of the Virgin as mother of God, declares that the Word is one and the same with the man whom he assumed and rejects the view that the man was gradually adopted into glory.[26] Elsewhere he denies that the Word adopted a man who already existed and speaks of a blending of two natures in the saviour. Whether or not the unnamed object of these admonitions is his 'Antiochene' contemporary Diodore of Tarsus,[27] it would surely have seemed to Diodore that only a hair's-breadth separated the orthodoxy of Laodicea from that of Cappadocia.

3. Confusion between the topographic and taxonomic use of proper names could be obviated if we substitute a contrast between two nouns universal application, flesh and man. The Word-man or Logos-*anthrôpos* model is said to affirm the presence of God in Christ without any diminution of his manhood, while the Word-flesh or Logos-sarx Christology tempers the paradox by depleting the humanity and putting God in place of the rational soul. The former, though

---

22 Gregory of Nyssa, To Theophilus. Yet Nestorius also urges that 'the body of the Son of God is the body of a man whose body and blood he has raised to his own *ousia*', according to Driver and Hodgson (1925), 29 (*Bazaar* 37).

23 Thus at *Against Eunomius* 3.4.46 (p. 152.7 Jaeger) he speaks of a transformation of the human into the divine; at 3.4.56 he writes that the meanness of human nature was exalted to the divine, and affirms a union or assimilation of natures.

24 *Oration* 37.2, trans. Beeley (2008), 128–9.

25 Beeley (2008), 137.

26 Beeley (2008), 129–30; on p. 129 Beeley adds 'it is worth noting that these letters are almost universally regarded as anti-Apollinarian treatises. However, on the central point of Christ's unity they are in fact more strongly anti-Antiochene than anti-Apollinarian'.

27 Beeley (2008), 130–31.

less rational, is generally held to be truer to the Gospel and more catholic in its promise of salvation; the Logos-sarx Christology can embrace at best two parts of our threefold nature, and can be praised for its sound intentions only so long as it rival fails to defend the unity of Christ. The antithesis, however, is imperfect, because the words 'man' and 'flesh' are not symmetrical in their application, or equally consonant with scriptural usage. John 1.14 declares that the Word became flesh, and, since there is no analogous testimony that the Word became man, it is presumptuous to say that one most hold more than a *logos-sarx* Christology to be orthodox. Moreover, there appears to be no misrepresentation of the biblical evidence in the statement that the Word assumed flesh, since 'flesh' is the collective noun for human nature in its fallen state; on the other hand, one cannot say without temerity that the Word assumed a man, since that would imply that the man called Jesus existed before the incarnation. If instead we say that he assumed not any particular man but humanity in the mass, the resulting model would not yield what twentieth-century admirers of the Antiochene Christology demand from it – an assurance that the captain of our salvation was a man like us, who consummated his individuality by the free subordination of his own will.[28]

Those who assume that flesh in Athanasius or Cyril excludes the reasoning soul do not approach the New Testament with the same prejudice. There they know that the flesh is human nature, conceived as that which is weaker than God but also a possible object of his love. It is better to have a heart of flesh than a heart of stone, but fatal to live by flesh and not in the Spirit. Flesh cannot be a synonym for body, since the body was good in the hour of its creation and those of the saints are destined to rise again to eternal life. At the same time, the body is the seat if not the source of the carnal appetites that enthral us in the fallen state, and Paul holds that redemption must be preceded by the wasting away of the outer man, until the 'body of death' is 'swallowed up by incorruption'. For this reason early commentators on Paul are apt to identify the flesh with the outer man in contradistinction to soul and spirit, which make up the internal complement to body at 1Thessalonians 5.23. Thus, as we saw in a previous chapter, neither the Valentinians nor their opponents seem to distinguish the resurrection of the body from that of the flesh; Apollinarius too is apt to equate Christ's flesh with his body, and his usage is imitated by his critics, the majority of whom would also understand the human spirit to be the hegemonic or reasoning faculty of the soul. It is nevertheless impossible that the biblical denotation of the term 'flesh' should have been forgotten when the apostolic writings are mined for texts in every controversy; it is one thing to refer to the body as flesh when we contrast it with the soul or the human intellect, another to make the term 'flesh' signify nothing more than body in conjunction with such terms as Word or 'spirit', when these are used in a sense peculiar to the New Testament. Whether the *Logos-sarx*

[28] This is in any case the thesis ascribed to the 'Alexandrian' Arius by Gregg and Groh (1981).

Christology excludes the soul, then, is a fact to be ascertained in the case of any given author; the words alone do not warrant this assumption.

4. The thesis that fidelity to different philosophers shaped the Christological traditions of Antioch and Alexandria perpetuates the geographical fallacy exposed in point (1) above. For this reason alone it fails, but it would be untenable even if 'Antiochene' and 'Alexandrian' were local eponyms rather than labels of convenience. Alexandria, we are told, was a seminary for Platonists, Antioch for Aristotelians; yet Antioch boasts not one great name in the history of Peripatetic scholarship. The bulkiest, and by common consent the ablest commentators on Aristotle in late antiquity were Simplicius and Philoponus, both Alexandrians, and the latter also a paladin of the Monophysite party, which held that Christ possessed one composite nature, not the two affirmed by the Council of Chalcedon. Philoponus seldom borrows from his own commentaries in dogmatic works, but a recent study has argued that the use of Aristotelian logic in Cyril was both rigorous and sustained. The conclusion has not been widely endorsed, and similar ingenuity could no doubt be employed in making a Platonist of Cyril. It has yet to be shown, however, that either philosophy could have made sense of the claim that the personal being called God the Word became identical with the personal being called Jesus. It is said that the man takes precedence in the Christology of Antioch and God the Word in that of Alexandria because Aristotle identified the real with the corporeal and Plato with the transcendent. But in neither city did Christians deny the corporeality of Christ or take the Platonic form for God. It is not the espousal of distinct philosophies that divides the two cities, but rather the fact that exposition in Alexandria follows scholastic principles, as though the text had no history, whereas the rhetoricians of Antioch construe the text with regard to the circumstances of composition and the calculated effect upon the audience. If there is an analogy to be drawn between exegesis and Christology, one might say that the Alexandrians demanded that the union of God and man in Christ be metaphysically intelligible, while the Antiochenes were content to proclaim that God and man became one in him for us.

The Whole Christ

After all these caveats, there remains a use for the term Antiochene, for teachers in the hinterland of Antioch built Christologies on principles imbibed from other teachers, which held widely enough to be regarded as catholic tenets of the Church. The positions of Diodore, Theodore, Nestorus and Theodoret are all marked by a strong aversion to any mingling of divine and human attributes, and to any diminution of Christ's humanity. All reject the mere juxtaposition of divinity and humanity that would result from the substitution of the Word for a human mind in Christ; all represent the human will in Christ as a coefficient of the Word, and thereby court the accusation that they are positing two Christs – a corollary that they all disown with vehemence, as it aligns them with the Gnostics and makes light of biblical testimonies to the unity of Christ. In intention the Antiochenes preach one Christ, both God and man, as all Christians did; in their refusal to compromise the integrity of Christ's manhood, however, some have found a presentiment of latter-day Christologies, in which the man Jesus all but eclipses God and his power to save is supposed to reside not so much in his resurrection or his conquest of the devil as in his willing surrender to infamy and affliction. On such an astigmatic reading of the original sources, it is easy enough to oppose the Antiochene Jesus of History to the Alexandrian Christ of faith.

No careful scholar today would entertain this benevolent caricature. When Antiochenes spoke of a voluntary union, they did not mean that the man Jesus voluntarily gave himself to God, but that God was present in him only by will – by his *eudokia* or good pleasure, as Theodore says with an allusion to the man's baptism,[29] and not by a natural bond that would make the divine susceptible to human passions. Nor, although they made less use than others of typology and allegory in their handling of the Old Testament, could any Antiochenes espouse the critical principles that inform most modern attempts to reconstruct the 'Jesus of history':[30] for them it is as much a historical fact that the Word became flesh as that the Son was ignorant of the final day. No more than their contemporaries were they exercised by questions about the inner life of Jesus, or the intelligibility of any man's knowing himself to be God while remaining subject to the finitude and inconstancy that waits on our condition. To Theodore it is necessary that Christ should be all that other humans are because he would otherwise be no saviour for humanity, and because his defeat of Satan in the wilderness would have no salvific value if he were merely a divine automaton.[31] It is in this episode that his difficulties in reconciling the unity of Christ's person with the fullness of his humanity become evident, for he understands the baptism as a consummation to which the man was led by the Word in order that the perfection of their intimacy would imbue the man with power to resist the wiles of his adversary. Even when we have granted the homilist a certain licence in the use of dramatic idiom, we may feel, with Theodore's critics in antiquity, that this is not the 'One Lord Jesus Christ' whom Paul proclaimed to the Corinthians, not the immutable subject of the Nicene Creed.

It is not my intention to argue here that Theodore fails the test of orthodoxy, in his own time or any other. It does appear, however, that he cannot be counted among the fathers of orthodoxy in the patristic era, since, unless they are construed with exceptional charity, his statements veer to both sides of the Chalcedonian

---

[29] See Matthew 3.17 and Theodore, *On the Incarnation* 7 at Swete II, 298, with Norris (1963), 221.

[30] See Young (1997), 179–82.

[31] See *Against Apollinarius* at Swete II, 316; with Abramowski (1992c); 31. Clayton (2007), 284–5 observes that Theodoret also understands the man as the proper subject of the temptation in his earlier works; he maintains that the same assumption is masked by a change of terminology in Theodoret's writings after his reconciliation with Cyril in 435.

norm. On the one hand, he seems scarcely to allow the Word to undergo the crucifixion, positing rather a moral solidarity between the Word and the man in whom he has hitherto resided:[32]

> It was not therefore the Lord himself who underwent the trial of death, but he was at his side and accomplished that which was proper to his nature, that is to say, that which is proper to the Creator who is above all things. He guided him through his sufferings to perfection, rendering him perfectly immortal, impassible, incorruptible and immutable for the salvation of a great number of those who elect to be united[33] with him.

On the other hand, an early paragraph of the same homily seems to succumb to the Alexandrian error of equating the humanity with the body, while at the same time it denies the identity of God the Word with the man assumed:[34]

> The man is the temple which he constructed and from which he made his domicile. That is why he said, *Destroy this temple in three days, and I shall raise it again* [John 2.19]. This the evangelist explains as follows: *he was speaking of the temple of his body*. Thus by the temple he meant his body, signifying that it was he who inhabited the temple.

In the eighteenth book of Theodore's lucubration against Eunomius there is a text which, had it been penned in Alexandria, would certainly have been held up as a specimen of 'Logos-sarx Christology':[35]

> Prosôpon is used in a twofold manner: either it signifies the hypostasis and what each of us is, or it is applied to honour and greatness and worship, in the following way. 'Paul' and 'Peter' signify the hypostasis and prosôpon of each of them (both); but the prosôpon of our Lord Christ indicates honour and greatness and worship. Because the God Logos revealed himself in the manhood, he joined the honour of his hypostasis with the visible. And therefore the 'prosôpon' of Christ signifies that it is (a prosôpon) of honour, not (a prosôpon) of the ousia of the two natures. [For honour is neither nature nor hypostasis, but a very great exaltation,

32 *Catechetical Homilies* 8.9, translated from the French of Debié (1996), 128–9. The original is preserved only in Syriac.

33 It is not clear that any difference in kind is acknowledged between the union of man and God in Christ and the union of believers with the Lord at 1Corinthians 6.7. But this is not a peculiarly 'Antiochene' shortcoming, since analogous confusion (if it is confusion) can be detected in Origen, *Against Celsus* 2.9.

34 *Catechetical Homily* 9.5, from Debié 122–3. Debié cites the apology of Devreesse (1948), 114, which appears simply to endorse the identification of the body with the man.

35 From Abramowski (1992c), 1–2 with some change in the punctuation.

> which is bestowed because of the revelation.][36] What purple robes or kingly vestments are for the king is, for the God Logos, the beginning which he has taken from us, inseparably, unalterably, without (spatial) removal in the worship [37]As the king, thus, does not have purple robes by nature, so the God Logos too does not have flesh by nature. If anyone asserts that the God Logos naturally has flesh, there occurs through him an alienation of the divine *ousia*, because he (sc. The Logos) is subjected to alteration by the addition of a nature. But if he does not have flesh by nature, how does Apollinarius say that the very same is partly consubstantial with the Father in his godhead and the same consubstantial with us in the flesh, so that he can make him composite? For he who is divided in natures is, and is found (to be) in nature, something composite.

It is not clear that this passage would be more orthodox by the Chalcedonian standard if, as some interpreters hold,[38] it portrayed the work of Christ as a synergy of hypostatic *prosôpa*, or centres of agency. In fact, Theodore is at some pains to warn us that he has used the term *prosôpon* in two senses: the *prosôpon* of a man would be his hypostasis, the locus of identity as it might be called today; the *prosôpon* of the Word, on the other hand, is not his incommunicable selfhood but a communication of dignity and honour. We are not told that a man may have a *prosôpon* of dignity, or that the words *prosôpon* and hypostasis can be used synonymously of the divine. In the simile the dominant hypostasis is that of the Word, who corresponds to the king; the robe, which stands for the flesh, is the receptacle of honour, and, while no doubt it has the hypostasis which is proper to a robe, this will be neither the hypostasis nor the *prosôpon* of the bearer. As the complement of the Word is invariably styled the flesh and not the manhood, and as it is likened throughout to a passive appendage of the true agent, it would not be illegitimate to deduce that Theodore made no room for a human will in Christ, were it not for the countervailing evidence of his other works.

'Two natures' is the watchword of the Christology that we call Antiochene. Before it became an oecumenical formula in 433, however, we do not hear of any thinker in this tradition who embraced the dictum 'consubstantial in Godhead with the Father, and with us in his humanity'. This excerpt reveals that, because it had been coined by Apollinarius, it seemed to Theodore to entail not so much a joining as a mutual adulteration of properties, an amalgam in which the nature of God succumbed to the frailties of the flesh, and the flesh was but two-thirds of a

[36] Abramowski believes that the terminology of this sentence is foreign to Theodore, and therefore brackets it as an interpolation.

[37] Note that Nestorius (*Bazaar* 21) constructs a different simile, in which the king puts off the robe and dons a soldier's livery, together with his privations. But he still holds that the Word attires the man in his own *prosôpon* (*Bazaar* 29, p. 23), and is regularly accused by Cyril of teaching only a common *prosôpon* of worship.

[38] Cf. Grillmeier (1975), 433.

man.[39] Nevertheless, whatever Apollinarius intended, it was from him, not from his critics, that the Church derived this canonical annotation to the doctrine of two natures. This fact alone may prompt us to suspect that the Alexandrian tradition, weighed without prejudice, will prove to have furnished more than half the matter of orthodoxy.

The Alexandrian Christ

As modern usage of the term 'Alexandrian' is more protean than that of 'Antiochene', it requires some hardihood to speak of a single tradition, let alone to name one man as its fountainhead. But the choice often falls on origin, and it is only just to observe that, if concern for the full humanity of Christ entails an interest in the workings of his inner life, there is no Antiochene author, and indeed no author anywhere in the early church, who pursued this study as vigorously as Origen and his Alexandrian progeny. The Jesus of the Fourth Gospel is at once the most exalted and the most susceptible to human passions, and the great commentaries on this gospel were composed in Alexandria. Commenting on the troubling of Christ's soul at John 13.21, Origen concludes that, while the Saviour possessed a human spirit no less than a human soul, they were not equally prone to grief and perturbation.[40] The passable but incorporeal soul of Jesus acts as a medium between the Word and his outer man, but it is the unconfused co-mingling of the Word with his spirit that cements the unity of his person. The consequence of this interpenetration is that the human spirit in Christ becomes immune to the shocks that would disturb the unregenerate. Commotion can originate in his spirit, and indeed may be engendered by the presence of the Word, when the man's participation in the divine omniscience imparts a presentiment of his own death; but what begins in the spirit is no longer felt as a turmoil *of* the spirit, and trepidation is experienced only in the soul. Interest in the psychology of temptation is pervasive in Origen, rare in other Christians except for his Alexandrian votary Didymus the Blind. His thoughts on the pains of Christ are not preserved, but we have literature enough from other quarters to show that questions of this kind were seldom canvassed if one had not received one's schooling in Alexandria. Not only, then, is it false to say that interest in the humanity of Christ was foreign to Alexandrian thought; it would be truer to say that interests matching those of today's theologians were almost an Alexandrian monopoly.

---

[39] Cf. Nestorius, *Bazaar* 20 at Driver and Hodgson (1925), 16: 'You do not confess that he is God in *ousia*, in that you have changed him into the *ousia* of the flesh, and he is no more man naturally, in that you have made him the *ousia* of God; and he is not God truly or God by nature, nor yet man truly and man by nature.' The interlocutor here is a hypothetical mouthpiece of the Cyrilline doctrine.

[40] For what follows see *Commentary on John* 32.218–28, pp. 355. 12–352.22 Preusschen.

It is urged none the less that Origen's influence languished even in his native city, and that, whereas the Antiochenes at least affirmed the presence of a human soul in Christ, the most illustrious representatives of Alexandrian thought neglect this element, so that the human soul and will become vestigial in their Christology. It is said of Athanasius, whom no-one could deny to be Alexandrian, that he understands the incarnation merely as the swaddling of the Word in a human body. We have seen above that, if one is sufficiently tendentious in the choice of excerpts, Theodore can be convicted of the same oversight; we have seen again that the *logos-sarx* Christology is nothing less than the biblical Christology, provided that by 'flesh' we mean the whole person in our present state of estrangement and corruption. Athanasius, then, is open to criticism only if sarx for him is synonymous with 'body'.[41] In his works there is no evidence that soul and flesh were antonyms to him, any more than to Paul; there is not even any passage which describes the human person as a trichotomy of body, soul and spirit (1Thessalonians 5.23), though it was so conceived by the Gnostics, Irenaeus, Tertullian and Origen before him. He could not, of course, deny that Paul had prayed for the Thessalonians in body, soul and spirit, but he was no more bound than any modern exegete to translate the adverbial datives into nominatives denoting three substantial entities. There are many theologians of our own day who have no use for the old concept of a separable soul, including some who deplore the 'Platonism' of Athanasius and other Alexandrians. It seems harsh, however, to blame for adhering to a model of human nature that he cannot be proved to have held, and then to blame him again for failing to meet the exigencies of this model in his Christology. That flesh means more than body to him can be demonstrated from his own usage in the Third Oration against the Arians. The body is the instrument through which the Word performs his mighty works and makes his Godhead known to the world; when grief or fear are imputed to him, however, it is not the body but the flesh that is said to feel them – the flesh that he makes his own in contradistinction to his eternal deity. It is hard to imagine what psychology Athanasius might have entertained that would have enabled him to predicate these emotions of a body without a soul.[42]

---

[41] It seems to me more plausible to argue with Weinandy (2007), 91–6 that 'flesh' in Athanasius encompasses all the elements of humanity than to confer an abnormal meaning on the term 'body', as Pettersen (1990a), 130–32 proposes. When the Word is said to employ the body as his instrument, the soul is ignored because it is not the vehicle of action; when grief or fear are in question, the flesh is spoken of rather than the body because it includes the seat of feeling.

[42] Hence the asseveration in his *Tome to the Antiochenes* that Christ is not a *sôma apsukhon*. This passage does not, however, declare that Christ possessed a rational or a human soul in opposition to any tenet held by Apollinarius, and could even be taken merely to affirm that the body of Christ was not "without life". The letter communicates the resolutions of a committee, which are likely to have been designed to accommodate a variety of opinions. Cf. Sellers (1940), 42. If, as Pettersen (1990b) contends, the letter is inspired by a Trinitarian debate, the assertion that Christ's body was ensouled has no other aim than to deflect polemical inferences which were drawn from the third oration of Athanasius against the Arians, in that age as in ours.

Modern trustees of the full humanity argue that it is our lot not only to suffer, but to suffer involuntarily. Texts from Athanasius, which imply that Christ's tribulation in the flesh was often lightened or destroyed by the intervention of the Word, have been invoked to prove that he took a 'docetic' view of the incarnation.[43] But if the Alexandrian is at fault here, so is Theodoret, the last mouthpiece of the Antiochene Christology in most textbooks, and the one whose writings survived his condemnation almost in their entirety. Defining what can be said of the Word on the Cross without blasphemy, this bishop and scholar not only hints that the Word is not the true subject of the Passion, but makes the tribulation of the flesh contingent on divine assent:[44]

> When we assert that the flesh or human nature suffered, we do not separate the divine nature. For just as it was united to the [human nature, flesh] when it hungered and thirsted and flagged, and indeed when it was actually sleeping, and when it was in the agony of the passion, not undergoing [or being the proper subject] of any of these things, but allowing this [human nature] to endure its natural sufferings, so it was united to it also when it was crucified, and it permitted the passion to be accomplished, so that by the passion it might undo death, not enduring any pain from the passion, but making the passion its own, as being that of its own temple and of the flesh united with it, by virtue of which those who believe have the status of members of Christ, and he himself is called the head of those who believe (*On the Impassibility of God the Saviour* 15, pp. 264–5 Ettlinger).

Antiochene and Alexandrian thinkers barely differ with respect to the human suffering of Christ. Neither school was willing to obviate the paradox of the incarnation by divorcing Christ the man from his divine yokefellow or by supposing the Word incarnate to be less prescient or more peccable than the Word as Second Person of the Trinity. No-one who wished to be faithful to the council of Nicaea could defend the Samosatene theory, according to which the man was not so much inhabited by the Word as animated from above. The ancient church was ignorant of the kenotic theory, according to which the Word divests himself of certain attributes when he descends to our estate; such a position, indeed, is tenable only if one believes that the Word abandoned the body after the ascension, or that in heaven he found some way of retaining the body without the *kenôsis* (or 'self-emptying') that had been forced upon him by his earthly ministry. But

---

43 See the muted criticism of Sellers (1940), 43, citing *Against the Arians* 3.56 and 3.57. On the integrity and authenticity of the third oration, see Meijering (1995) against Kannengiesser (1993).

44 Clayton (2007), 197–9 finds that even in his maturest writing Theodoret is apt to distinguish the body which died from the Word who remains immortal, and that at most he contrives some phrases which could be read in a Cyrilline sense if one were ignorant of the author.

if the divine in its plenitude is joined to the flesh, it follows, for the Antiochenes no less than for their critics, that the man thus constituted will be governed at all times by an infallible counsellor. The notion that he might have sinned or erred, that our salvation hung on his undetermined choices, was as unpalatable to Theodore and Theodoret as to any other Christian of the fourth century. Since it was a commonplace in this era that sin is engendered by the infirmities of our carnal nature, all parties tend to arrive at the conclusion that he was tempted as we are, but not to the same extreme. If a modern theologian feels obliged to judge his colleagues of the fourth century, he must either condemn them all or excuse them all, with the rider that, as we have seen, it was not impossible for a virtuoso of 'Alexandrian' thought to propose that Christ experienced certain pains more keenly *because* he was God.

The Apollinarian Christ

The paradigm of Alexandrian thought, if one subscribes to modern taxonomies, was, as we have noted, not an Alexandrian either by birth or by adoption. Apollinarius, bishop of Laodicea in Syria, was at one time a friend of Athanasius, and, like him, an incorruptible champion of the Nicene Trinity. It was he, if the letters preserved in his name are genuine, who persuaded Basil of Caesarea to take the *homoousion*, in preference to the formula *homoios kat' ousian*, as his canon of orthodoxy.[45] For him, therefore, the Word who condescended to wear our flesh in the incarnation was possessed of all the attributes of divinity. From this premises arose the familiar difficulty of explaining how the creature and the creator could form one person, together with one that followed from his conviction that the human mind as we know it cannot retain its freedom and remain free of sin. In a treatise on the three persons which can be confidently ascribed to him, though it comes down under another name, he described the incarnate Word as a 'mind invincible to the passions'.[46] Quotations from his works in other sources reveal that the Word acquires this character by supplanting the created mind that would have exercised hegemonic functions in a common human agent. Although he was accused of having substituted the Word for the entire soul, this is not a position demanded by his own reasoning or clearly substantiated by his own words. 'Flesh' and 'body' are at times coterminous in his usage, but he also posits as soul as the seat of passion in human beings and, since he wishes the Word to remain exempt from passion, it would only have marred his theory to make it perform the functions of this lower element. The aim of Apollinarius is to explain the impeccability of the man Jesus, not to circumscribe the perfections of the Word.

For this reason he would not have been moved by Theodore's objection that, as the human mind is troubled by the affections of the carnal nature, so the Word, if he

[45] See Basil, *Letters* 361–3, Prestige (1956) and Chapter 5 above.

[46] *Articles of Faith* 30, p. 178 Lietzmann.

takes the place of a mind in Christ, cannot hope to remain immune to the pains of creature-hood. He would answer that, on the contrary, it is because the Word, and only the Word, is immune to the pains of creature-hood that the Word, and only the Word, can perform the hegemonic functions To Gregory of Nyssa, who protests that only free obedience can be meritorious, he could answer that a common mind cannot remain obedient to God without coercion, whereas a man whose mind was the Word would always freely choose the good. Not so lightly dismissed are two criticisms brought against him by Gregory Nazianzen: that in excluding a human mind from Christ he excludes all fallen minds form the economy of salvation (Letter 101.32), and that his blending of the two natures revives the old heresy that Christ took his flesh not from Mary but from heaven (101.16). Although it might be argued that the first is not to the purpose and the second calumnious, both could be answered only by the adoption of new postulates, or of postulates which had not received any magisterial sanction since they were first enunciated. The assertion that God died on the Cross and the doctrine of the communication of idioms were novelties in the time of Apollinarius, yet both were to become desiderata of orthodox Christology.

1. By communication of idioms theologians mean the attribution to a single subject of the qualities peculiar to each nature. The orthodox application of the principle excludes the attribution to either nature of the qualities peculiar to the other. While the locution itself is not attested before the sixth century, Apollinarius clearly observes the orthodox communication of idioms. Rebutting the charge that his teaching superimposes human properties on the divine, he appeals to the common use of terms which pertain to immiscible elements of the human person. Soul, he contends, is evidently a thing distinct from body, yet we predicate of the whole person what in fact is true of the soul alone, and are equally ready to predicate of the whole person what in fact is true of body alone. We say without impropriety that the man thinks, not that his soul thinks, that he feels a blow and not that his body feels it. Thus when Apollinarius styles Christ the man from heaven, this should not be taken to signify that his body or his flesh came down from heaven, but that the one who came down from heaven, namely the Word, is now also a man. What is true of God the Word is true of the man that he became, and the converse also holds; it does not, however, follow that whatever is true of both these logical subjects will be true of both the natures, and it will never be true that the characteristic properties of one nature are characteristic of the other.

2. Nazianzen's maxim, foreshadowed in Tertullian, is 'what he has not assumed he has not saved'. Gregory of Nyssa contrives a simile to the same effect: 'the leaven of Christ's obedience begins its work in his own flesh, but must permeate the entire mass of humanity, bringing health to every component of our nature, before the promise of redemption is fulfilled'.[47] Once their presuppositions are granted, this refutation of Apollinarius is unanswerable; the defendant, however, is not obliged to grant them, since the work ascribed to the Word here is attributed in

[47] See *Catechetical Oration* 32, alluding to Romans 9.21.

his own works to the sanctifying power of the Holy Spirit.[48] Like other theologians who maintain that the fall has stolen the power of obedience from humanity, he regards atonement not so much as a work performed in us as a work performed on our behalf. Its efficacy depends on its being performed by God, as immortality is God's prerogative, and he alone was therefore bound to survive the death that he chose to undergo:[49]

> The death of a human being does not undo death, nor does the one who does not die rise again. From all of which (he says), it is clear that it was god himself who died, in as much (he says) as it was not possible for Christ to be mastered by death.

Since Melito of Sardis in the second century, no-one had said that God died on the Cross so plainly as Apollinarius dared to say it; not until the sixth century, in fact, did it become a talisman of good Churchmanship to say 'One of the Trinity has suffered.'[50]

From these positions three more were deduced by Apollinarius, to the perplexity or dismay of some contemporaries, though fifty years after his death all three had received the imprimatur of an oecumencial council.

3. Mary is the Theotokos, or Mother of God. This title is first attested in Greek, with a tacit invocation of the communication of idioms, in Alexander of Alexandria's refutation of Arius.[51] On its next appearance it furnishes Gregory Nazianzen with an argumentum *ad hominem* against Apollinarius: if Mary is the mother of God, we cannot suppose that the flesh of Christ originates in heaven, for what, in that case, could Mary be said to have borne?[52] We know that the term was not only accepted by Apollinarius[53] but vigorously promoted by his adherents in Constantinople, for when Nestorius came there he discovered that it had fallen into bad repute because of their advocacy. Nestorius himself, who barely seems to grasp the communication of idioms, was at no time prepared to admit without reserve that a mortal woman could be the mother of the Word.

4. The worship of the exalted Christ is directed to a single subject, not to two of which one receives by association the honours due to the other.[54] Theodore, in the passage quoted above, maintains that the Saviour's flesh is united to the

---

48 See Fr. 76 Lietzmann and On Union 10ff (p. 189 Lietzmann).

49 Fr. 96 Lietzmann (p. 229), from Gregory of Nyssa, *Antirrheticus* 52.

50 On the origin and reception of this formula see Grillmeier (1995), 317–43.

51 Theodoret, *Church History* 1.4.54 (letter to Alexander of Thessalonica). On the cult of Mary before Cyril see Shoemaker (2008).

52 See *Letter to Cledonius* 101.16, with Beeley (2008), 129 and 136.

53 Two fragments of an encomium on Mary are recorded: Lietzmann (1904), 209–10 (Frs 11–12).

54 Fr. 84 Lietzmann: 'Nothing is so united to God as the flesh that was assumed. Those things that are not so united are not so worthy of worship; but there is nothing so worthy of worship as the flesh of Christ.' At Fr. 47 he adds the qualification that it is as God that

Godhead by a communication of honour, just as after Nicaea some thought it enough that the Son and the Father should receive parity of honour, whether or not the theologians grant the same measure of divinity to both. As Athanasius urged that it would be idolatry to revere the Son unless he were the true equal of the Father, so Apollinarius argues that the man Jesus could receive no cult if he were not also God.

5. Christ is consubstantial (*homoousios*) with the Father in respect of his divinity, and with us in respect of his manhood. Theodore's animadversions on this formula have been noted above. He is not our only witness, for we have a clear Greek statement of it in another text now commonly assigned to Apollinarius, though preserved under the pseudonym of Julius, Bishop of Rome:[55]

> Thus he is consubstantial with the Father by virtue of the invisible Spirit, the flesh being also bound up with the name because it is united to that which is consubstantial with God; and again he is consubstantial with human beings, the Godhead being bound up with the body because it has been united with that which is consubstantial with us (*On the Union* 8, p. 188 Lietzmann).

In his letter to Epictetus, which is likely to be an earlier composition, Athanasius had stated at different points that the Word incarnate is consubstantial with the Father and that his manhood is consubstantial with ours;[56] nevertheless, it is not Athanasius but Apollinarius who has made a figure from the disjointed limbs.

Here then are five presentiments of orthodoxy in Apollinarius, though not all his interlocutors thought them orthodox. Antecedents, where they are retrievable, are most likely to be discovered in Alexandria; but, as we shall see, on all five points the mind of Alexandria was to coincide with that of the church at large in the mid-fifth century, and the testimonies of Melito and Nazianzen indicate that this may have been the mind of the Church already in the time of Apollinarius.

The Genealogy of the Formula of Reunion

Notwithstanding the condemnation of Apollinarius at the Second Oecumenical Council in 381, the Christological controversy of his day was, for the most part, a war of pamphlets. It became a war between bishoprics in 428, when Nestorius, an Antiochene monk, was installed as patriarch in Constantinople.[57] Here, by

Christ is adored before the foundation of the world. Here and at *Anakephalaiosis* 28 (p. 245 Lietzmann) he says 'man', not 'flesh', as Cyril invariably does.

55 See Lietzmann (1904), 104–5 and 134–5 on the provenance of this text.

56 See especially Chapter 4, p. 828 De Montfaucon, though the letter is more concerned to deny that the body is consubstantial with the Godhead than to affirm that it is consubstantial with ours.

57 For the history see McGuckin (2004), 53–125.

his own account, he found the city divided by the liturgical salutation of Mary as Theotokos, or Mother of God, and, having permitted sermons to be preached against the term under his authority, proposed his own substitute Christotokos, or 'mother of Christ'.[58] No theological writing by Nestorius survives from this early phase of his career, but if his latest manifesto, the *Bazaar of Heraclides*, is a fair digest of the views that he held as patriarch, he conceived the incarnation as a union, not of two natures or hypostases, but of two *prosôpa* or concretions of attributes, one human, one divine.[59] The two *prosôpa* coalesced while the natures remained distinct, and Mary was the mother of this joint *prosôpon*, not the mother of the eternal Word. The vocabulary seems to derive from Theodore, though it is not clear that *prosôpo*n is used in either of the senses that he defined. If it signifies the hypostasis or identity of a subject, it would appear that Nestorius contemplates a union of two subjects, each existing antecedently, which no bishop of that time could have defended if he wished to keep his see. If instead the joint *prosôpon* is one of dignity and honour, there is merely a specious union, which, even in the parlance of the ancient Church, would justly be called docetic. If the joint *prosôpon* is a hypostasis, the man and the Word are one and there is no ground for denying Mary the appellation 'Mother of God'.

Such at least was the reasoning of Cyril, patriarch of Alexandria, whose polemics were acidified by personal grievances against the see of Constantinople and its incumbent.[60] Two letters to Nestorius having failed to secure his recantation, Cyril wrote the third as an ultimatum, listing the errors of Nestorius, quoting the Nicene Creed of 325 as his canon and appending twelve propositions which he required Nestorius to anathematize. In the interim, he and Nestorius had each acquainted Celestine, Bishop of Rome, with the other's heresies. Celestine took Cyril's part, and when the Emperor Theodosius ordered that a council be held at Ephesus in 431, its purpose in the eyes of both Alexandria and Rome was to oust a heretic from the see of Constantinople. Nestorius had distributed Cyril's anathemas to the bishops of the east, and an indignant party, led by John of Antioch, set out to vote against his deposition. Whether because of their procrastination or because of Cyril's intrigues, the council proceeded without them and Nestorius was deposed. When John of Antioch's complement arrived they set up a council of their own, deposing Cyril; this measure was reciprocated, and all the three great sees of the east were without a patriarch until Alexandria and Antioch signed a Formula of Reunion in 433.

The formula did not supersede the previous resolutions of the council. It has been common for twentieth-century scholars to treat the Council of Ephesus as though

---

58 *Bazaar*, p. 99 Driver and Hodgson.

59 See *Bazaar* 27–9, pp. 21–3 Driver and Hodgson, with Driver and Hodgson (1925), 402–10. A union merely by *skhêma* or relation is, however, excluded at *Bazaar* 23, p. 18.

60 On the fecundity of Cyril's use of title Theotokos before the Council of Ephesus see Young (2003). On the intrigues which exacerbated his quarrel with Nestorius, see Schwartz (1928).

it were perceived by all observers as an abortive project, awaiting the correctives of Chalcedon. The mere fact that no argument was advanced for the reinstatement of Nestorius is a measure of the finality that was accorded to the decisions of the council. Few bishops in good standing with the majority of their colleagues after 433 would have thought that they had a right to uphold the Antiochene positions which had been repudiated in Cyril's letters. In its acclamation of these letters, the council endorsed a hypostatic union of God with his flesh in contrast to a union of *prosôpa*, refused to divide the adoration of Christ between the Word and his human acolyte and commended Cyril's use of the Nicene Creed to prove that the one who abides eternally with the Father is identical with the one who became incarnate. It even bound the Church to the first anathema of Cyril's third letter, rebuking those who shrink from the title 'Mother of God'; to the fourth, which forbids the division of Christ's words and sayings between distinct hypostases or *prosôpa*; and to the twelfth, which makes it a heresy to deny that God the Word has tasted death upon the Cross.

In applauding Cyril's letters to Nestorius, the Council endorsed the five principles which had come to mature expression in the work of Apollinarius. The name of the man himself now stood for nothing but the confusion of two natures in a soulless Christ, and Cyril escaped the odium of discipleship by asseverating, more than once, that Christ took flesh endowed with a rational soul. There is no doubt, on the other hand, that after the Council Cyril bruised his own cause by repeating the phrase 'one nature of the Word enfleshed' from a text by Apollinarius that had been smuggled into the Athanasian corpus.[61] But of this document he and his coadjutors at Ephesus seem to know nothing, and if it was an Apollinarian web that caught Nestorius it was woven of catholic threads. All five notes of Apollinarian teaching, as we defined it in the last section, are sounded again in the council's vindication of Cyril:

1. Cyril hints at a communication of idioms when he protests in his second letter that the Word was not born of Mary in the sense that his divine nature took its origin from her but in the sense that he became one hypostasis with the *anthropinon*, the human, that he united to himself (*Second Letter* 4, p. 7 Wickham). In the third letter he likens the relation between the Word and his flesh to that between soul and body: as soul as soul and body are unlike substances which constitute a single person, so the Word and his flesh make up one man without prejudice to the salient qualities of either. The father of this conceit, as we have seen, was Apollinarius, which is not so much a proof that Cyril knowingly purloined the thoughts of a heretic as an instance of the rule that an idea does not always perish when a teacher is condemned.

2. In his twelfth anathema (*Third Letter*, p. 33 Wickham), Cyril invites Nestorius to disown those who will not admit that God the Word tasted death for our salvation

---

[61] See *Letter to Eulogius*, p. 63 Wickham; *First Letter to Succensus* 7, p. 77 Wickham; *Second Letter to Succensus* 3, p. 87 Wickham. On the provenance of the quotation see Wickham (1983), 62–3 n.3.

(cf. Hebrews 3.15). The locution 'tasted death' is perhaps more biblical than 'died', but Cyril may have adopted it as a prudent circumlocution, since the theopaschite motto, 'one of the Trinity has suffered', would have tried the conscience even of an Alexandrian delegate at Ephesus. By going further with Apollinarius he could have met the later standard of orthodoxy; The 'Antiochene' retort to the twelfth anathema intimates that he had already gone too far.[62]

3. The Council ratifies Cyril's defence of 'Mother of God' as an oecumenical title. Posterity also canonised Cyril's gloss in his letter to John of Antioch. Like Gregory Nazianzen, and no doubt with the same intention of rebutting Apollarius, he urges that if the flesh came down from haven and not from Mary, she would not be the mother even of Christ's humanity. But then he goes on to explain in what sense God himself is the subject of the nativity: 'When we say that God the Word, having come down from heaven, emptied himself, assuming the form of a slave and became the Son of man, while remaining what he was, this is God.'[63] That is to say that Mary is truly the mother of the Word, though not according to his divinity; and this is what Nestorius would not consent to say.

4. There is much debate as to whether the popular cry against Nestorius was prompted more by zeal for the integrity of Christ's person or by devotion to his mother.[64] This question has been apt to obscure the one that divided Cyril and Nestorius, which concerns the relation between the eternal glory of the Word and the veneration of the exalted Son of Man. The maxim of Nestorius, 'I worship the one who was borne for the sake of the one who bore him', had been corrected by Apollinarius long before Cyril had occasion to denounce it in his third letter to the patriarch (p. 21), and the Council of Ephesus was therefore obliged to vindicate the old heretic against the new heresy.

5. The twofold consubstantiality is not affirmed in any letter by Cyril before the one addressed to John of Antioch which celebrates the Formula of Reunion and brings the Council of Ephesus to a happy issue for everyone but Nestorius. The theory that he put on the harness of Antioch in this document has been in fashion since it was first composed,[65] and will require examination at some length. We may begin by quoting the most substantial paragraph of the formula:

> We confess then our Lord Jesus the Christ, the Son of God only-begotten, perfect God and perfect man from a rational soul and a body, begotten of the Father before the ages according to his divinity, but in the last days [born] the same one for our sakes and for our salvation from Mary the Virgin according

---

62 See Percival (1991), 217: 'If anyone, in confessing the sufferings of the flesh, ascribes these also to the Word of god as to the flesh in which he appeared, and does not distinguish the dignity of the natures; let him be anathema'. Percival attributes these anathemas to Nestorius, but the author is almost certainly Theodoret.

63 Letter to John of Antioch, pp. 169–70 Bindley.

64 See now Price (2008).

65 It is perpetuated, for example in Wessel (2004), 268–73.

> to his humanity; the same being consubstantial with the Father according to his divinity and consubstantial with us according to his humanity. For there was a union of two natures. In the light of this understanding of the unconfused union, we confess the holy Virgin to be Mother of God[66] inasmuch as God the Word became flesh and man, and from his very conception united to himself the temple that he had taken from her. And as to the evangelical and apostolic sayings about the Lord, we know that men proficient in theology make some common, with respect to one *prosôpon*, while dividing others, with respect to two natures; and those that befit God they expound according to the divinity of Christ and the lowly according to his humanity (p. 168.66–82 Bindley).

Cyril had scented heresy in the word 'temple' when he was writing against Nestorius, though in his *Commentary on John*, completed a few years before the accession of Nestorius to the see of Constantinople, he had found no occasion to quarrel with a metaphor that the evangelist puts into the mouth of Christ.[67] It is difficult to believe that his acceptance of this usage in the Formula of Reunion was the fruit of a second, but equally honest, change of heart; to most scholars his subscription indicates either that he was ready to keep his present opinion under curfew for the sake of his bishopric or that, once he had achieved his political end, he relinquished a pose which he had assumed from policy rather than conviction. Yet he can be acquitted both of dishonesty and of tergiversation, if we distinguish the flesh and the body, as Paul taught the Church to do. If the Word became flesh, it is illogical to maintain that the flesh is the temple of the Word; it is, however, not only logical but consonant with the teaching of the apostles to maintain that the body of Christ was a temple – not only because the evangelist makes him say as much, but because every Christian is enjoined by Paul to treat his own body as a temple of the Spirit. Thus, where John spoke of a shrine without a deity, Paul identifies its denizen as the third person of the Trinity (1Corinthians 6.19), through whose presence (as the Gospel tells) Christ himself has promised to make his home in the believer (John 16.17–23). The person of Christ, however, is not that of a common man in whom the spirit dwells, but that of the Word begotten as a man through the overshadowing of Mary by the Spirit; his body is thus the temple of the Word. Of the flesh this cannot be asserted, because the flesh is that which the Word became, not a part of his humanity but the condition of being human: the flesh is coextensive with the divinity, and no more than the latter can it be regarded as a mere envelope to the Word.

The formula of reunion goes on to affirm that Christ is consubstantial with the Father in his divinity, and with us in his humanity. Enough has been said above to explode the common view that this was an Antiochene counterpoint to

---

[66] Price (2008), 95 observes: 'the Antiochene approval of Theotokos was not a concession to Cyril, but simply reflected the fact that Nestorius' criticism of the tile had never won the approval of his Syrian colleagues'.

[67] *Patrologia Graeca* 73, 162b on John 1.14.

the monophysitic teaching of Alexandria. Theodore, as we have seen, quotes this as the paradox of an adversary; Cyril, in a comment which was canonised with the Formula of Reunion, cites the letter of Athanasius to Epictetus. But we have seen the doctrine of twofold consubstantiality in its cradle; if Apollinarius was the first to propound it, it is an Alexandrian tenet in the modern sense, but in no conceivable sense Antiochene.

What of the final article, that the words and sayings of Christ may be predicated either according to his humanity or according to his divinity? A false dissonance is suggested by the translation of Percival – still for many English readers the standard one –in which divine and human properties are distributed between different subjects.[68] This would be a contradiction of Cyril's fourth anathema, but, if that was calculated to permit what it did not preclude, it was perfectly consistent with the assignation of unlike predicates *to the same subject* under two descriptions. Any miscegenation of divine and human epithets is excluded in Cyril's letters – more plainly, as we have seen, than in certain passages of Gregory of Nyssa. It would be difficult, none the less, to be any plainer in this matter than Gregory's whetstone Apollinarius, as we have seen. Once again there are no grounds for pronouncing the sentence more Antiochene than Alexandrian, in the ancient or in the modern application of these terms.

The Deposition of Eutyches

The formula of reunion did not restore Nestorius to his see. There was no secession on his behalf, no orchestrated resistance to the verdict of the Council. Cyril was required to explain how he came to sign the Formula of Reunion, both by those who would have put their own signatures to it and by those who feared that it contravened the teaching of his previous ebullitions against Nestorius. The invectives of Theodoret, however, were anomalous and proved costly to the author,[69] who in any case conferred more dignity upon his see than he derived from it. When a synod met again to judge a position held in Cyril's name, it was four years after his death and fifteen years after the reconciliation with Antioch in 433.

---

[68] Percival (1991), 252: 'other things they divide as to the two natures, and attribute the worthy ones to god on account of the divinity of Christ and the lowly ones on account of his humanity [to his humanity].' If the brackets were removed the translation would be perfect. Bindley (1899), 275 has 'to the divinity' and 'to the humanity', which is bad translation and worse theology; McGuckin (2004), 345 renders impeccably 'according to the humanity' and 'according to the divinity', but adds in a needless footnote that 'this is meant as an attack on Cyril's fourth anathema'.

[69] See Clayton (2007), 144–53 on his repudiation of Cyril's twelve anathemas, an exercise which tempts him to play down the suffering of the Word (as he does elsewhere) and even to adopt the locution 'God-bearing man' in opposition to the 'Apollinarian' notion of Christ as 'man-bearing God', which was also Cyrilline and became Chalcedonian.

The inquisitor in 448 was Flavian, Bishop of Constantinople, and the defendant Eutyches, an archimandrite under Flavian's jurisdiction. In his own mind the latter was redeeming the true Christology of Cyril from its adulterous liaison with a doctrine of two natures; to Flavian, the Formula of reunion represented the mind of Cyril and the Church. So far as our evidence goes, it seemed to him that he was upholding the oecumenical consensus, and hence the more complete account of Cyril's own position, not that he was defending the Antiochene half of the Formula against an Alexandrian usurpation.

Eutyches believed that he could not keep faith with Cyril or with Christ by admitting more than one nature after the incarnation.[70] He could not, like Apollinarius, conceive of this as a nature which was jointly consubstantial with the Father and with our humanity. Whereas Apollinarius was widely accused of having made God a prisoner to the flesh, Eutyches was supposed to have fallen into the opposite error of allowing the Godhead to absorb the manhood, so that one that one could hardly speak even of 'one nature enfleshed'. If there is any colourable precedent for this theory, it is to be found in the harshest critic of Apollinarius, Gregory of Nyssa, though, as we have seen, his letter to Theophilus does not maintain that the manhood is extinguished but rather that it is so irradiated by the uncreated glory of the Word as to become indiscernible.[71] One text which would have enabled Eutyches to lay this egg in Cyril's nest was the eleventh anathema of the final letter to Nestorius, where divine properties are accorded to Christ's flesh:

> If anyone does not confess the flesh of the Lord to be life-giving, and to belong to the very Word of the Father, but [confesses it instead] to be that of some other who is conjoined to him in honour or indeed merely possesses a divine indwelling, and not to be rather lifegiving,as we have said, because it belongs to the Word who has power to give life to all, let him be anathema (*Third Letter to Nestorius*, anathema 11, p. 32 Wickham).

Theodoret's rejoinder to this anathema does not suggest that the ancients were as ready as modern critics to see a reference to the eucharist here;[72] the integrity of the risen and exalted Christ is a theme that Greek theologians were able to discuss without pre-empting the ecclesiological controversies of the Reformation. But this is a difficult aphorism for any catholic theologian after 433 if 'flesh' is a synonym

---

70 Cyril affirms two natures before the union and one incarnate nature after the union at *First Letter to Succensus* 7, pp. 75–7 Wickham; but the word 'incarnate' carries an important qualification, as he notes in *Second Letter to Succensus* 3, p. 89 Wickham. The assertion of two natures is a vicious error only when it implies that 'a man has been connected with God only in equality of honour' (*Letter to Acacius*, 17, p. 55 Wickham). See further McGuckin (2004), 206–12.

71 *To Theophilus against Apollinarius*, pp. 128–30 Mueller.

72 See Percival (1991), 217, where reference is made to the resurrection but not the eucharist. See Chadwick (1951) for the application to the sacrament.

for 'human nature', for then an exchange of properties between natures would be implied, not the 'communication of idioms' which confers the antithetical characteristics of the two natures on one person. 'Flesh' is the name of the palpable element in our constitution, and, since it therefore denotes what is common to all of us, it can also stand for the mass or aggregate of human beings, and for the pliable and deciduous condition of a human being outside the body of Christ. There is a sense in which we are our flesh, another sense in which we possess it, and for Paul a sense in which it possesses us. There is no logical dichotomy between a man and his flesh, as there is between the human individual and his human nature. It is the flesh, not the nature, that feels, the flesh, not that nature that decays; the flesh is thus understood in Cyril's time to be that 'corruptible' which 'puts on incorruption' in the resurrection of Christ and those who come after him. This, as we have noted in Chapter 2, is a distortion of Pauline nomenclature, an accommodation to Valentinian usage, which to malign interpreters might connote the same mingling of immiscibles of which Apollinarius was accused. Cyril's meaning, however, is that the relation between the Word and his flesh is as intimate as that which obtains between the inner and the outer man, and hence more intimate than any possible relation between unlike and unmingled natures. The corollary of the eleventh anathema is that the man is glorified while remaining man, not that the properties which make him human are overwhelmed by the divine.

Cyril does indeed concede in his letters after 433 that Christ may be said to suffer in his human nature if this is a periphrasis for his suffering in the flesh;[73] at the same time he prefers his own usage not only because it is biblical, but because he is conscious that the two locutions are not always interchangeable in common or ecclesiastical parlance. To predicate both divine and human natures of one subject is to make him a dyad, a juxtaposition of contraries; Cyril preaches not so much a union of opposites as the complementarity of Word and flesh. Humanity cannot be identified with or predicated of divinity; flesh, on the other hand, is predicated of a subject or an aggregate of subjects, and if the Word becomes flesh, the subject of which flesh is predicated can be no other than the Word. The predication is not one of identity, yet it does not preclude identity. The flesh is not the species, not the nature of humanity considered in abstraction, not even the quiddity of the man if this is strictly another thing than the man himself; it is that which constitutes his being, not only as man, but as *this* man and no other. For this reason, as Apollinarius had already argued,[74] it can be said of a man, or of human beings considered in the aggregate, that they are flesh, although the flesh can also be treated as a concomitant to the soul, which is also the man. The man may be identified, grammatically if not logically, either with his soul or with his flesh,

[73] See *Letter to Eulogius*, p. 65 Wickham; *Second Letter to Succensus* 5, p. 93 Wickham That 'flesh' means 'man' is affirmed, for example at *On the Creed* 14, p. 111 Wickham.

[74] See for example Fr. 25, p. 211 Lietzmann.

though neither of these can be predicated of, or identified with the other.[75] That his simile was anticipated by the great heresiarch is, as Cyril protests,[76] no reason for disowning it. In the spirit of Tertullian, when he purloins the word *probolê* from the Valentinians,[77] Cyril derives a circumspect analogy from a false conceit, with the caveat that the flesh with which the Word unites himself is more than body, and that the Word and the soul resemble each other only in their relation to their instruments: the uncreated Word, in this Christology, does not go bail for any created element in Christ.

On the one hand, then, the anathema does not enjoin an Apollinarian confusion of natures: to reinforce the arguments of the last paragraph, we need only add that the charge against Apollinarius was that his God inherits the frailty of his human envelope, whereas Cyril's Word is always an active power, who remains impassible even when he suffers, and whose quickening presence irradiates the flesh without consuming it.[78] On the other hand, it is certainly true that his usage of the word flesh is too protean to lend itself to a neat dichotomy between person and nature, or even between the individual and the collective. His teaching can be translated into the language of the formula of reunion,[79] more readily than that of his interlocutors in 433, but he spoke that language as a foreign tongue. He was, as most of the Fathers are, a homilist and a commentator; decrees and formulations of great councils could lay down a canon of interpretation and eke out the vocabulary of the scriptures where they required elucidation, but to treat the creeds themselves and not the scriptures as the matter of theology would be to study the constellations without the stars. If Cyril's use of the term 'flesh' seems equivocal to us, that is because he is imitating the polyphony of the written Word of God, itself a continuing incarnation at the centre of all liturgical performance. Only one who despised the plenitude of revelation would subject the God-given term that 'the Word became flesh' to our provisional categories of logic.

However he construed this anathema, Eutyches could not believe that a man who was God could share one nature with mortal and fallen specimens of humanity. He could be induced to subscribe to Cyril's formula that Christ was of two natures, and the synod did not force him to accept the (much less Cyrilline) addendum that he was 'in two natures' after the union. They did require him, without success, to join the Cyril of 433 in affirming the twofold consubstantiality of the Saviour.

---

75 For the union of soul and body as an analogue to that of Word and flesh see *Third Letter to Nestorius* 8, p. 23 Wickham; *First Letter to Succensus* 7, p. 77 Wickham; *Second Letter to Succensus* 3, p. 89 Wickham.

76 See *Letter to Eulogius* with McGuckin (2004), 183.

77 See *Against Praxeas* 8.1 and Chapter 3 above.

78 See for example Keating (2005), 20–53, though, as Daley (2002), 143 observes, the divinization of Christ's flesh is also a tenet of Apollinarius: see Fr. 160 Lietzmann amongst others.

79 For a cogent demonstration of the Chalcedonian character of his thought see Weinandy (2003), 43–53.

It will not be necessary to repeat the demonstration that this formula was not of Antiochene provenance: when Apollinarius coined it, it became a hostage to infamy, and might have remained so but for the restoration of peace between Antioch and Alexandria in 433.

The Council of Chalcedon

But Eutyches appealed to the throne, and the president of the council that convened at Ephesus in 449 was Dioscorus, Cyril's nephew and an enemy to the Formula of reunion. By this time the bickering of the frogs was loud enough to wake the stork. Leo of Rome, who had been the right hand of Celestine at the time of the Council of Ephesus, was a vigilant inspector of proceedings and prerogatives that threatened to compromise the hegemony of the Petrine see. When Flavian of Constantinople sent him a formal account of the deposition of Eutyches at the Home Synod of 448, Leo replied with an unsolicited statement of orthodoxy, designed at one to confirm and to amend the judgment of the patriarch. This letter, since known regularly as the 'Tome to Flavian', was not in fact sent directly to its nominal recipient, since at the time of its dispatch a new synod had been convened at Ephesus to review the deliberations of the Home Synod. Leo's envoys wished the Tome to be read publicly at Ephesus, but the president of the council, Dioscorus of Alexandria, refused a hearing to his western colleague, who had not had the foresight to choose as his courier anyone competent to take a full part in a disputation between Greek speakers. No word would have been uttered at this gathering on behalf of Rome had not one member of Leo's delegation exclaimed *contradicitur* 'we object' when he saw that Dioscorus intended to carry the argument by force. Hilary's remonstrance was transcribed by the stenographers in Greek characters, and while it failed to save Flavian from the violence which was later said to have caused his death, it was cited in Rome to prove that the his deposition had been lawfully countermanded. Protesting that there had been no true assize but a 'conspiracy of robbers' (*latrocinium*), Leo demanded that the remedial council at Chalcedon should include the recitation and endorsement of his *Tome*.[80]

The *Tome* begins with a soft rebuke to Flavian for his failure to seek direction from the Roman see when the controversy with Eutyches first erupted. Leo builds on this intimation of primacy by adducing not the Nicene Creed but its western counterpart, the so-called Apostles' Creed, as the test of orthodoxy. Like others, but unlike the Symbol of 325, this creed affirms that Christ was born of Mary and conceived by the Holy Spirit (Chapter 2);[81] in like vein, Leo goes on to juxtapose scriptural attestations of the humanity of Christ with the evidence that he was more than human. He was born as man, but adored by the Magi as God; his hunger and grief were human, but his healing and feeding of others manifested his divinity

80 For these events see Price and Gaddas (2005), vol. 1, 30–37.

81 See Westra (2002), 210–11, with further observations on Leo, Letter 31.

(Chapter 4). The conjunction of the two natures can not only be proved empirically from the gospels, but can be shown to have been necessitated by the very purpose of his descent. Humankind could not have been redeemed from the devil had not the one who overcame the devil possessed all the elements of humanity; at the same time, no human who had once fallen into sin could have vanquished Satan, and no human who is the offspring of two fallen parents can remain free of sin (Chapter 3). Hence it was ordained that the deliverer should unite the two natures, inheriting from his mother all that constitutes humanity in its pristine state, while being protected by his divine paternity from the trespasses which have marred the image of God in his mortal kin (Chapter 3). This notion of salvation as the conquest of the devil by his prisoner savours of Theodore more than of Cyril or the majority of western theologians;[82] on the other hand, it is accompanied in Leo by a belief in the indelible universality of sin which, while it certainly does not lack eastern patrons, is more evident in Cyril, the Cappadocians and Chrysostom than in accredited representatives of 'Antiochene' Christology.[83] Since the time of Leo it has almost been a rule in western thought that soteriology shapes Christology[84] – that is to say, that the constitution of the God-man is supposed to have been determined by the object of his ministry. Since it was in fact the Nicene symbol of 325, not the Apostles' Creed, which declared that Christ became man 'for our salvation',[85] it cannot be said that this synthesis of doctrines was more characteristic of one half of the empire than another in the fifth century; it would, however, be true to say that no earlier document reasons so economically from the mission to the two natures. Theodore could demonstrate that the defeat of Satan must be a human work, and Apollinarius that only God could survive the crucifixion; Cyril has little to say on the atonement in his letters to Nestorius, but Leo's soteriology fuses two positions which, while they were not strictly antithetical, had hitherto been tied to antithetical Christologies.

Yet heresy was still heresy to Leo, and the anathema of a council irreversible when it was ratified by one of his predecessors. Fifteen years after the formula of reunion, Nestorianism was such a bugbear to him that he detected its shadow even in the arch-Monophysite Eutyches. At the end of the *Tome*, he complains that the easterners failed to exact from Eutyches a confession that the Saviour performed

---

82 See Abramowski (1992c), 31.

83 Cyril, Doctrinal *Questions and Answers* 6, pp. 200–203 Wickham; Gregory of Nyssa, *On the Three Days' Interval and Great Catechism* 16; Chrysostom, Homilies on Hebrews 12.7.

84 So Wiles (1989), 157. But in the east the question 'whom do I worship?' has never meant only 'how shall I be saved?', and it would be as true to say that all Christology is doxology.

85 The seminal inquiry into the genesis of this creed is Kelly (1972), 100–166 and 368–97. For survey of critical responses see Westra (2002), 22–72, and for the argument that the creed owes its present form to Marcellus, see Kinzig and Vinzent (1999). On Leo's use of the Roman creed which is the prototype of our Apostles' Creed, see Bindley (1899), 206.

his ministry in two natures (Chapter. 6). Instead he was permitted to affirm that Christ was incarnate 'from two natures' –a Cyrilline formula, but one which to Leo implies that before the union there existed not only the Word but a man whom the Word was to adopt. To hold this was to resurrect the doctrine of two sons which Cyril and Celestine had laid to rest at Ephesus:

> But when Eutyches responded to your interrogation by saying 'I confess that our Lord was from two natures before the union, but I confess one nature after the union', I am amazed that this absurd protestation of his was not rebuked by the impeachment of any of the judges, and that an utterance of such exceeding folly and blasphemy was passed over as though the hearing of it had given no offence.[86] After all it is just as impious to say that the only-begotten Son of God was from two natures before the union as it is sacrilegious to assert one single nature in him after the Word became flesh (pp. 203, 279–89 Bindley).

That is to say, Leo understands the formula 'from two natures' to imply that the man assumed had existed already before his assumption. This is as much a libel on Cyril as on his self-appointed champion. Both, in affirming a union from two natures, were teaching not that the Word assumed a particular man, but that the flesh which he took from Mary was the flesh that we all inherit from Adam and not of some new texture. But if Leo is a poor heresiologist, this does not make him a heretic in the eyes of anyone who holds the Ephesian definition of orthodoxy. In this epilogue Leo proves himself as hostile to Nestorius, or at least to the popular caricature of his teachings, as any prelate of the east.

Chalcedon and Leo's Tome

Before we ask what it was in Leo's Tome that divided the east, we must speak of the venue at which it was at last to obtain a hearing. The Council of Chlcedon was convened in 451 to undo what had beeen ill done at Ephesus in 449, but not to meddle with the oecumenical decisions of 431. After deposing the patriarch Dioscorus,[87] it restored the supporters of Flavian, including Bishop Theodoret of Cyrrhus, who had lost their sees at the Latrocinium, and agreed upon the following definition:

---

[86] As Price and Gaddas (2005), 23 n.68 point out, it appears that Leo not only misconstrued the words 'from two natures', but fails to acknowledge that Eutyches had been required to affirm 'one nature after the union'. On the other hand, it remains true that the synod of 448 was prepared to recognise two natures before the union and that Leo abhors this formula.

[87] Price and Gaddas (2005), vol. 1, 25–37.

> Following the holy Fathers, we confess one and the same Son, our Lord Jesus Christ, and this we all teach with one voice, the same perfect in divinity, the same perfect in humanity, truly God and truly human, the same from a body and a rational soul, consubstantial with the Father according to his divinity and the same consubstantial with us according to his humanity, in all like us excepting sin [Heb 4.15]; begotten from the Father before the ages according to his divinity, and born in these last times the same for us and for our salvation from the virgin Mary, mother of God, according to his Godhead, one and the same Christ, Son, Lord, Only-Begotten, acknowledged as one person [*prosôpon*] in two natures, unconfusedly, unchangeably, indivisibly, inseparably, the difference of natures in no way being confounded by the union, since on the contrary the particularity of each nature is preserved and comes together into one person or hypostasis.[88] He is not parted or divided into two persons, but one and the same Son and Only-Begotten God, Word, Lord Jesus Christ.[89]

At the core of this proclamation are clauses from the Formula of Reunion, which have been discussed sufficiently in this chapter.[90] Equally Cyrilline is the affirmation of one hypostasis or *prosôpon* in the Only-begotten; the argument that *prosôpon* is the Antiochene or Nestorian term would be cogent only if it were use in such a way as to modify or overrule the nomenclature of Cyril. The contrary is true, for it is Nestorius who maintains the logical primacy of the two *prosôpa*, even in such a late text as the *Bazaar of Heraclides*. By treating the terms *prosôpon* and hypostasis as synonyms, and by refusing to countenance two of either, the Council signifies its assent to Cyril's fourth anathema, which is aimed against those who allot the sayings and titles of Christ to two distinct hypostases or *prosôpa*. The proviso that the natures are indivisibly and inseparably united is the essence of Cyril's teaching, and although the balancing predicates 'unconfusedly' and 'unchangeably' have been traced to the works of Theodoret,[91] there is nothing that gives them the lie in Cyril's writings. It was not the compatibility of Cyril with Nestorius, or Cyril with Theodore, that became a topic of inextinguishable debate in the eastern church; those who disowned the council in Cyril's name accused it of having admitted a wooden horse, not from Antioch but from Rome.[92]

---

88 Richard (1945b), 278–9 suggests that the conjunction of *prosôpon* and hypostasis is intended to supply an unambiguous equivalent to the Latin persona, which has already been translated by both terms in Trinitarian discourse.

89 Lines 131–49 at Bindley (1899), 233.

90 The parallel formulae are reduced to a table by Diepen (1953), 109.

91 These adverbs furnish headings for two of the three books in the *Eranistes* of Theodoret. Bindley (1899), 241 cites Tertullian, *Against Praxeas* 27 and ps.-Athanasius, *Against Apollinarius* 1.10.

92 See Price and Gaddas (2005), vol. 2, p. 139 (session 4.114), where reconciled dissidents note that they had met phrases in Leo's Tome which 'struck us as implying a separation or division for those who wished to think this way, that is whatever Leo's intent

The easterners at Chalcedon seem to have acquiesced with little demur in the substitution of 'in two natures' for 'from two natures',[93] though they were conscious that the latter form of words had been canonised in Cyril's letters and had recently proved acceptable to a meeting of bishops outside Alexandria. The cancer, according to Leo's critics, was in the very stomach of his argument, for in Chapters 3 and 4 of the Tome, he employs terms which, for all their biblical pedigree, suggest that the divine and human agencies in Christ are to be assigned to two different agents. On is the form of God, the other the form of a servant; but whereas Paul had spoken in the Philippian Hymn of a single person relinquishing the higher form to take on the lower, and hence to be 'found in fashion as a man (Philippians 2.7), Leo personifies each form, declaring that each 'performs the acts that are proper to it'.[94] Cyril's fourth anathema in the third letter to Nestorius had denounced those who distribute the sayings and titles of Christ between tow distinct hypostases or *prosopa*; the Formula of Reunion had suffered the sayings and titles to be predicated '*according to* the humanity' or '*according to* the divinity', but never *of* one nature in contradistinction to the other. Leo thus violates one formulation without the sanction of the other. We may feel that his infelicity is redressed by his strictures on Eutyches in the postscript, with the ancillary misquotation of 1John 4.3, an injunction not to deny Christ which he reads as an admonition not to divide him.[95] But, while self-contradiction might be a proof of insolvency rather than fraud, it could hardly restore the intellectual credit of the pontiff. It is easy to see why partisans of Cyril at Chalcedon took offence at the adoption of Leo's dictum that 'the peculiar traits of each nature are retained',[96]

had been in stating that each nature retains its property and that each form discharges the work that is proper to it, the result was a charter for Nestorianism.

[93] Bindley (1899), 240 notes that 'from two natures' still appears in the Greek text of the Acts, although the supersession of this by 'on two natures' at the insistence of the Romans is recorded. Evagrius Scholasticus, *Church History* 2.4 confirms the reading 'in two natures'. Although it has been suggested that one version of the decree read 'from two natures and in two natures, there is no evidence in favour of this conjecture.

[94] *Tome* Chapter 4, p. 199n, Bindley. Bindley (1899), 211 notes that it was defended from Cyril's Second Letter to Succensus, but Cyril had nowhere spoken of the two natures as two agents.

[95] Bindley (1899), 213 observes that this is the reading of the Vulgate, but its only Greek congener comes from the pen of an author hostile to Nestorius and writing between the councils of Ephesus and Chalcedon: Socrates, *Church History* 7.32. Westcott (1886), 163–5 reports that the Vulgate reading is attested in a number of Latin texts before Leo, including the translation of Irenaeus; Socrates, on the other hand, defends it against the consensus of Greek manuscripts. There is also a Latin testimony that this reading was disputed by Nestorius. If there has been any corruption of the Biblical text in the orthodox interest, it originated in the Latin west.

[96] Adopted from Chapter 3 of the *Tome*, p. 198.93 Bindley. Price and Gaddas (2005), vol. 2, 17 n.43 observe that in the following clause, which also echoes the *Tome*, the term *persona* is amplified to *prosôpon kai hypostasin* in deference to Cyril's partiality for the latter noun.

for they had reason to apprehend that transposition from the passive to the active would turn two natures into two persons. For them it was enough to affirm, with Cyril, that the sufferings of the Word were experienced not in his divine nature but in the flesh that he took from Mary, and that this flesh was not exempt from the common pangs of grief and hunger. It is probable that no Greek at Chalcedon would have wished to read more than this into the few words from Leo's *Tome* that they consented to knead into their own proclamation of the faith.

Leo's *Tome* was therefore not intended to rehabilitate any teaching that had been proscribed at the oecumenical council of Ephesus. If he veers towards a doctrine of two persons in the middle, he catches a different wind in the epilogue; when he steers a firm course, his Christology is consistent with the Formula of Reunion, which after 433 was as much a norm for Alexandria as for Antioch. He rejects the Cyrilline shibboleth 'from two natures', but without showing any knowledge of its provenance; like Cyril and his own mentor Celestine, he is correcting the standard of orthodoxy in Constantinople, which was never a satellite of 'Alexandrian' theology. If we imagine that the *Tome* had never been written, we shall not be at a loss to think of a formula that would have sufficed to chasten Dioscorus, vindicate Flavian and unmask the errors of Eutyches. The Council would have needed to do no more than rehearse the Formula of Reunion – or more cogently, the letter from Cyril in which this was embedded – and an oecumenical gathering could have not failed to perceive that Flavian was the most Cyrilline of the three protagonists. Leo's *Tome* did not resolve any theological conflict that had not been resolved already before Chalcedon; by its use of terms which lent themselves to an invidious construction, it ulcerated the sores that had been inflicted on the Alexandrian church by the deposition of its patriarch Dioscorus. The Tome of Leo and two or three of Cyril's letters were jointly acclaimed in the Chalcedonian Definition of 451; but from that time on, thinkers of stature in Antioch as in Egypt were to conclude, after close perusal of the canonised texts, that the orthodoxy of Ephesus was no longer the diagnostic of catholicity in Rome.

The Canonicity of Cyril's Letters

We have yet to establish which of Cyril's letters were deemed canonical at the Council of Chalcedon. That one was the letter to John of Antioch, celebrating the reconciliation of the two patriarchs under the formula of reunion is beyond doubt. The evidence regarding the canonisation of Cyril's letters to Nestorius, on the other hand, is not of a piece, for the acts of the council suggest one answer, the Definition another. The acts record the reading and acclamation of the second letter, which Cyril addressed in his own name to his adversary. The Definition, however, speaks of synodical letters to Nestorius and the bishops of the east (p. 232.110 Bindley). By the latter they mean the conciliatory epistle to John of Antioch; the former designation does not fit the second salvo against Nestorius so well as the third, which purports to convey the judgment of a whole synod. It is commonly held that only the second letter to Nestorius was canonised, the third having received that status in 553 from the Second Council of Constantinople, which wrongly believed itself to be endorsing a decision already taken at Chalcedon.[97] Since it was the anathemas to the third letter that inflamed the east against Cyril, the conclusion that this document lacks the sanction of the Fourth Oecumenical Council satisfies those who regard Chalcedon as a palliative for the wounds of 431. On this view, the Second Council of Constantinople in 553 was a repristination of Ephesus, estranging those whom its predecessor had aimed to reconcile.

Nevertheless, however the machinery of this council may have functioned, it had little power to deny the authority of either letter. Both had been recited to applause at Ephesus in 431, and in the preamble to the Chalcedonian Definition this is the latest of the three oecumenical councils whose decisions bind the Church. Nothing was promulgated at Chalcedon that was manifestly at variance with the third letter to Nestorius – unless it be the proviso that the two natures are united without confusion, which might be thought to contradict Cyril's attribution of divinity to the flesh of Christ in his eleventh anathema. We have seen already, however, that Cyril's usage of the term 'flesh' in this and other texts is an instance of his partiality for Biblical terms where these appeared to say to him all that his critics were attempting to say in words of their own invention. It ought by now to be evident that in Cyril's view no doctrine could be uttered with the sanction of the church if it did not possess the authority of the scriptures. This is also a premisis for Leo, who adopts the noun forma to signify that which constitutes the humanity or divinity of Christ because this is the term that Paul employs in his Philippian hymn, which celebrates the descent of one who was in the form of God to the *skhêma* or fashion of a man that he might assume the form of a slave. The same text explains the presence in the *Bazaar of Heraclides* of a theory (not embraced without misgiving by Nestorius) that the Word became man not in nature but in *skhêma*. The constitution on Christ's two natures issued by the Council of Chalcedon in 451 would have been a document without parallel if it had been imposed on the church as a self-authenticating mandate which, like an act of the British parliament, needed only to be proclaimed to become the law. But the Chalcedonian Definition appears to have cut the hermeneutic knot by fiat only when it is pared down to its last quarter, where the delegates turn from the iteration, commendation and censure of earlier witnesses to frame their own epitome of the doctrine which they declare to be already universal. These paragraphs incorporate sentences from Cyril's letter acclaiming the Formula of Reunion and from the Tome of Leo; in the preamble, these two texts are canonized, together with one or two of Cyril's letters to Nestorius and the creeds of 325 and 381. If the intent behind the declaration is to be understood, it cannot be read alone.

---

[97] Bindley (1899), 237, though at 160 he admits that the letter had already been acclaimed at the oecumenical Council of Ephesus in 431.

Concluding Remarks

From what has been said, it is evident that the historian cannot use the name 'Chalcedon', as systematic theologians often do, to signify only the twelve-line torso that comprises the new confession of two natures in the one Christ. If this were the whole definition, it would lend itself as wax to the good intentions of those scholars who wish to shape it into a hybrid of Alexandrian and Antiochene Christology; in itself it would so meagre as to justify the complaint of one shrewd critic that it does not tell us even whether the risen Christ is male or female.[98] But this and other lacuna in the formula are supplied by the Nicene Creed and itself Constantinopolitan offspring, which the delegates at Nicaea reproduced as the indispensable preamble to any statement of their own. The same definition canonizes at least two letters by Cyril intimating that the words of the council admitted of no construction that was inimical to his teachings or propitious to teachings that he had condemned. It was neither the aim nor a consequence of this council to restore the credit of Theodore, and it had no choice but to sanction the anathemas that the third oecumenical council had pronounced upon Nestorius; since they took the Formula of reunion as a paradigm, there was nothing in their own words that they could not trace back to Cyril except for a phrase or two that was conscious derived from the Tome of Leo. Had a different provenance been sought for the affirmation of double consubstantiality,[99] it would not have been in the Antiochene tradition, but in its hostile interlocutor, Apollinarius of Laodicea. He had fallen under the censure of the church before any charge was laid against Theodore or Nestorius, but, whereas every doctrine that was peculiar to these last two was rejected at Chalcedon, this assembly not only ratified his teaching that 'the same' being who was man was also God, but prepared the way for a vindication of his dictum that the Word was the proper subject of the passion, a doctrine which was not espoused by the writers whom we commonly style 'Antiochene', and which even Cyril cannot affirm without periphrasis.

---

[98] Coakley (2002), 163. It remains true, as she urges, that the definition fails to construct a metaphysic of the incarnation, though I do not know why she requires it to say expressly whether the word hypostasis has the same sense throughout, or whether the hypostasis 'is identical with the pre-existent logos'. Even if affirmative answers were not implied in the document, they are given in Cyril's letters, where some attempt is made to 'say what happens to the *physeis* at Christ's death and in his resurrection'.

[99] Richard (1945a) denies the authenticity of a passage in a catena which attributes it to Amphilochius of Iconium.

Epilogue

It has been observed[1] that ancient heresiologists espoused a 'discourse of difference', which the scholarship of the last two hundred years has been all too ready to perpetuate, and even to refine. Irenaeus, the earliest polemicist whose works survive, exultantly casts Simonians against Valentininians, Marcionites against Basilideans, Nicolaitians against Encratites; in the works of his successors, even the satellites of the great heresiarchs were subject to capricious reduplication, so that Ptolemaeus, Secundus and Theodotus become Ptolemaeans, Secundians and Theodotians by the mere addition of a suffix. Only such devices could engender the eighty sects which Epiphanius of Salamis compared to the eighty concubines whom Solomon contrasted with his one unspotted dove. Modern commentators are increasingly reluctant to accept the taxonomies of these catholic witnesses, but are happy to divide the Christian world of the first five centuries into larger agglomerates, few of which are named or even silently attested in any contemporary source.'Gnostic' is now the most infamous of these supervenient categories, but 'Origenist' is another term that has been extended in modern books to both 'orthodox' and 'heterodox' experiments which never fell within the protean usage of the epithet before Origen's condemnation in 553. False notions of *monarchia* in the Godhead are denounced by a number of catholic polemicists, but none of them is aware of a 'monarchian' movement, let alone of the ramification of this into dynamic and modalistic monarchianism. We are warned, with almost valetudinarian rigour, against the application of the terms 'heresy' and 'orthodoxy' to any side in debates of the first three centuries, since no gathering of prelates in this period could be truly oecumenical or pretend to the force of law. It is, however, the authors who impose this quarantine who are most likely to maintain that there was never a single church, that it was only under imperial duress that the archipelago took on the semblance of a continent, and that even this illusion could not last because the attempt to bring about unity by violence forestalled any peaceful commerce of ideas. The Arian controversy has been renamed the 'Search for the Christian Doctrine of God', but many historians, following the example of ancient partisans, continue to represent it as a struggle between congealing factions rather than as an interlocking series of two-handed jousts and collective disputations. The troubles which came to a head at the third and forth oecumencial councils are still apt to be regarded as symptoms of an inveterate feud between the schools of Antioch and Alexandria, and the failure of the ancients to record the earlier stages of this feud is ascribed to the blindness induced by more parochial enmities. In short, it is assumed that it was not possible for anyone in the first

---

[1] King (2008), 79.

five centuries to be simply a Christian, as there was always a choice to be made hermetic and discordant 'Christianities'.

The bellwethers of this modern historiography have been Protestants by culture if not conviction; the picture of ancient Christendom which emerges from their studies is not proved to be false because it manifestly prefigures the dissolution of the western church into a loose confederacy of denominations, each imparting only its own theology to its ordinands. It can indeed be argued that to think of the Church as one thing in antiquity is to set one's face against the last 150 years of scholarship on the New Testament, in which it has become mandatory for scholars of all confessions to think of Mark as writing only for the Marcan community, Paul for Paulines, the authors or compilers of Q for Ebionites and John perhaps for an early school of Gnostics. But while this may be a sound heuristic principle for commentators, it cannot mirror any ancient Christian's notion of his own churchmanship.[2] Even in our own age of cheap paper, it would be a prodigal author who wrote only for those within hearing; in the ancient world, an author who let his work pass out of his hands lost all control of its circulation, and the community for which he wrote was simply the sum of those who chanced to read him. The likeliest readers of any gospel, in ancient as in modern times, were the readers of other gospels, and an evangelist who believed all proclamations but his own to be defective or erroneous would evidently wish his own to be read by those whom others had deceived. Most believers have in fact found it possible to suppose that all the canonical evangelists held one gospel; whether their intent supplementary or polemical, it is certain that all four of the canonical evangelists wrote ostensibly for the world, and not for one conventicle. The same is true of catholics in the next century who were openly polemical: to Ignatius and Irenaeus the church which they defended was not one denomination, but the saving ark, while the dissidents were the flotsam of a transient cataclysm. Among later heretics, those who, like Eunomius, confess that they cannot speak for the majority arc anomalous; more commonly all parties to a debate purport to be upholding truths which are universally received within the Episcopal communion. This communion, for its adherents, is coterminous with the church, and so, for those whom we call 'pro-Nicene' or 'Neo-Nicene' is allegiance to the first oecumenical council. Athanasius was no more a mere 'Nicene' than a mere 'Athanasian' in his own eyes, and Eusebius of Caesarea opposed him in the name of oecumenical consensus, not in his own name or in that of Origen. The participants in the controversy that followed the Nicene Council were not so often schools and sects as individuals, each professing to enunciate the doctrine of the same church.

This observation accounts for the assimilative capacity of early catholic doctrine. For a Roman Catholic to adopt a palpably Lutheran doctrine today would be to compromise his allegiance to his own magisterium; in the climate of the fourth century an argument patronized by Athanasius might be strengthened by an infusion of Eusebian or 'homoiousian' reasoning. Of course an Athanasius would

---

[2] See further Bauckham (1998).

continue to represent every contradiction of his own view as the cant of some benighted coalition, while a Eusebius would continue to maintain that only the intrigues of a few malcontents had robbed the church of peace. It was the Athanasian temper (which no bishop fails to share in some degree) that led the episcopate to built permeable dykes against heterodoxy from the outset; it is well known that the dykes became less permeable when reinforced by sacerdotal interdicts, civil penalties and the arcane machinery of the inquisition. The Athanasian temper, as we have seen, has also guided the historian; we might wonder, then, if the academic categories that it spawns have proved so friable and delusive, whether it might also be time for those few churches which retain a strong magisterium to forgo the pursuit of heresy and permit unbridled liberty of belief. The predictable answer is none the less a persuasive one: no church stands long unless it is perceived to stand for something, and no truth can be secured unless its guardians have some means of disarming error. Not only the Curia but the academy requires its theologians to decide that this is false because that is true. The majority of academics, however – and perhaps now the majority of churchmen – would be bound to deplore any measure which abridged freedom of debate, and would concur with the emollient recommendations of Hans Küng.[3]

> The one essential thing is understanding: the 'unmasking and refutation' of heretical doctrines, which from the time of Irenaeus was always regarded as the main aim of the Christian heresiologists, generally makes true understanding impossible. Heresies fulfill the function of preventing the Church from becoming rigid and paralyzed *(sic)* in its life and its teaching; they can preserve it from idle complacency and vain self-satisfaction; they can keep it spiritually in motion, drive it forwards, and challenge it to keep ever more faithful to the Gospel. Heresy should be seen, not primarily as a challenge to the unity of Church fellowship, but as a challenge to the Church to discover a new, purer and deeper unity.

The episcopate of the early church did not set out to act as Küng prescribes, but we have seen that its thought grew ripe by the absorption of ideas which it had once found indigestible. No tenet that was manifestly grounded in the scriptures could be extinguished without a trace, and it would not have been impossible for the same church to accommodate contradictory inferences from the same text without deeming any of them heretical. The canon of rabbinic apophthegms would be slight indeed if all but one pronouncement on any topic had been anathematized; a Buddhist will choose a sect, but may believe that it is necessary for other sects to occupy other point in the grid of possible beliefs.[4] Even the Roman Catholic Church does no declare Scotus a heretic because it now favours the doctrines of Aquinas. The Subtle Doctor is safe in the shadow of the Angelic Doctor; Valentinus, on the other hand, he was eclipsed by Irenaeus,

---

3 Küng (1968), 254, 255 and 257.

4 See Takakusu (1956).

the homoiousians by the homoousians, Apollinarius and by the Chalcedonian Definition. But even a body that has been eclipsed will not cease to exert the force of gravity on the one that is interposed.

Bibliography

Primary Texts

Acta Concilii Aquiliensis

See Zelzer (1982) in second bibliography.

Apollinarius

See Lietzmann (1904) in second bibliography.

Augustine

De Civitate Dei (*City of God*), ed. B. Dombart and A. Kalb, 2 vols (Turnhout: Brepols, CCSL 47–8, 1955)

De Libero Arbitrio (*On Free Will*), ed. W.M. Green (Vienna: Tempsky, CSEL 74, 1956).

De Vera Religione (*On True Religion*), ed. W.M. Green (Vienna: Tempsky, CSEL 77, 1961).

Athanasius

Contra Arium (*Against the Arians*) I and II, in *Werke* I.1, vol. 1, ed. M. Tetz (Berlin: De Gruyter, 1998).

Contra Arium (*Against the Arians*) III, in *Werke* I.1, vol. 2, ed. M. Tetz and D. Wyrwa (Berlin: De Gruyter, 2000).

Contra Gentes and *De Incarnatione*, ed. and trans. R.W. Thomson (Oxford: Clarendon Press, 1971).

*De Syn*odis (*On Synods*), in *Werke* II.2, vols 8–9, ed. H.-G. Opitz (Berlin: De Gruyter, 1940–1941).

Epistula ad Epictetum (*Letter to Epictetus*), in B. de Montfaucon, *S. Athanasii Opera Dogmatica Selecta* (Leipzig: Weiger, 1853), 820–43.

Epistula de Sententia Dionysii (*On the Opinion of Dionysius*), in B. de Montfaucon, *S. Athanasii Opera Dogmatica Selecta* (Leipzig: Weiger, 1853), 92–139.

Athenagoras

Legatio and *De Resurrectione*, ed. and trans. W. Schoedel (Oxford: Clarendon Press, 1972).

Basil of Caesarea

Letters, ed. and trans. J. Deferrari, 4 vols (New York: Heinemann, Loeb Classical Library, 1928).

Chalcedonian Definition

See Bindley (1899), 229–43 in second bibliography.

Clement of Alexandria

Protrepticus und Paedagogus, ed. O. Stählin and U. True (Berlin: Akademie Verlag, GCS, 1972).
Stromata I–VI, ed. O' Stählin, L. Früchtel and U. Treu (Berlin: Akademie Verlag, 1985).
Stromata Buch VII–VIII, Excerpta ex Theodote, Eclogae Propheticae, Quis Dives Salvetur, Fragmente, ed. O. Stählin and H. Früchtel (Berlin: Akademie Verlag, 1970).

Clement of Rome

For all texts attributed to him see Lightfoot in second bibliography, part 1, vol. 2 (1890).

Constantine

Oration to the Saints, in Eusebius, *Werke* I, ed. I.A. Heikel (Leipzig: Hinrichs, GCS, 1902).

Cyril of Alexandria

In Ioannis Evangelium (*Commentary on John*), Libri I–VI, ed. J. Aubert, *Patrologia Graeca* 73 (Paris: Migne, 1859).
Letters. See Wickham (1983) in second bibliography.

Epiphanius

Panarion, 3 vols, ed. K. Holl and J. Dummer (Berlin: Akademie Verlag, 1980–1985).

Eunbomius

The Extant Works, ed. R. Vaggione (Oxford: Clarendon Press).

Eusebius of Caesarea

Demonstratio Evangelica (*Gospel Demonstration*), ed. I.A. Heikel (Leipzig: Hinrichs, GCS, 1913).
Ecclesiastical History ed. and trans. H.J. Lawlor and J.E. Oulton, 2 vols (New York: Heinemann, Loeb Classical Library, 1926–1932).
Gegen Marcell (*Against Marcellus*); *Über die Kirchliche Theologie* (*Ecclesiastical Theology*), ed. E. Klostermann and G.C. Hansen (Berlin: Akademie Verlag, GCS, 1972).
De Vita Constantini (*Life of Constantine*), ed. B. Bleckman (Turnhout: Brepols, 2007).

Gregory of Nazianzus

*Oratione*s 27–31, ed. P. Gallay (Paris: Cerf).

Gregory of Nyssa

De Anima (*On the Soul*), see Ramelli in second bibliography.
Opera I, ed. W. Jaeger (Leiden: Brill, 1960).
Opera II, ed. W. Jaeger (Leiden: Brill, 1960).
Opera III.4, ed. F. Mueller (Leiden: Brill, 1958).
Opera V, ed. J. Mc Donough and P. Alexander (Leiden: Brill, 1962).
Opera VI, ed. H. Langerbeck (Leiden: Brill, 1960).

Hilary of Poitiers

Liber de Synodis (*On Synods*), ed. by monks of the Benedictine order in *Patrologia Latina* X (Paris: Migne, 1845), 471–545.

Hippolytus

Refutatio Omnium Haeresium (*Refutation of all Heresies*), ed. M. Marcovich (Berlin/New York: De Gruyter).

Ignatius

For his genuine letters see Lightfoot in second bibliography, part 2, vol. 2 (1889).

Irenaeus

Contre les Hérésies (*Against Heresies*), ed. and trans. A. Rousseau and J. Doutreleau, 5 double vols (Paris: Cerf, 1965–1982).

Jerome (Hieronymus)

Epistulae (Letters), ed. I. Hilberg, 3 vols (Vienna: Tempsky, CSEL 54–6, 1910–1918).

Justin Martyr

Apologiae (*Apologoes*), ed. M. Marcovich (Berlin: De Gruyter, Patristische Texte und Studien, 1994).
Dialogue cum Tryphone, ed. M. Marcovich (Berlin: De Gruyter, Patristische Texte und Studien, 1997).

Leo the Great

For *Tome to Flavian* see Bindley (1899), 195–215 in second bibliography.

Marcellus of Ancyra

Fragmente, ed. M. Vinzent (Leiden: Brill, 1997).

Marius Victorinus

Opera Theologica, ed. A. Locher (Leipzig: Teubner, 1976).

Methodius

Werke, ed. N. Bonwetsch (Leipzig: Hinrichs, GCS, 1917).

Nag Hammadi Codices

See Robinson (2000) in second bibliography.

Nestorius

Bazaar of Heraclides. See Driver and Hodgson (1925) in second bibliography.

Novatian

Opera quae supersunt, ed. G. Diercks (Turnhout: Brepols, CCSL 4, 1972).

Origen

De Principiis (*First Principles*), ed. P. Koetschau (Leipzig: Hinrichs, GCS, 1913).
De Resurrectione (*On the Resurrection*), see Bonwetsch (ed.), Methodius: *Werke*, 217–424.

Die Homilien zur Genesis, Exodus und Leviticus, ed. W. Baehrens (Leipzig: Hinrichs, GCS, 1920).
Die Homilien zur Samuel I, zum Hohelied (On the Song of Songs) und zur den Propheten, ed. W. Baehrens (Leipzig: Hinrichs, GCS, 1925).
Entretien avec Héraclide et les evêques (*Dialogue with Heraclides*), ed. J. Scherer (Cairo: Institut Français d'Archéolgie, 1960).
Gegen Celsus (*Against Celsus*) and *Die Schrift von Gebiet* (*On Prayer*), ed. P. Koetschau (Leipzig: Hinrichs, GCS, 1988).
Johanneskommentar (*Commentary on John*), ed. E. Preuschen (Leipzig: Hinrichs, GCS, 1899).
Philokalie 1–20: *Sur les Écritures*, ed. and trans. M. Harl (Paris: Cerf, 1983).
Philokalie 21–7: *Sur le libre arbitre*, ed. and trans. E. Junod (Paris: Cerf, 1976).

Pamphilus

Apologia pro Origene (*Apology for Origen*), see Rowekamp in second bibliography.

Philo of Alexandria

Works, ed. and trans. by various hands, 12 vols (New York: Heinemann, Loeb Classical Library, 1929–1953).

Philostorgius

Kirchengeschichte (*Church History*), ed. J. Bidez (Leipzig: Hinrichs, GCS, 1913).

Socrates Scholasticus

Kirchengeschichte (*Church History*), ed. G.C. Hansen and M. Sirinjan (Berlin: Akademie Verlag, GCS, 1995).

Sozomen

Kirchengeschichte (*Church History*), ed. G.C. Hansen (Berlin: Akademie Verlag, GCS, 1960).

Tatian

Oratio ad Graecos, ed. and trans. M. Whittaker (Oxford: Clarendon Press, 1982).

Tertullian

Opera Omnia, ed. A. Gerlo, 2 vols (Turnhout: Brepols, CCSL 1–2, 1954).

Theodore of Mopsuestia

In Epistulas Beati Pauli, ed. H.B. Sweete, 2 vols (Cambridge: Cambridge University Press, 1880, 1882). Fragmentary works in vol. 2.

Theodoret of Cyrus

Eranistes, ed. with supplementary texts by G. Ettlinger (Oxford: Clarendon Press, 1975).

Historia Ecclesiastica (Church History), ed. L. Parmentier and F. Scheidweiler (Leipzig: Hinrichs, GCS, 1954).

Theophilus of Antioch

Ad Autolycum (*To Autolycus*), ed. R.M. Grant (Oxford: Clarendon Press, 1970).

Abbreviations

CCSL = Corpus Christianorum Scriptorum Latinorum
CSEL = Corpus Scriptorum Ecclesiasticorum Latinorum
GCS = Die Griechischen Christlichen Schriftsteller
HTR = *Harvard Theological Review*
JEH = *Journal of Ecclesiastical History*
JTS = *Journal of Theological Studies*
ZAC = *Zeitschrift für Antikes Christentum*

Academic Literature

Abramowski, L. (1992a), 'Dionysius of Rome (6.268) and Dionysius of Alexandria (d. 164/5) in the Arian Controversy of the Late Fourth Century', English trans, in Abramowski, *Formula and Context* (Aldershot: Ashgate), XI, 1–35.

——— (1992b), 'The Synod of Antioch 324/5 and its Creed', English trans. in Formula and Context (as above), III, 1–12.

——— (1992c), 'The Controversy over Diodore and Theodore in the Interval between the two Councils of Ephesus', in *Formula and Context*, II, pp. 1–37.

——— (2007), '*Audi ut dico*. Literarische Beobachtungen und chronologische Erwägungen zu Marius Victorinus und den 'platonisierenden' Nag Hammadi Traktaten', *Zeitschrift für Kirchengeschichte* 117, 145–68.

Anatolios, K. (1997), 'The Body as Instrument: A Re-evaluation of Athanasius' Logos-Sarx Christology', *Coptic Church Review*, 78–84.

——— (1999), *Athanasius. The Coherence of his Thought* (London: Routledge).

Arnold, D.W.H. (1991), *The Early Episcopal Career of Athanasius of Alexandria* (Notre Dame: University of Notre Dame Press).

Ashwin-Siejkowski, P. (2008), *Clement of Alexandria. A Project of Christian Perfection* (Edinburgh: T. and T. Clark).
Aulen, G. (1951), *Christus Victor* (London: Macmillan).
Ayres, L. (2004), *Nicaea and its Legacy* (Oxford: Clarendon Press).
Bammel, C.P. (1989), 'Adam in Origen', in R. Williams (ed.), *The Making of Orthodoxy* (Cambridge: Cambridge University Press).
Barnes, T.D. (1985), *Tertullian. A Historical and Literary Study*, 2nd edition (Oxford: Clarendon Press).
——— (1993), *Athanasius and Constantius* (Cambridge: Cambridge University Press).
——— (2001), 'Constantine's *Speech to the Assembly of the Saints*: Date and Place of Delivery', *JTS* 52, 26–36.
Barrett, C.K. (1982), *Studies in John* (London: SPCK).
Bauckham, R. (1998), *The Gospel for all Christians* (Grand Rapids: Eerdmans).
Bauer, W. (1971), *Orthodoxy and Heresy in Earliest Christianity* (Philadelphia: Fortress Press).
Bechtle, G. (1999), *The Anonymous Commentary on Plato's Parmenides* (Bern: Haupt).
Behr, J. (2000), *Asceticism and Anthropology in Irenaeus and Clement* (Oxford: Clarendon Press).
Bindley, T.H. (1899), *The Oecumenical Documents of the Faith* (London: Methuen).
Borsch, F.H. (1967), *The Son of Man in Myth and History* (London: SPCK).
——— (1970), *The Christian and the Gnostic Son of Man* (London: SPCK).
Boulnois, M.-O. (2003), 'The Mystery of the Trinity according to Cyril of Alexandria', in T. Weinandy (ed.), *The Theology of Cyril of Alexandria: A Critical Appreciation* (London/NY: T. and T. Clark), 75–111.
Bousset, W. (1911), Valentinus, in *Encyclopedia Britannica*, 11th edition, vol. 27, 852–7.
Braun, R. (1962), *Deus Christus. Recherches sur le vocabulaire doctrinal de Tertullien* (Paris: Fondation de Lettres et Sciences d'Alger).
Bray, G. (1999), *Ancient Christian Commentary on Scripture. New Testament: VII 1 and 2 Corinthians* (Downers Grove, IL: Inter-Varsity Press).
Brent, A. (1995a), *Hippolytus and the Roman Church in the Third Century* (Leiden: Brill).
——— (1995), 'Was Hippolytus a Schismatic?', *VC* 49, 215–44.
Brewer, H. (1909), *Das sogennante Athanasianische Glaubensbekunden: ein Werk der heilige Ambrosius* (Paderborn: Schöningh).
Bright, W. (1882), *Notes on the First Four Oecumenical Councils* (Oxford: Clarendon Press).
Buchinger, J. (2005), *Pascha bei Origenes* (Innsbruck: Verlag Tyrolia).
Bultmann, R. (1956), *Primitive Christianity in its Original Setting* (London: Thames and Hudson).

Burgess, R.W. (2000), 'The Date of the Deposition of Eustathius of Antioch', *JTS* 51, 150–60.

Cadiou, R. (1935), *La Jeunesse d'Origène* (Paris: Beauchesne, 1935).

Caird, G. B. (1956), *Principalities and Powers. A Study in Pauline Theology* (Oxford: Clarendon Press).

Cameron, A. and Hall, S. (1999), *Eusebius: Life of Constantine* (Oxford: Clarendon Press).

Casey, R.P. (1934), *Theodotus: Excerpta ex Theodoto* (London: Christophers. Texts and Documents 1).

Cerfaux, L. (1954), *Recueil Lucien Cerfaux* (Paris: Duculot and Gembloux).

Cerrato, J. (2001), *Hippolytus between East and West* (Oxford: Clarendon Press).

Chadwick, H. (1947), 'Origen, Celsus and the Stoa', *JTS* 48, 34–49.

——— (1950), 'The Silence of Bishops in Ignatius of Antioch', *Harvard Theological Review* 43, 169–72.

——— (1951), 'Eucharist and Christology in the Nestorian Controversy', *JTS* 2, 145–64.

——— (1958), 'Ossius of Cordova and the Presidency of the Council of Antioch, 325', *JTS* 9, 292–304.

Clark, E.A. (1992), *The Origenist Controversy* (Princeton: Princeton University Press).

Clayton, P.B. (2007), *The Christology of Theodoret of Cyrus* (New York: Oxford University Press).

Coakley, S. (2002), 'What Does Chalcedon Solve and What Does it Not? Some Reflections on the Status and Meaning of the Chalcedonian Definition', in S.T. Davies, G. Kendall and G. O'Collins (eds), *The Incarnation* (Oxford: Oxford University Press), 143–63.

Crouzel, H. (1973), 'A Letter from Origen to "Friends in Alexandria"', in D. Neireins and M. Schutka (eds), *Essays in Honour of George Vasilievich Florovsky* (Rome: Pontifical Institute), 135–50.

——— (1978), 'L'Hadès et la Géhenne selon Origène', *Gregorianum* 59, 291–331.

——— (1989), 'Theological Construction and Reason: Origen on Freewill', in B. Drewery and R. Bauckham (eds), *Scripture, Tradition and Reason* (Edinburgh: T. and T. Clark), 239–65.

Daley, B. (2002), 'Nature and the Mode of 'Union': Late Patristic Models for the Personal Unity of Christ', in S.T. Davies, D. Kendall and G. O'Collins (eds), *The Incarnation* (Oxford: Oxford University Press), 164–1946.

Daniélou, J. (1973), *Gospel Message and Hellenistic Culture*, trans. J.A. Baker (London: Dartman, Longman, and Todd).

——— (1974), *The Origins of Latin Christianity*, trans. J.A. Baker (London: Dartman, Longman and Todd).

Davies, W.D. (1965), *Paul and Rabbinic Judaism* (London: SPCK).

Debié, M., trans. (1996), *Théodore de Mopsueste, Homélies Catéchétiques* (Paris: Migne/Breplos).

Dechow, J. (1977), *Dogma and Mysticism: Epiphanius of Salamis and the Legacy of Origen* (Macon, Georgia).
De Lubac, H. (1949), *L'Exégèse Mediévale. Les Quatre Sens de l'Écriture*, première partie, vol. 1 (Paris: Aubin).
DeSimone, R.J. (1970), *The Teaching of Novatian the Roman Presbyter on the Trinity* (Rome: Instititum Patristicum).
Devreesse, R. (1948), *Essai sur Théodore de Mopsueste* (Vatican: *Studi e Testi* 141).
Diepen, H.M. (1953), *Les trois chapîtres au Concile de Chalcédoine* (Oosterhout: Éditions de Saint Michel).
Dillon, J. (1986), 'Plutarch and Second-Century Platonism', in A.H. Armstrong (ed.), *Classical Mediterranean Spirituality* (New York; Crossroads), 213–29.
——— (1999), 'Monotheism in the Gnostic Tradition', in M. Frede and P. Athanassiadi (eds), *Pagan Monotheism in Late Antiquity* (Oxford: Clarendon Press), 69–79.
Dodd, C.H. (1935), *The Bible and the Greeks* (London: Hodder).
Döllinger, H. (1876), *Hippolytus and Callistus*, trans. A. Plummer (Edinburgh: T. and T. Clark. German publication 1853).
Drecoll, V. (1999), *Die Entwicklung der Trinitätslehre des Basilius von Caesarea: Seiin Weg von Homöusianer zu Neunizänischer* (Göttingen).
Driver, G.R. and L. Hodgson (1925), *Nestorius: The Bazaar of Heraclides* (Oxford: Clarendon Press).
Duckworth, C. and E. Osborn (1985), 'Clement of Alexandria's Lost Hypotyposes: An Eighteenth-Century French Sighting', *JTS* 36, 67–84.
Edwards, M.J. (1989), 'Gnostics and Valentinians in the Church Fathers', *JTS* 40, 25–40.
——— (1990a), 'Neglected Texts in the Study of Gnosticism', *JTS* 41, 26–50.
——— (1990b), '"Atticizing Moses? Numenius, the Fathers and the Jews", *Vigiliae Christianae* 44, 64–75.
——— (1993), 'Ammonius, Teacher of Origen', *JEH* 44, 169–81.
——— (1995), 'Origen's Two Resurrections', *JTS* 46, 502–18.
——— (1998), 'Did Origen Apply the Word *Homoousios* to the Son?', *JTS* 49, 658–70.
——— (1999), *Ancient Christian Commentary on Scripture VIII: Galatians, Ephesians, Philippians* (Downers Grove: Inter-Varsity Press).
——— (2001), 'Pauline Platonism: The Myth of Valentinus', *Studia Patristica* 35, 205–21.
——— (2002), *Origen against Plato* (Aldershot: Ashgate).
——— (2006), 'Nicene Theology and the Second God', *Studia Patristica* 40, 191–5.
——— (2008a), review of E. Prinzivalli (ed.), *Il Commento a Giovanni di Origene. Il testo e ì suoìi contesti* (Rome 2004), *JTS* 59, 349–54.
——— (2008b), 'Origen's Platonism. Questions and Caveats', in *ZAC* 12, 20–38.
Elliott, J.K. (1993), *The Apocryphal New Testament* (Oxford/New York: Oxford University Press).

Elliott, T.G. (1992), 'Constantine and the "Arian Reaction" after Nicaea', *JEH* 43, 169–94.

Elm, S. (1997), 'The Dog that did not bark: doctrine and political in the conflict between Theophilus of Alexandria and John Chrysostom of Constantinople', in L. Ayres and G. Jones (eds), *Christian Origins: Theology, Rhetoric and Community* (London: Routledge), 68–93.

Evans, E.E. (1948), *Tertullian: Adversus Praxean* (London: SPCK).

Fairbairn, D. (2003), *Grace and Christology in the Early Church* (Oxford: Clarendon Press).

Festugière, A.J. (1949), *La Révélation d'Hermès Trismégiste, II: Dieu Cosmique* (Paris: Gabalda).

Freedman, H. and Simon M. (1977), *The Mishnah Rabbah*, vol 1: *Genesis* (Oxford: Oxford University Press).

Frend, W.H.C. (1954), 'The Gnostic Sects and the Roman Empire', *JEH* 5, 25–37.

Gaston, L. (1987), *Paul and the Torah* (Vancouver: University of British Columbia Press).

Gelzer, H. (1995), *Patrum Nicaenorum Nomina* (Stuttgart: Teubner. Original printing 1898).

Gerber, S. (2001), 'Calixt von Rom und der monarchianische Streit', *ZAC* 5, 213–37.

Goehring, J. (2001), 'The Provenance of the Nag Hammadi Codices Once More', *Studia Patristica* 35, 234–53.

Görgemanns, H. and H. Karpp, eds (1993), *Origenes: Vier Bücher über den Prinzipien* (Darmstadt: Wissenschftliche Buchgesellschaft).

Grant, R.M. (1964), 'Tatian (*Oration* 30) and the Gnostics', *JTS* 15, 65–9.

Green, B. (2008), *The Soteriology of Leo the Great* (Oxford: Clarendon Press).

Greer, R. and Mitchell, M. (2007), *The Belly-Myther of Endor* (Atlanta: Society of Biblical Literature).

Gregg, R.C. and D.E. Groh (1981), *Early Arianism: A View of Salvation* (Philadelphia: Fortress Press).

Grillmeier, A. (1975), *Christ in Christian Tradition* vol. 1 (London: Mowbray).

——— (1995), *Christ in Christian Tradition*, vol. 2.2 (London: Mowbray).

Gunton. C. (1993), *The One, the Three and the Many* (Cambridge: Cambridge University Press).

Gwynn, D. (2007), *The Eusebians* (Oxford: Clarendon Press).

Hadot, P. (1996), 'Porphyre et Victorinus: Questions et Hypothèses', supplement to Tardieu (1996).

Hall, S.G. (1991), *Doctrine and Practice in the Early Church* (London: SPCK).

Hanson, R.P.C. (1972), 'Did Origen Apply the Word *Homoousios* to the Son?', in J. Fontaine and C. Kannengiesser (eds), *Epektasis. Mélanges Patristiques offerts à Cardinal Daniélou* (Paris), reprinted in Hanson, *Studies in Christian Antiquity* (Cambridge: Cambridge University Press, 1983), 292–303.

——— (1988), *The Search for the Christian Doctrine of God* (Edinburgh: T. and T. Clark).

Harl, M. (1963), 'Recherches sur l'origénisme d'Origène', *Studia Patristica* 2, 373–405.
——— (1987), 'Le pré-existence des âmes chez Origène', in L. Lies (ed.), *Origeniana Quarta* (Innsbruck), 238–58.
Harnack, A. von (1931), *Lehrbuch der Dogmengeschichte*, vol. 1, 5th edition (Tübingen).
——— (1990), *Marcion. The Doctrine of the Alien God* (Durham, NJ: Labyrinth).
Harris, J.R. (1923), 'Athena, Sophia and the Logos', *Bulletin of the John Rylands Library* 7, 55–72.
Harvey, W. (1857), *Sancti Irenaei libros quinque* (Cambridge: Cambridge University Press).
Heather, P. (2005), *The Fall of the Roman Empire* (Harmondsworth: Penguin).
Heine, R.E. (1998), 'The Christology of Callistus', *JTS* 49, 56–91.
Hess, H. (2005), *The Early Development of Canon Law and the Council of Sardica*, 2nd edition (Oxford: Clarendon Press).
Hick, J. (1968), *Evil and the God of Love* (London: Fontana).
Hill, C. (2004), *The Johannine Corpus in the Early Church* (Oxford: Clarendon Press).
Hübner, R. (1999), *Der Paradoxe Eine* (Leiden: Brill).
Hunt, E.J. (2003), *Christianity in the Second Century. The Case of Tatian* (London: Routledge).
Hurtado, L. (2003), *Lord Jesus Christ* (Grand Rapids: Eerdmans).
Jackson, H.M. (1985), *The Lion becomes Man. The Gnostic Leontomorphic Creator and the Platonic Tradition* (Atlanta: Scholars Press).
Jacobsen, A.L. (2008), 'Genesis 1–3 as Source for Origen's Anthropology", *VigChr* 62, 313–32.
Jonas, H. (1971), *The Gnostic Religion* (Boston: Beacon Press).
Jung, C.G. (1967), *Alchemical Studies* (New York: Bollingen Foundation).
Kalvesmaki, J. (2008), 'Italian *versus* Eastern Valentinianism?', *VigChr* 62, 79–89.
Kannengiesser, C. (1993), 'Athanasius' So-Called "Third Oration" against the Arians', *Studia Patristica* 26, 375–88.
Keating, D. (2005), *The Appropriation of Divine Life in Cyril of Alexandria* (Oxford: Clarendon Press).
Kelly, J.N.D. (1972), *Early Christian Creeds* (London: SCM Press).
——— (1995), *Golden Mouth: The Story of John Chrysostom* (Grand Rapids: Baker).
King, K.L. (2003), *What is Gnosticism?* (Cambridge, Mass: Harvard University Press).
——— (2008), 'Which Early Christianity?', in S. Harvey and D. Hunter (eds), *Oxford Handbook to Early Christian Studies* (New York: Oxford University Press), 66–85.
Kinzig, W. (1994), 'The Title of the New Testament in the Second and Third Centuries', *JTS* 45, 519–44.

Kinzig, W. and M. Vinzent (1999), 'Recent research on the Origin of the Creed', *JTS* 50, 535–59.

Knöpf, R. (1901), *Ausgewähtle Martyracten* (Tübingen: Mohr).

Kokkinos, N. (1989), 'Crucifixion in A.D. 36: The Keystone for dating the Birth of Jesus', in E.J. Vardaman and E.M. Yamauchi (eds), *Chronos, Kairos, Christos: Nativity and Chronological Studies Presented to Jack Finegan* (Winona Lake: Eisenbrauns), 233–63.

Kopecek, T. (1970), *A History of Neo-Arianism*, 2 vols (Philadelphia: Philadelphia Patristic Foundation).

Kruger, M. (1996). *Ichgeburt. Origenes und die Entstehung der christlichen Idee der Widerkörperung in der Denkbewegung von Pythagoras bis Lessing* (Hildeshiem: Olms).

Küng, H. (1968), *The Church*, trans. R. and R. Ockenden (London: Search Press).

Lampe, P. (2003), *From Paul to Valentinus* (London: T. and T. Clark).

Lang, U.M. (2000), 'The Christological Controversy at the Synod of Antioch in 268/9', *JTS* 51, 54–80.

——— (2001), *John Philoponus and the Controversies over Chalcedon in the Sixth Century* (Leuven: Peeters, 2001).

Lietzmann, H. (1904), *Apollnarius von Laodicea und seine Schüle* (Tübingen: Mohr).

Lightfoot, J.B. (1885–1890), *The Apostolic Fathers*, 5 vols (London: Macmillan).

Logan. A.H.B. (1992), 'Marcellus of Ancyra and the Councils of 325: Antioch, Anycra, Nicaea', *JTS* 43, 425–46.

——— (1996), *Gnostic Truth and Christian Heresy* (Peabody, Mass.: Hendrickson).

Löhr, W. (1996), *Basilides und seine Schüle* (Tübingen: Mohr).

Loofs, F. (1924), *Paulus von Samosata* (Tübingen: Mohr).

Lowry, W. (1938), 'Did Origen Stuyle the Son a ktisma?', *JTS* 39, 39–42.

McGuckin, J. (2004), *The Westminster Handbook to Origen* (Louisville: Westminster John Knox Press).

McLynn, N. (1994), *Ambrose of Milan. Church and Court n a Christian Capital* (Berkeley: University of California Press).

Macmullen, R. (2006), *Voting about God in Early Christian Councils* (New Haven: Yale University Press).

Macrae, G. W. (1970), 'The Jewish Background of the Gnostic Sophia Myth', *Novum Testamentum* 12, 86–101.

Majercik, R. 'Porphyry and the Gnostics', *CQ* 55, 277–92.

Markschies, C. (1992), *Valentinus Gnosticus* (Tübingen: Mohr).

——— (2000a), *Alta Trinita Beata* (Tübingen: Möhr).

——— (2000b), 'New Research on Ptolemaeus Gnosticus', *ZAC* 4, 225–54.

Marshall, J. (2003), 'The Objects of Ignatius' Wrath and Jewish Angelic Mediators', *JEH* 56 (2005), 3–27.

May, G. (1994), *Creatio ex Nihilo* (Edinburgh: T. and T. Clark).

Meijering, E.P. (1995), 'Zur Echtheit der Dritte Rede des Athanasios gegen die Arianer', *Vigiliae Christianae* 48, 135–56.

Moingt, J. (1967), *Théologie trinitaire de Tertullien, 2: Substantialité et individualité* (Paris).

Molland, E. (1950), 'Irenaeus of Lugdunum and the Apostolic Succession', *JEH* 1, 12–28.

Moreschini, C. and Tommasi, C. (2007), *Opere teologice di Mario Vitorino* (Turin).

Morin, G. (1932), 'L'origine du symbole d'Athanase: témoignage inédit du S. Césaire d'Arles', *Revue Benedictine* 44, 207–19.

Musurillo, H. (1972), *Acts of the Christian Martyrs* (Oxford: Clarendon Press).

Nautin, P. (1947), *Hippolytus et Josippe* (Paris: Cerf).

——— (1949), *Hippolyte: Contre les Hérésies* (Paris: Cerf).

——— (153), *Le Dossier d'Hippolyte et de Meliton* (Paris: Cerf).

——— (1974), 'Les fragments de Basilide sur la souffrance et leur interpretation par Clément d'Alexandrie et Origène', in *Mélanges d'histoire et de religion offerts à Henri-Charles Puech* (Paris), 393–403.

——— (1977). *Origène: sa Vie et son Oeuvre* (Paris: Cerf).

Nédoncelle, M. (1948), '*Prosôpon* et *persona* dans l'antiquité classique', *Revue des Sciences Religieuses* 22, 277–99.

Newman, J.H. (1845), *Essay on the Development of Doctrine* (London: Longmans).

Norris, R.A. (1963), *Manhood and Christ. At Study in the Christology of Theodore of Mopsuestia* (Oxford: Clarendon Press).

O'Brien, 'Plotinus on Matter and Evil', in L. Gerson (ed.), *The Cambridge Companion to Plotinus* (Cambridge: Cambridge University Press), 171–95.

Orbe, A. (1969), *La Antropologia de San Ireneo* (Madrid: Editoriale Catolica).

——— (1991), 'Origenes y los monarquianos', *Gregorianum* 72, 39–73.

Osborn, E.F. (1994), 'Arguments for Faith in Clement of Alexandria', *Vigiliae Christianae* 48, 1–24.

——— (1997), *Tertullian, First Theologian of the West* (Cambridge: Cambridge University Press).

——— (2005), *Clement of Alexandria* (Cambridge: Cambridge University Press).

Pagels, E. (1979), *The Gnostic Gospels* (New York: Random House).

Parvis, P. (2007), 'Justin, Philosopher and Martyr', in S. Parvis and P. Foster (eds), *Justin Martyr and his Worlds* (Minneapolis: Fortress Press), 22–37.

Parvis, S. (2006), *Marcellus of Ancyra and the Lost Years of the Arian Controversy* (Oxford: Clarendon Press).

Pearson, B.A. (1981), 'Jewish Elements in *Corpus Hermeticum* I (*Poimandres*)', in R. van den Broek and M.J. Vermaseren (eds), *Studies in Gnosticism and Hellenistic Religion* (Leiden: Brill), 336–48.

——— (2007). *Ancient Gnosticism. Traditions and Literature* (Minneapolis).

Pétrement, S. (1991), *A Separate God. The Christian Origins of Gnosticism* (London: Longmans).

Pettersen, A. (1990a), *Athanasius* (London: Geoffrey Chapman).

——— (1990b), 'The Arian Context of Athanasius of Alexandria's *Tomus ad Antiochenos* VII', *JEH* 41, 183–98.

Prestige, G.F. (1956), *The Correspondence of Basil and Apollinaris* (London: SPCK).

Price, R. (2008), 'The Theotokos and the Council of Ephesus', in C. Maunder (ed.), *The Origin of the Cult of the Virgin Mary* (London: Continuum, 2008), 89–104.

Price, R. and M. Gaddis (2005), *Acts of the Council of Chalcedon* (Liverpool: Liverpool University Press).

Quispel, G. (1948), 'Gnostic Man: the Doctrine of Basilides', *Eranos Jahrbuch* 17.

——— (1980), 'Ezekiel 1.26 in Jewish Mysticism and Gnosis', *Vigiliae Christanae* 34, 1–13.

Ramelli, I. (2007), *Gregorio di Nissa, Sull'Anima e la Resurrezione* (Milan: Bompiani).

Rashdall, H. (1919), *The Idea of Atonement in Christian Theology* (London: Macmillan).

Richard, M. (1945a), 'Le fragment XXII d'Amphiloche d'Iconium', *Mélanges E. Podechard* (Lyon), 199–210.

——— (1945b), 'L'introduction du mot "Hypostase" dans la théologie de l'incarnation', *Mélanges de Science Religieuse* 2, 5–32 and 245–70.

——— (1964), 'Une paraphrase grecque résumée du commentaire d'Hippolyte sur le cantique des cantiques', *Muséon* 77, 137–54.

——— (1965), 'La Lettre de S. Irénée à au Pape Victor', *Zeitschrift für die Neutestamentliche Wissneschaft* 56, 260–82.

Robertson, J. (2007), *Christ as Mediator. Studies in the Theology of Origen, Eusebius, Marcellus of Ancyra and Athanasius* (Oxford: Clarendon Press).

Robinson, J.A.T. (1952), *The Body. A Study in Pauline Theology* (London: SCM Press).

Robinson, J.M., ed. (1990), *The Nag Hammadi Library* (San Francisco: Harper).

——— ed. (2000), *The Coptic Gnostic Library*, 5 vols (Leiden: Brill).

Rousseau, A. and L. Doutreleau (1982), *S. Irénée, Contre Les Héresies Livre II*, 2 vols (Paris: Sources Chrétiennes).

Röwekamp, G., ed. and trans. (2005), *Pamphilus von Caesarea: Apologia pro Origene* (Turnhout: Brepols).

Russell, N. (2004), *The Doctrine of Deification in the Greek Patristic Tradition* (New York: Oxford University Press).

Ste-Croix, G. de (2006), 'The Council of Chalcedon', in *Christian Persecution, Maryrdom and Orthodoxy* (New York: Oxford University Press), 259–319.

Sanday, W. and A. Headlam (1907), *Critical and Exegetical Commentary on the Epistle to the Romans* (Edinburgh: T. and T. Clark).

Schoedel, W.R. (1985), *Ignatius of Antioch. A Commentary on the Letters* (Philadelphia: Fortress Press).

Scholem, G. (1974), 'Jaldabaoth Reconsidered', in *Melanges d'histoire des religions offerts à Henri-Charles Puech* (Paris: Presses Universitaires), 405–21.

Schwartz, E. (1928), *Cyrill und der Mönch Victor* (Vienna: Akademie der Wissenschaften).
Scott, A.B. (1991), *Origen and the Life of the Stars* (Oxford: Clarendon Press).
Scott, W.B. (1925), *Hermetica*, vol. 2 (Oxford: Clarendon Press).
Sellers, R.V. (1928), *Eustathius of Antioch and his Place in the Early History of Christian Doctrine* (Cambridge: Cambridge University Press).
——— (1940), *Two Ancient Christologies* (London: SPCK).
Shoemaker, S. (2008), 'The Cult of the Virgin Mary in the Fourth Century: A Fresh Look at Some New and Old Sources'. C. Maunder (ed.), *The Origin of the Cult of the Virgin* Mary (London: Continuum), 71–87.
Siddals, R. (1987), 'Logic and Christology in Cyril of Alexandria', *JTS* 38 (1987), 341–67.
Simonetti, M. (1965), *Studi sull'Arianesimo* (Rome: Pontifical Institute).
Skarsaune, O. (1987), 'A Neglected Detail in the Creed of Nicaea (325)', *Vigiliae Christianae* 41, 54–74.
Smith, M. (1981), 'History of the Term *Gnôstikos*', in B. Layton (ed.), T*he Rediscovery of Gnosticism*, vol. 2 (Leiden: Brill), 796–807.
Stead, G.C. (1961), 'The Significance of the *Homoousios*', *Studia Patristica* 3 (Berlin: *Texte und Untersuchungen* 78), 397–412.
——— (1963), 'Divine Substance in Tertullian', *JTS* 14, 38–58.
——— (1964), 'The Platonism of Arius', *JTS* 15, 16–37.
——— (1969), 'The Valentinian Myth of Sophia', *JTS* 20, 75–104.
——— (1977), *Divine Substance* (Oxford: Clarendon Press).
——— (1978), 'The *Thalia* of Arius and the Testimony of St Athanasius', *JTS* 29, 20–52.
——— (1980), 'In Search of Valentinus', in B. Layton (ed.), *The Rediscovery of Gnosticism*, vol. 1 (Leiden: Brill), 75–95.
——— (1988), 'Athanasius' Earliest Written Work', *JTS* 39, 76–91.
——— (1998), 'The Word "From Nothing"', *JTS* 49, 671–84.
Steenberg, M.C. (2008), *Irenaeus on Creation. The Cosmic Christ and the Saga of Redemption* (Leiden: Brill).
Stewart-Sykes, A. (2002), 'Bread and Fish, Water and Wine', in G. May and K. Greschat (eds), *Marcion und seine Kirchengeschichtliche Wesung* (Berlin: De Gruyter), 207–20.
Struttwolf, H. (1999), *Die Trinitätslehre und Christologie des Eusebs von Caesarea* (Göttingen: Vandenhoeck and Ruprecht).
Studer, B. (1993), *Trinity and Incarnation* (Edinburgh: T. and T. Clark).
——— (1998), *Schola Christiana* (Paderborn: Schöningh).
Takakusu, J. (1956), *The Essentials of Buddhist Philosophy* (Honolulu: Office Appliance Company).
Tardieu, M. (1984), *Écrits Gnostiques. Codex de Berlin* (Paris: Cerf).
——— (1996), *Recherches sur la formation de l'Apocalypse de Zostrien et les sources de Marius Victorinus* (Bures-sur-Yvette:Groupe pour l'Étude de la Civilisation du Moyen Orient).

Tarrant, H. (2000), *Plato's First Interpreters* (London: Duckworth).
——— (2003), *Proclus. Commentary on the Timaeus* (Cambridge: Cambridge University Press).
Tennant, F.R. (1968), *Sources of the Doctrine of the Fall and Original Sin* (New York: Schocken. Original publication 1903).
Thomson, R.W. and Howard-Johnston, J. (1999), *The Armenian History attributed to Sebeos*, vol. 1. *Translation and Notes* (Liverpool: Liverpool University Press).
Tiessen, T. (1993), *Irenaeus on the Fate of the Unevangelized* (London/NJ: Scarecrow Press).
Torrance, I.R. (1988), *Christology after Chalcedon* (Norwich: Canterbury Press).
Torrance, T.F. (1995), *Divine Meaning. Studies in Patristic Hermeneutics* (Edinburgh: T. and T. Clark).
Tzamalikos, P. (2006), *Origen: Cosmology and Ontology of Time* (Leiden: Brill).
Urbach, E.E. (1975), *The Sages. Their Concepts and Beliefs* (Cambridge, Mass.: Harvard University Press).
Vaggione, R. (2000), *Eunomius of Cyzicus and the Nicene Revolution* (Oxford: Clarendon Press).
Van den Hoek, A. (1997), 'The Catechetical School of Early Christian Alexandria and its Philonic Heritage', *HTR* 90, 59–87.
Wallace-Hadrill, D.M. (1982), *Christian Antioch* (Cambridge: Cambridge University Press).
Weinandy, T. (2003), 'Cyril and the Mystery of the Incarnation', in Weinandy (ed.), *The Theology of Cyril of Alexandria: A Critical Appreciation* (London/NY: T. and T. Clark), 23–54.
——— (2007), *Athanasius. A Theological Introduction* (Aldershot: Ashgate).
Welch, L. (1994), '*Logos-Sarx*? Soul and the Eucharist in the Early Thought of Cyril of Alexandria', *St Vladimir's Seminary Quarterly* 38, 271–92.
Wessel, S. (2004), *Cyril of Alexandria and the Nestorian Controversy* (Oxford: Clarendon Press).
Westcott, B.F. (1886), *The Epistles of St John* (Cambridge/London: Macmillan).
Westra, L.H. (2002), *The Apostles' Creed. Origins, History and Some Early Commentaries* (Turnhout: Brepols).
Whittaker, J. (1969), 'Basilides and Negative Theology', *HTR* 62, 367–71.
——— (1975), 'The Historical Background of Proclus' Doctrine of the *authupostaton*', *Entretiens Hardt* 21: *De Jamblique à Procle* (Geneva: Foundation Hardt), 193–232.
Wickham, E.L. (1983), *Cyril of Alexandria: Select Letters* (Oxford: Clarendon Press).
Widdicombe, P. (1994), *The Fatherhood of God from Origen to Athanasius* (Oxford: Clarendon Press).
Wiles, M.F. (1976), *Working Papers in Christian Doctrine* (Cambridge: Cambridge University Press).

Wiles, M.F. (1989), 'Eunomius: hair-splitting dialectican or defender of the accessibility of salvation?', in R.D. Williams (ed.), *The Making of Orthodoxy* (Cambridge: Cambridge University Press), 157–72.

——— (1993), 'A Textual Variant in the Creed of the Council of Nicaea', Studia Patristica 26, 428–35.

Williams. D.H. (1998), 'Constantine and the "Fall" of the Church', in L. Ayres and G. Jones (eds), *Christian Origins: Theology, Rhetoric and Community* (London: Routledge), 117–38.

Williams, M.A. (1996). *Rethinking 'Gnosticism'. An Argument for Dismantling a Dubious Category* (Princeton, NJ: Princeton University Press).

Williams, R.D. (12000), *Arius: Heresy and Tradition* (London: Dartman, Longman and Todd).

Wordsworth, C. (1890), *Saint Hippolytus and the Church of Rome* (London: Rivingtons).

Young, F.M. (1971), 'A Reconsideration of Alexandrian Christology', *JEH* 22, 103–14.

——— (1997), *Biblical Exegesis and the Formation of Christendom* (Cambridge: Cambridge University Press).

——— (2003), 'Theotokos: Mary and the Pattern of fall and redemption in the Theology of Cyril of Alexandria', in T. Weinandy (ed.), *The Theology of Cyril of Alexandria: A Critical Appreciation* (London/NY: T. and T. Clark), 55–74.

Zachhuber, J. (1999), *Human Nature in Gregory of Nyssa* (Leiden: Brill).

——— (2000), 'The Antiochene Synod of AD 343 and the Beginnings of Neo-Nicenism', *ZAC* 4, 83–101.

——— (2001), 'Basil and the Three-Hypostasis Tradition: Reconsidering the Origins of Cappadocian Theology', *ZAC* 5, 65–85.

——— (2003), 'Nochmals: Der "38. Brief" des Basilius von Cäsarea als Werk des Grego von Nyssa', *ZAC* 7, 73–90.

Zelzer, M. (ed.) (1982), *Gesta Concilii Aquiliensis*, in CSEL 82.3 (Vienna: Tempsky), 313–68.

Zisioulas, J. (1988), *Being as Communion* (London: SCM).

Zuntz, G. (1955), 'On the Hymns in the *Corpus Hermeticum*', *Hermes* 90, 68–92.

Index